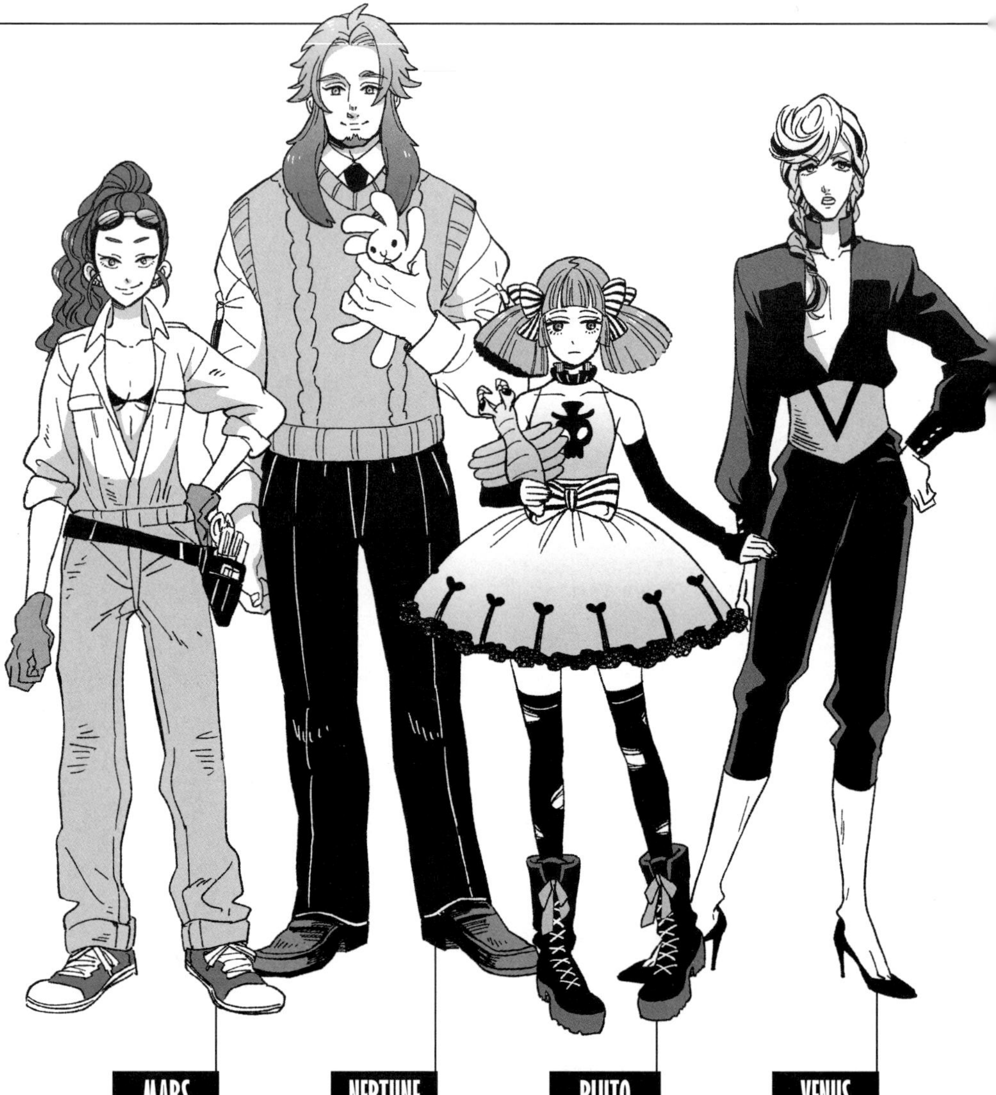

MARS

An engineer. Tests whether the animal designs will actually function in the physical world. The hardest worker in the office.

NEPTUNE

A designer. His masterpiece: the kangaroo.

PLUTO

A designer. Her masterpiece: the poisonous frog.

VENUS

A designer. Nicknamed "Ven." Their masterpiece: the bird.

HEAVEN'S DESIGN TEAM

CONTENTS

CHARACTER PROFILES —————— 002

PROPOSAL 1 —————— 005

PROPOSAL 2 —————— 025

PROPOSAL 3 —————— 045

PROPOSAL 4 —————— 065

PROPOSAL 5 —————— 085

PROPOSAL 6 —————— 105

PROPOSAL 7 —————— 125

THE ENCYCLOPEDIA OF REAL ANIMALS
021 · 041 · 061 · 081 · 101 · 121 · 141

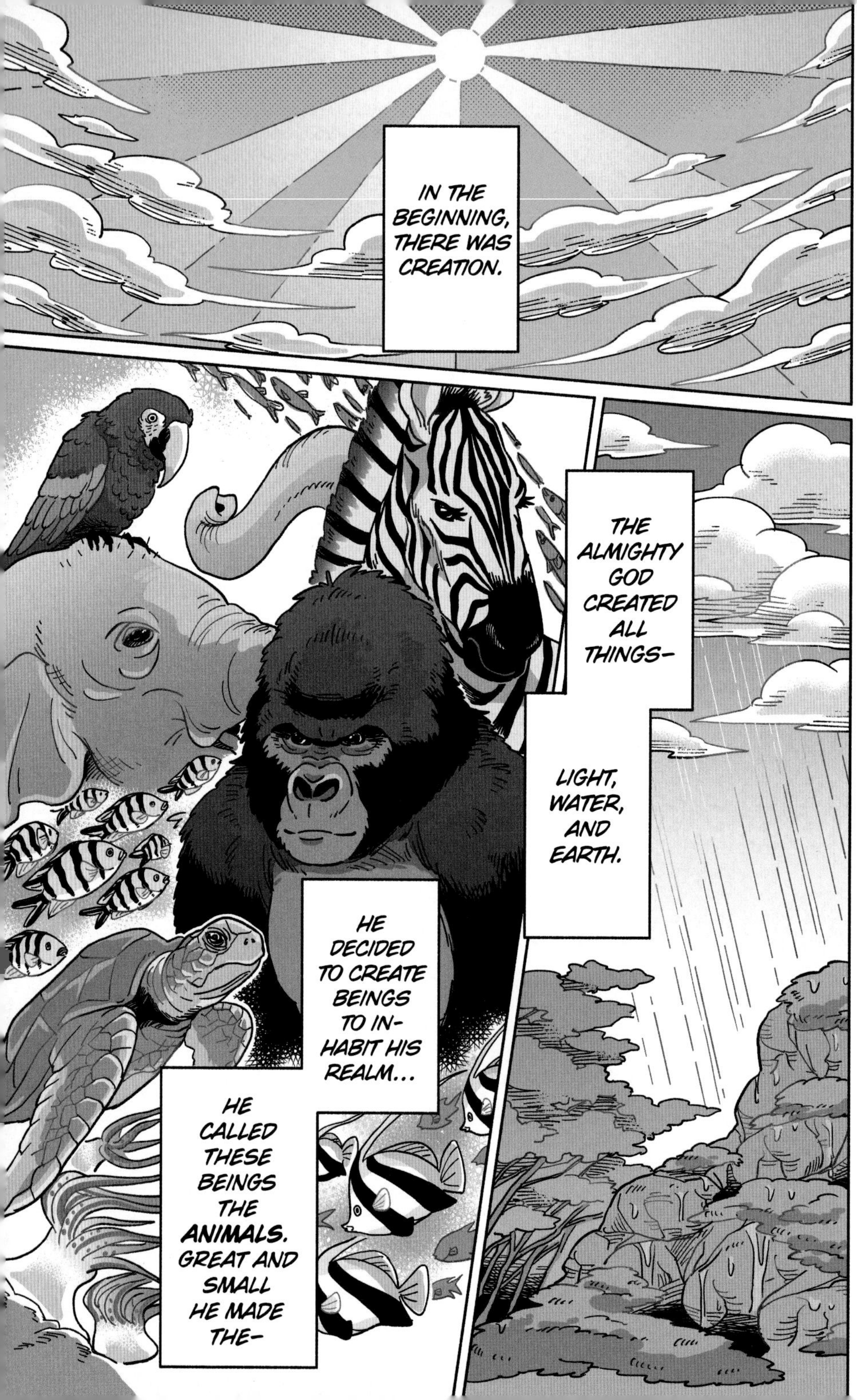
IN THE BEGINNING, THERE WAS CREATION.
THE ALMIGHTY GOD CREATED ALL THINGS-
LIGHT, WATER, AND EARTH.
HE DECIDED TO CREATE BEINGS TO IN-HABIT HIS REALM...
HE CALLED THESE BEINGS THE ANIMALS. GREAT AND SMALL HE MADE THE-

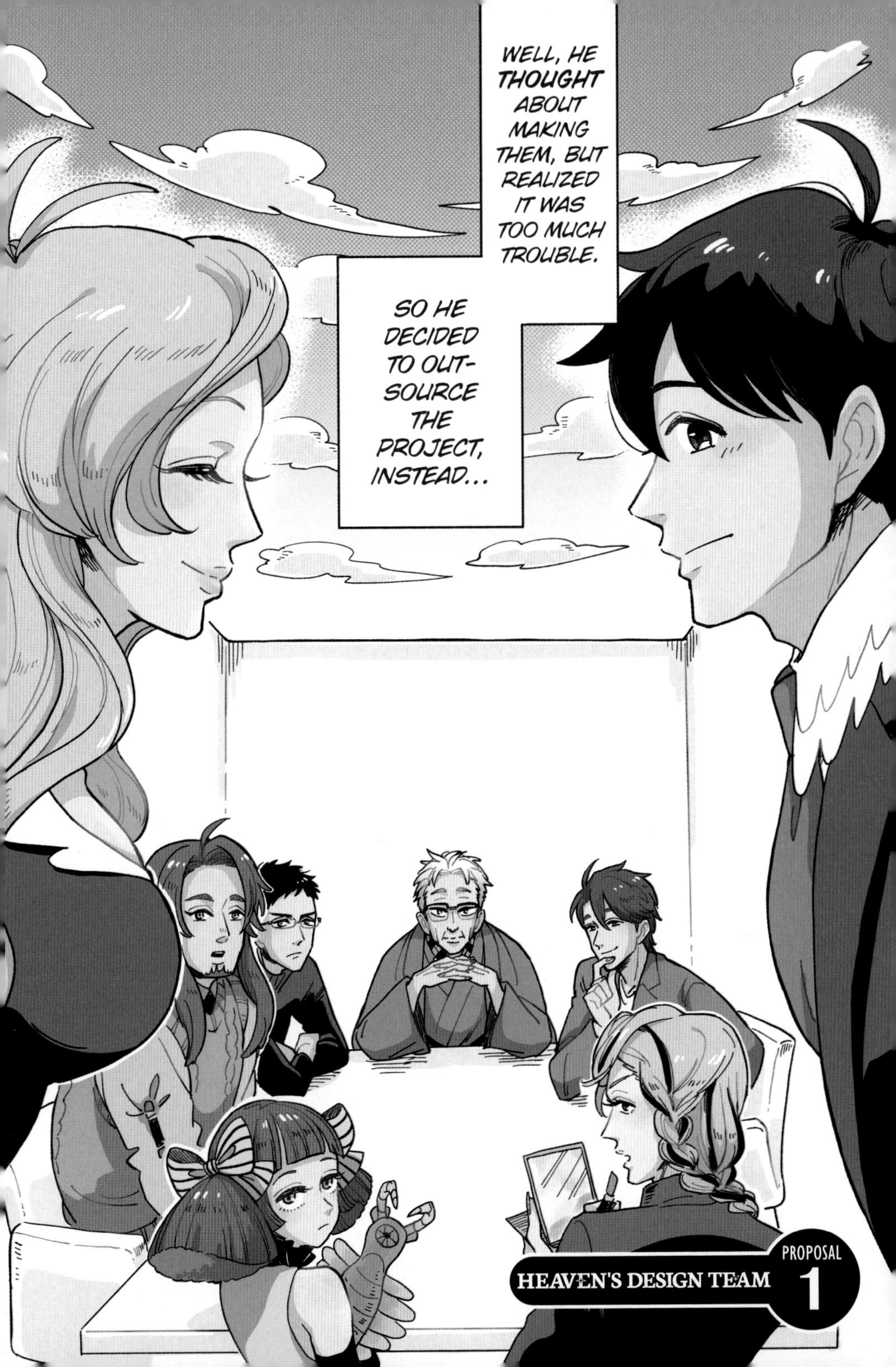
WELL, HE THOUGHT ABOUT MAKING THEM, BUT REALIZED IT WAS TOO MUCH TROUBLE.
SO HE DECIDED TO OUT-SOURCE THE PROJECT, INSTEAD...
HEAVEN'S DESIGN TEAM
PROPOSAL 1

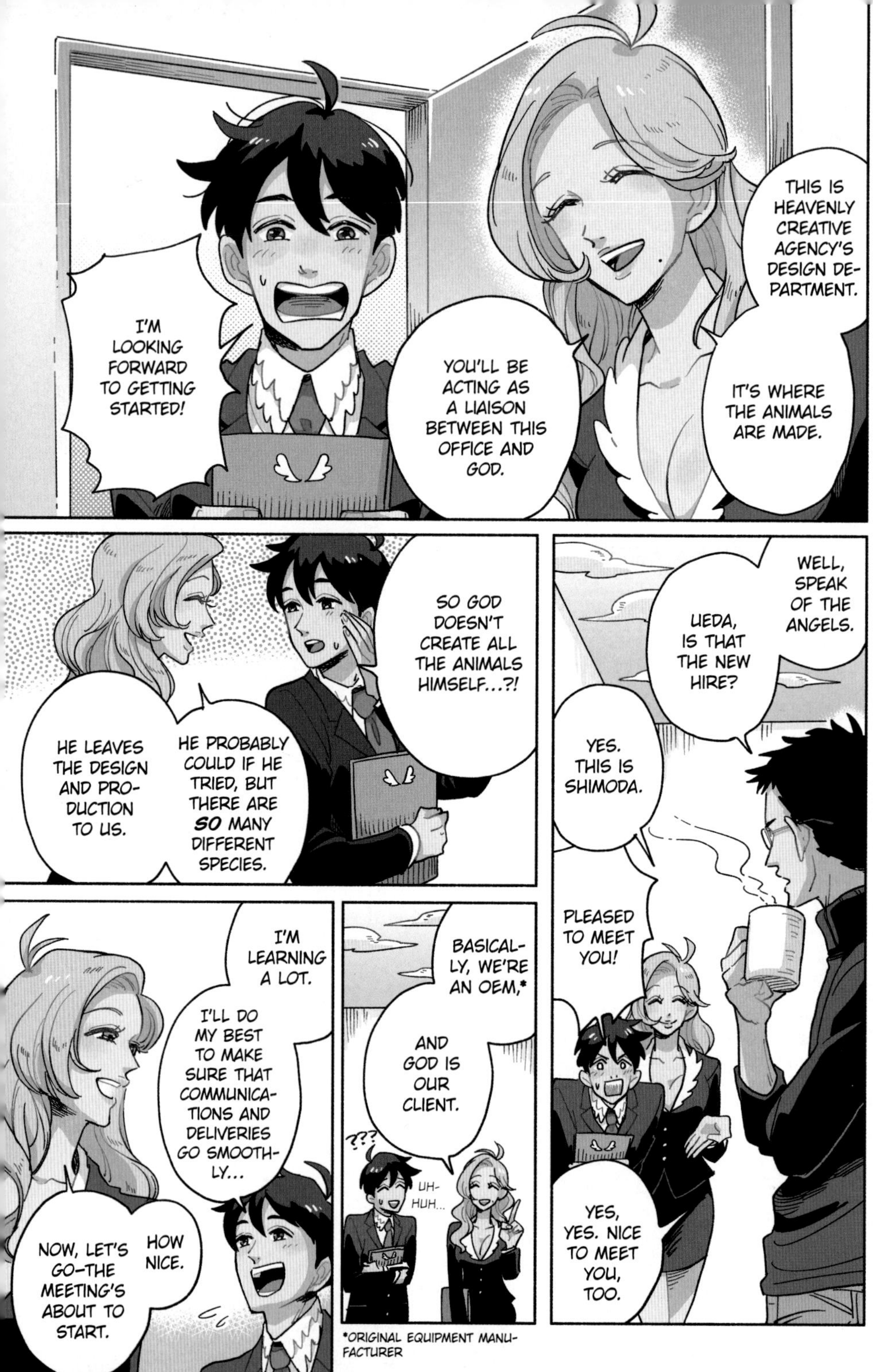
THIS IS HEAVENLY CREATIVE AGENCY'S DESIGN DE-PARTMENT.
IT'S WHERE THE ANIMALS ARE MADE.
YOU'LL BE ACTING AS A LIAISON BETWEEN THIS OFFICE AND GOD.
I'M LOOKING FORWARD TO GETTING STARTED!
WELL, SPEAK OF THE ANGELS.
UEDA, IS THAT THE NEW HIRE?
YES. THIS IS SHIMODA.
PLEASED TO MEET YOU!
YES, YES. NICE TO MEET YOU, TOO.
SO GOD DOESN'T CREATE ALL THE ANIMALS HIMSELF...?!
HE PROBABLY COULD IF HE TRIED, BUT THERE ARE SO MANY DIFFERENT SPECIES.
HE LEAVES THE DESIGN AND PRO-DUCTION TO US.
BASICAL-LY, WE'RE AN OEM,*
AND GOD IS OUR CLIENT.
???
UH-HUH...
I'M LEARNING A LOT.
I'LL DO MY BEST TO MAKE SURE THAT COMMUNICA-TIONS AND DELIVERIES GO SMOOTH-LY...
HOW NICE.
NOW, LET'S GO—THE MEETING'S ABOUT TO START.

*ORIGINAL EQUIPMENT MANU-FACTURER

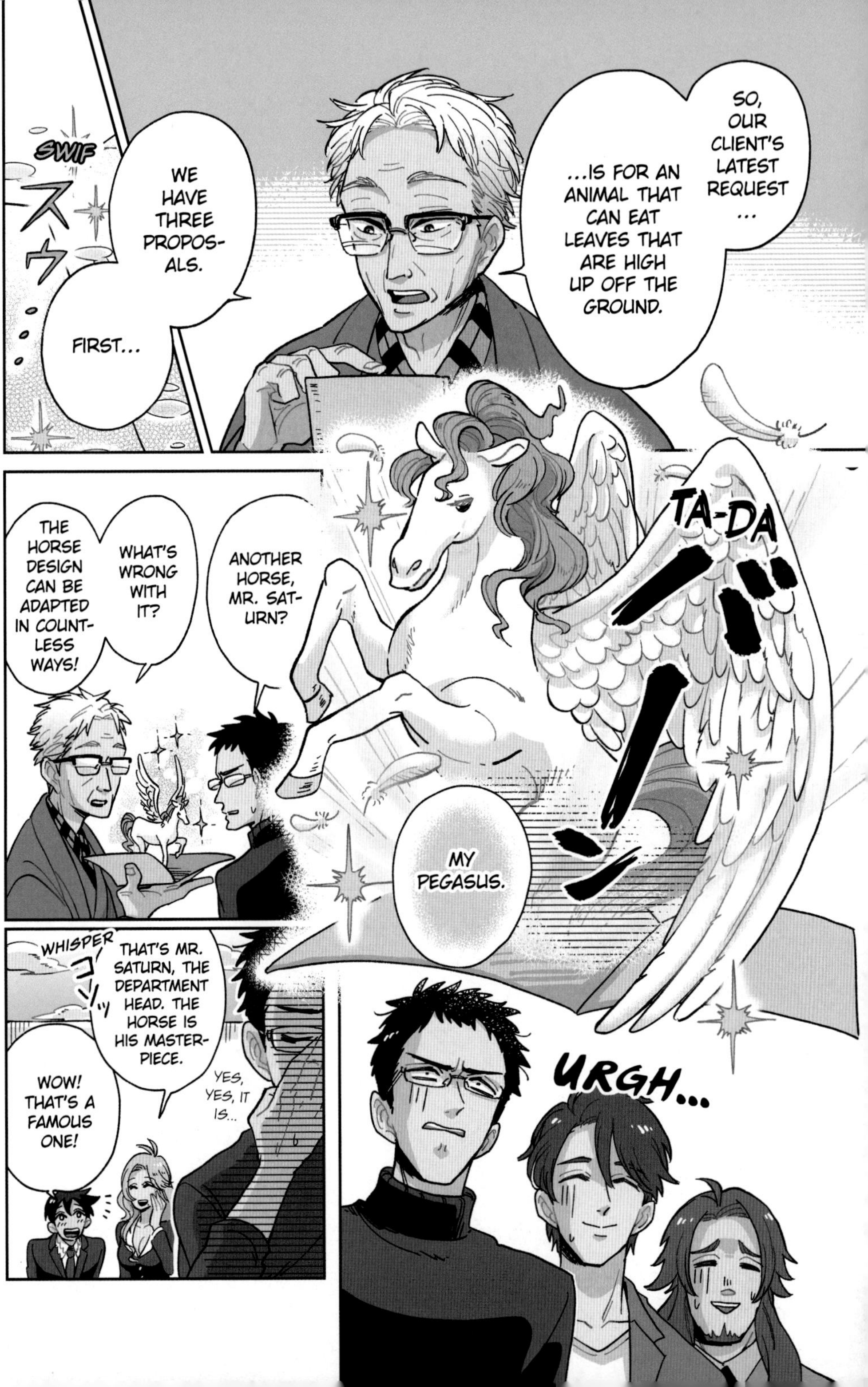
SO, OUR CLIENT'S LATEST REQUEST...
...IS FOR AN ANIMAL THAT CAN EAT LEAVES THAT ARE HIGH UP OFF THE GROUND.
SWIF
WE HAVE THREE PROPOSALS.
FIRST...
TA-DA
MY PEGASUS.
ANOTHER HORSE, MR. SATURN?
WHAT'S WRONG WITH IT?
THE HORSE DESIGN CAN BE ADAPTED IN COUNTLESS WAYS!
URGH...
WHISPER
THAT'S MR. SATURN, THE DEPARTMENT HEAD. THE HORSE IS HIS MASTERPIECE.
YES, YES, IT IS...
WOW! THAT'S A FAMOUS ONE!

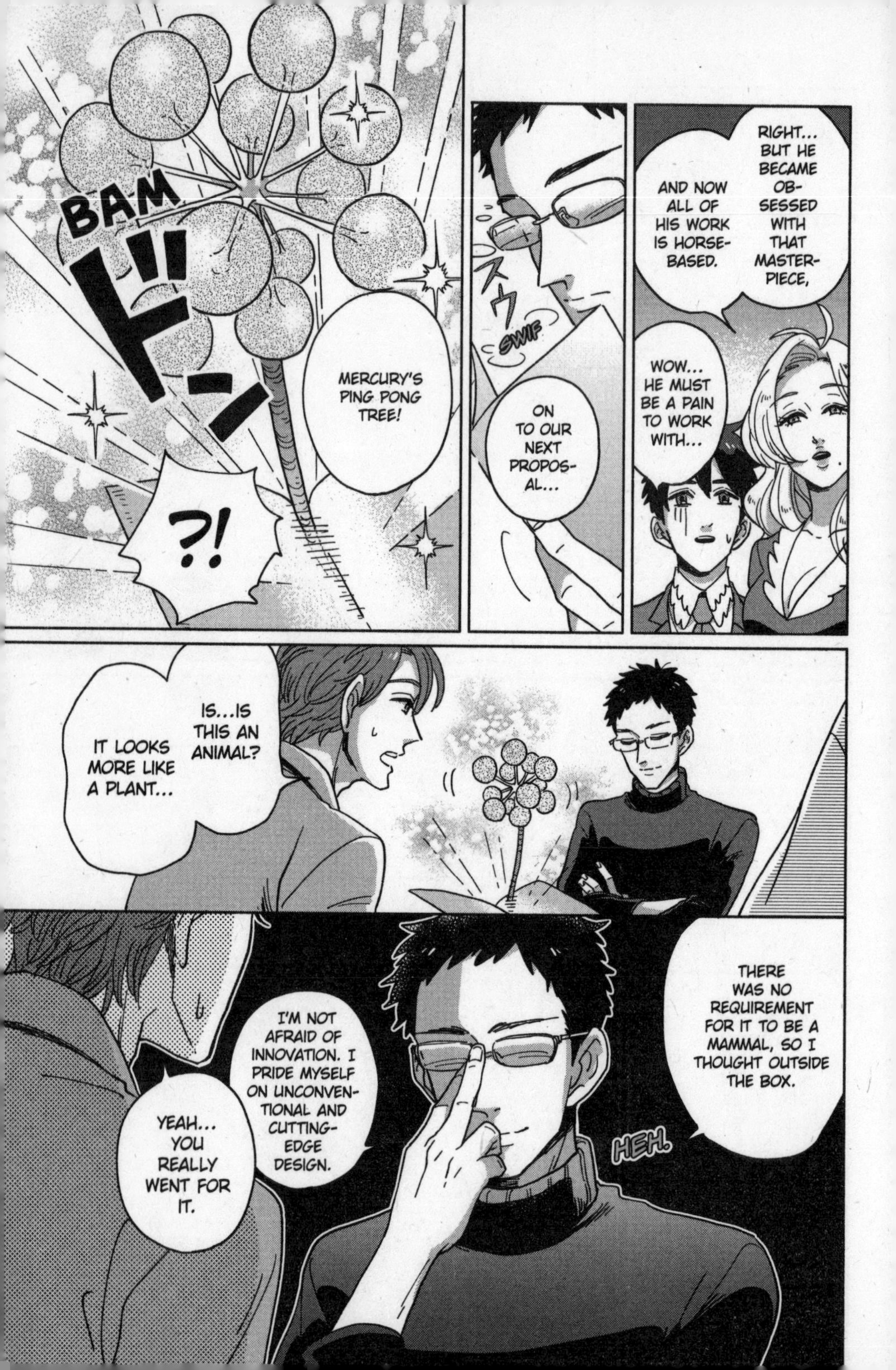
RIGHT... BUT HE BECAME OB-SESSED WITH THAT MASTER-PIECE,
AND NOW ALL OF HIS WORK IS HORSE-BASED.
WOW... HE MUST BE A PAIN TO WORK WITH...
スゥ
SWIF
ON TO OUR NEXT PROPOS-AL...
BAM
MERCURY'S PING PONG TREE!
?!
IS...IS THIS AN ANIMAL?
IT LOOKS MORE LIKE A PLANT...
THERE WAS NO REQUIREMENT FOR IT TO BE A MAMMAL, SO I THOUGHT OUTSIDE THE BOX.
HEH.
I'M NOT AFRAID OF INNOVATION. I PRIDE MYSELF ON UNCONVEN-TIONAL AND CUTTING-EDGE DESIGN.
YEAH... YOU REALLY WENT FOR IT.

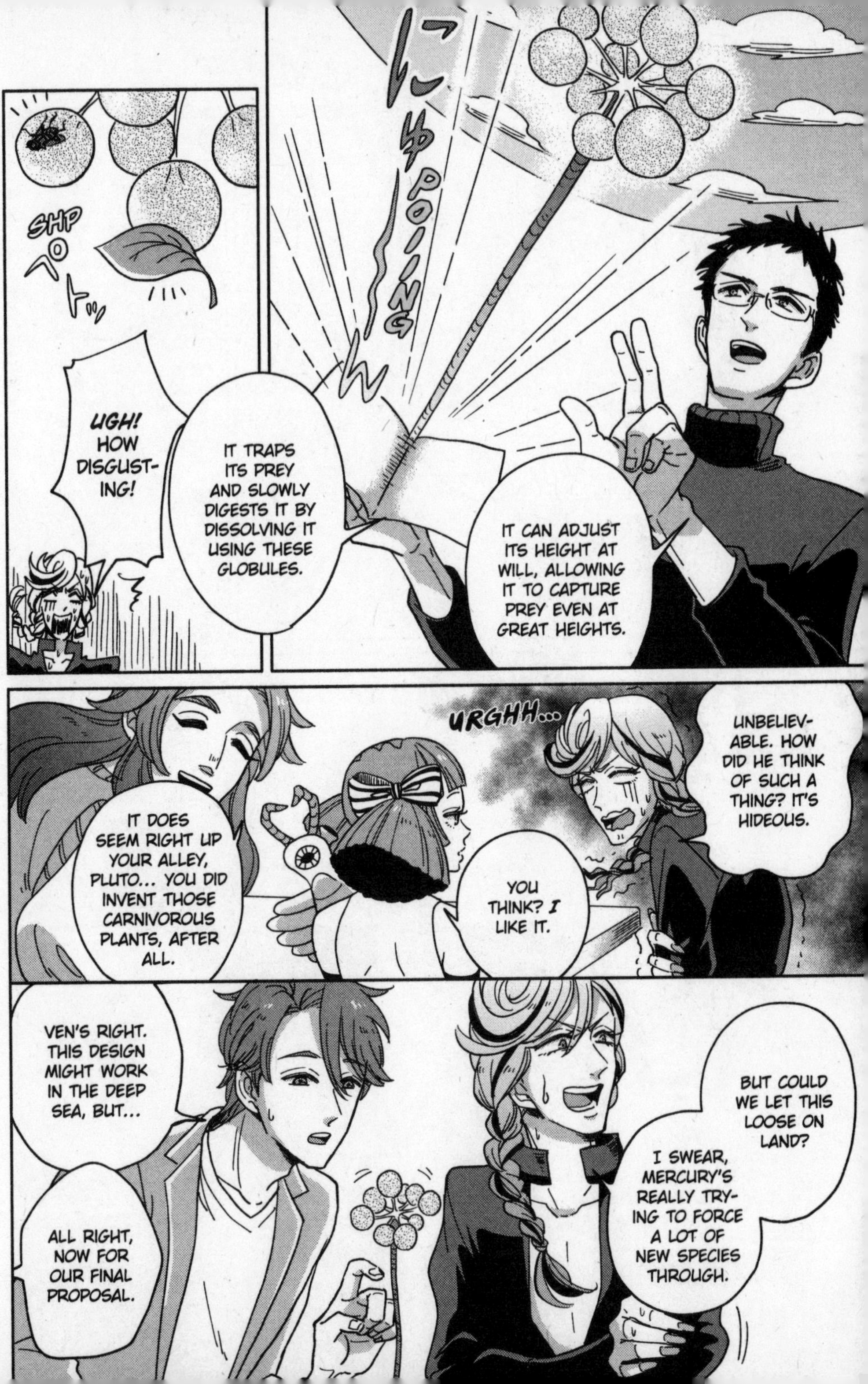
POIIING
IT CAN ADJUST ITS HEIGHT AT WILL, ALLOWING IT TO CAPTURE PREY EVEN AT GREAT HEIGHTS.
IT TRAPS ITS PREY AND SLOWLY DIGESTS IT BY DISSOLVING IT USING THESE GLOBULES.
SHP
UGH! HOW DISGUST-ING!
UNBELIEV-ABLE. HOW DID HE THINK OF SUCH A THING? IT'S HIDEOUS.
URGHH...
YOU THINK? I LIKE IT.
IT DOES SEEM RIGHT UP YOUR ALLEY, PLUTO... YOU DID INVENT THOSE CARNIVOROUS PLANTS, AFTER ALL.
BUT COULD WE LET THIS LOOSE ON LAND?
I SWEAR, MERCURY'S REALLY TRY-ING TO FORCE A LOT OF NEW SPECIES THROUGH.
VEN'S RIGHT. THIS DESIGN MIGHT WORK IN THE DEEP SEA, BUT...
ALL RIGHT, NOW FOR OUR FINAL PROPOSAL.

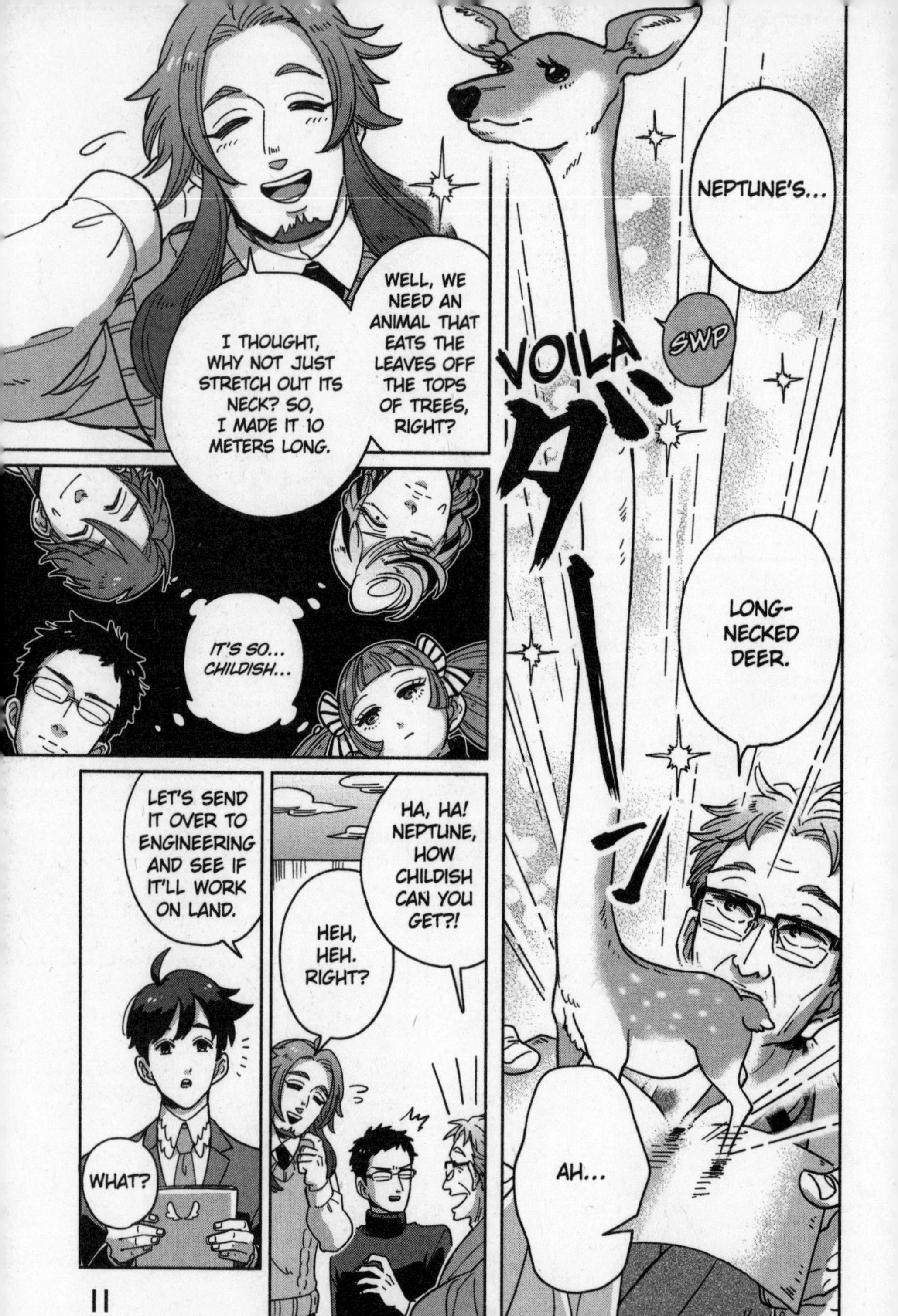
NEPTUNE'S...
SWP
VOILA
LONG-NECKED DEER.
AH...
WELL, WE NEED AN ANIMAL THAT EATS THE LEAVES OFF THE TOPS OF TREES, RIGHT?
I THOUGHT, WHY NOT JUST STRETCH OUT ITS NECK? SO, I MADE IT 10 METERS LONG.
IT'S SO... CHILDISH...
HA, HA! NEPTUNE, HOW CHILDISH CAN YOU GET?!
HEH, HEH. RIGHT?
LET'S SEND IT OVER TO ENGINEERING AND SEE IF IT'LL WORK ON LAND.
WHAT?

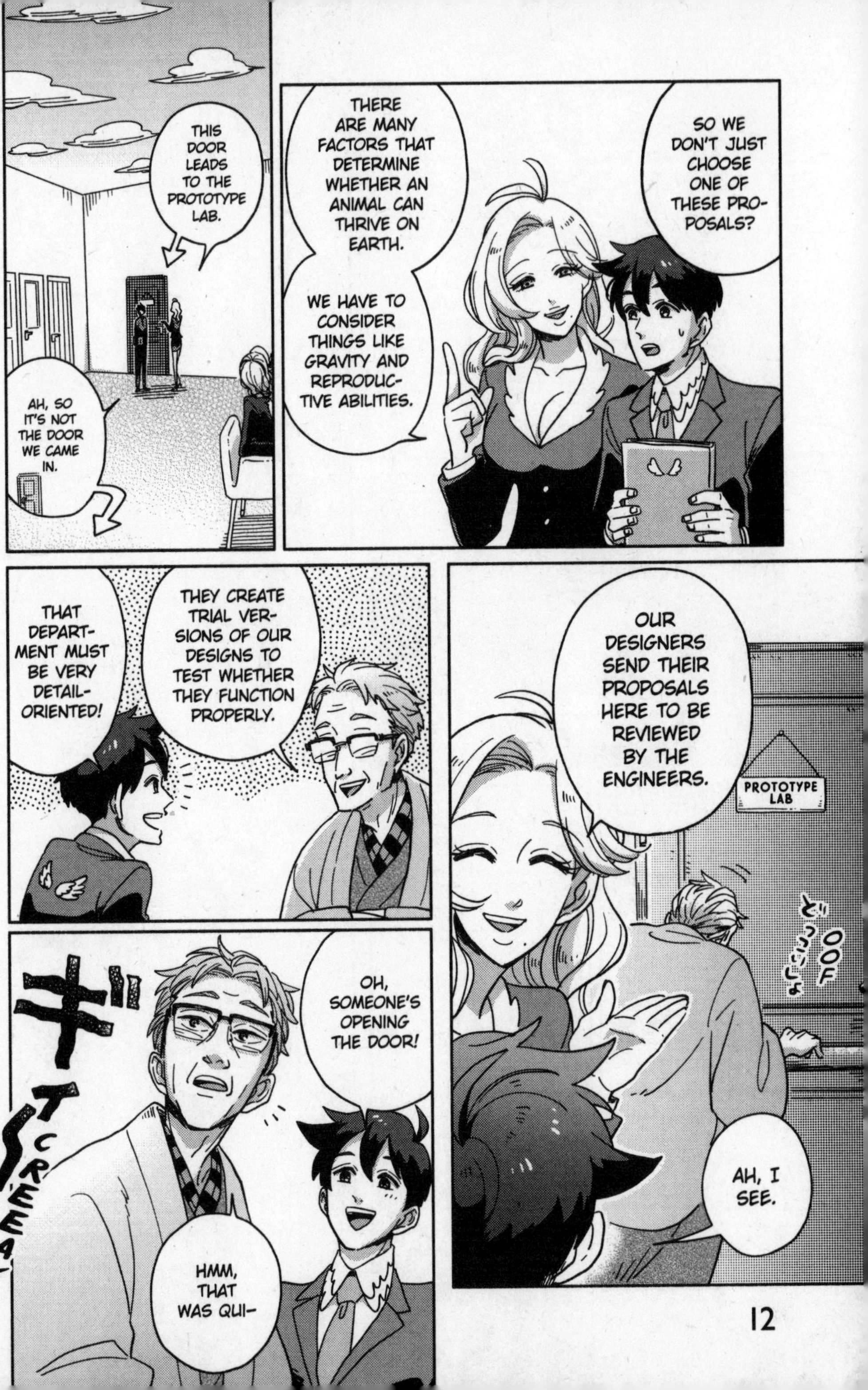
SO WE DON'T JUST CHOOSE ONE OF THESE PRO-POSALS?
THERE ARE MANY FACTORS THAT DETERMINE WHETHER AN ANIMAL CAN THRIVE ON EARTH.
WE HAVE TO CONSIDER THINGS LIKE GRAVITY AND REPRODUC-TIVE ABILITIES.
THIS DOOR LEADS TO THE PROTOTYPE LAB.
AH, SO IT'S NOT THE DOOR WE CAME IN.
OUR DESIGNERS SEND THEIR PROPOSALS HERE TO BE REVIEWED BY THE ENGINEERS.
PROTOTYPE LAB
OOF
どっこいしょ
AH, I SEE.
THEY CREATE TRIAL VER-SIONS OF OUR DESIGNS TO TEST WHETHER THEY FUNCTION PROPERLY.
THAT DEPART-MENT MUST BE VERY DETAIL-ORIENTED!
OH, SOMEONE'S OPENING THE DOOR!
HMM, THAT WAS QUI-
ギ
CREEAK

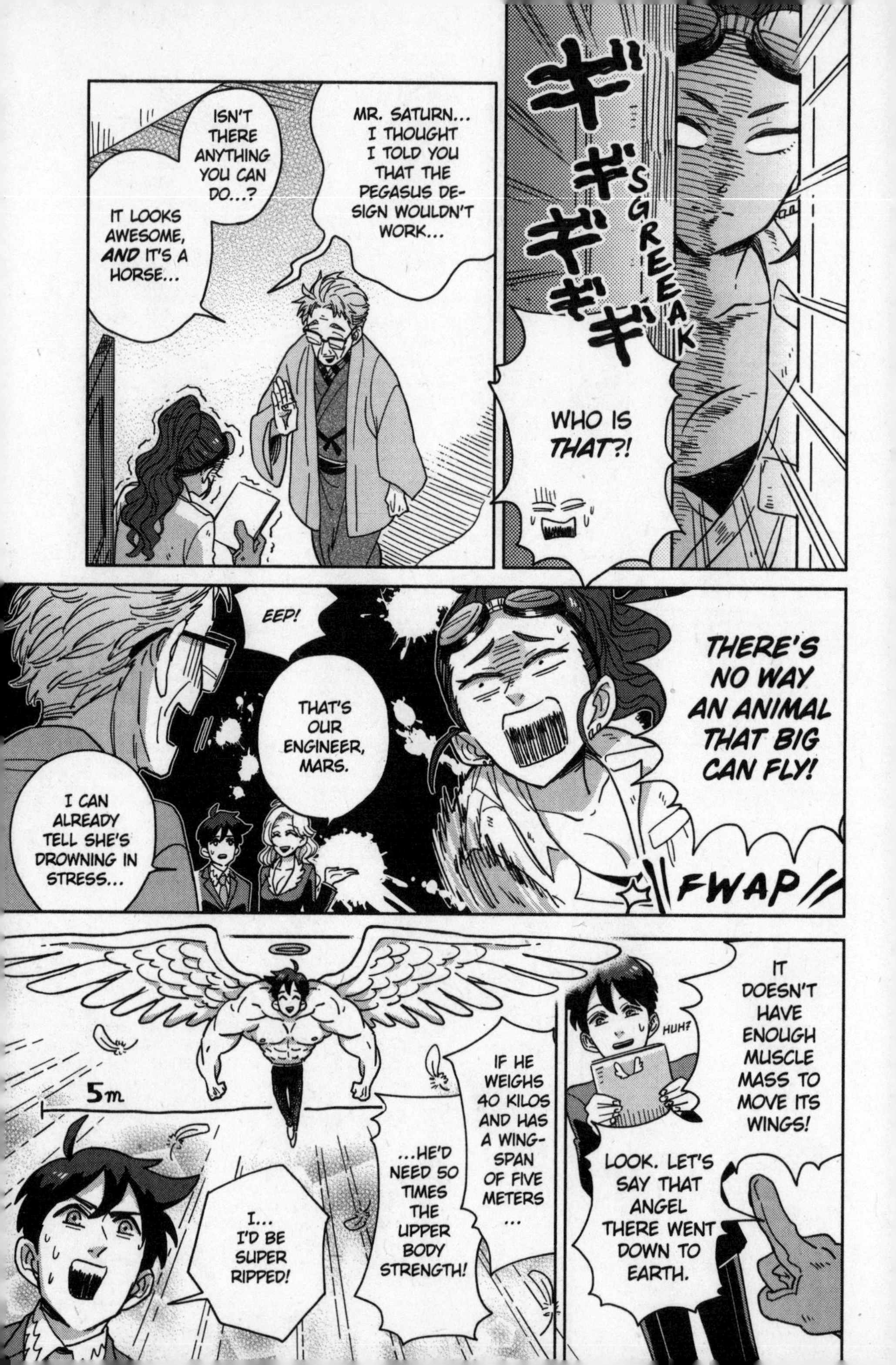
ギギギギ
SGREEAK
WHO IS *THAT*?!
MR. SATURN... I THOUGHT I TOLD YOU THAT THE PEGASUS DESIGN WOULDN'T WORK...
ISN'T THERE ANYTHING YOU CAN DO...?
IT LOOKS AWESOME, **AND** IT'S A HORSE...
THERE'S NO WAY AN ANIMAL THAT BIG CAN FLY!
FWAP
EEP!
THAT'S OUR ENGINEER, MARS.
I CAN ALREADY TELL SHE'S DROWNING IN STRESS...
IT DOESN'T HAVE ENOUGH MUSCLE MASS TO MOVE ITS WINGS!
HUH?
LOOK. LET'S SAY THAT ANGEL THERE WENT DOWN TO EARTH.
IF HE WEIGHS 40 KILOS AND HAS A WINGSPAN OF FIVE METERS...
...HE'D NEED 50 TIMES THE UPPER BODY STRENGTH!
5m
I... I'D BE SUPER RIPPED!

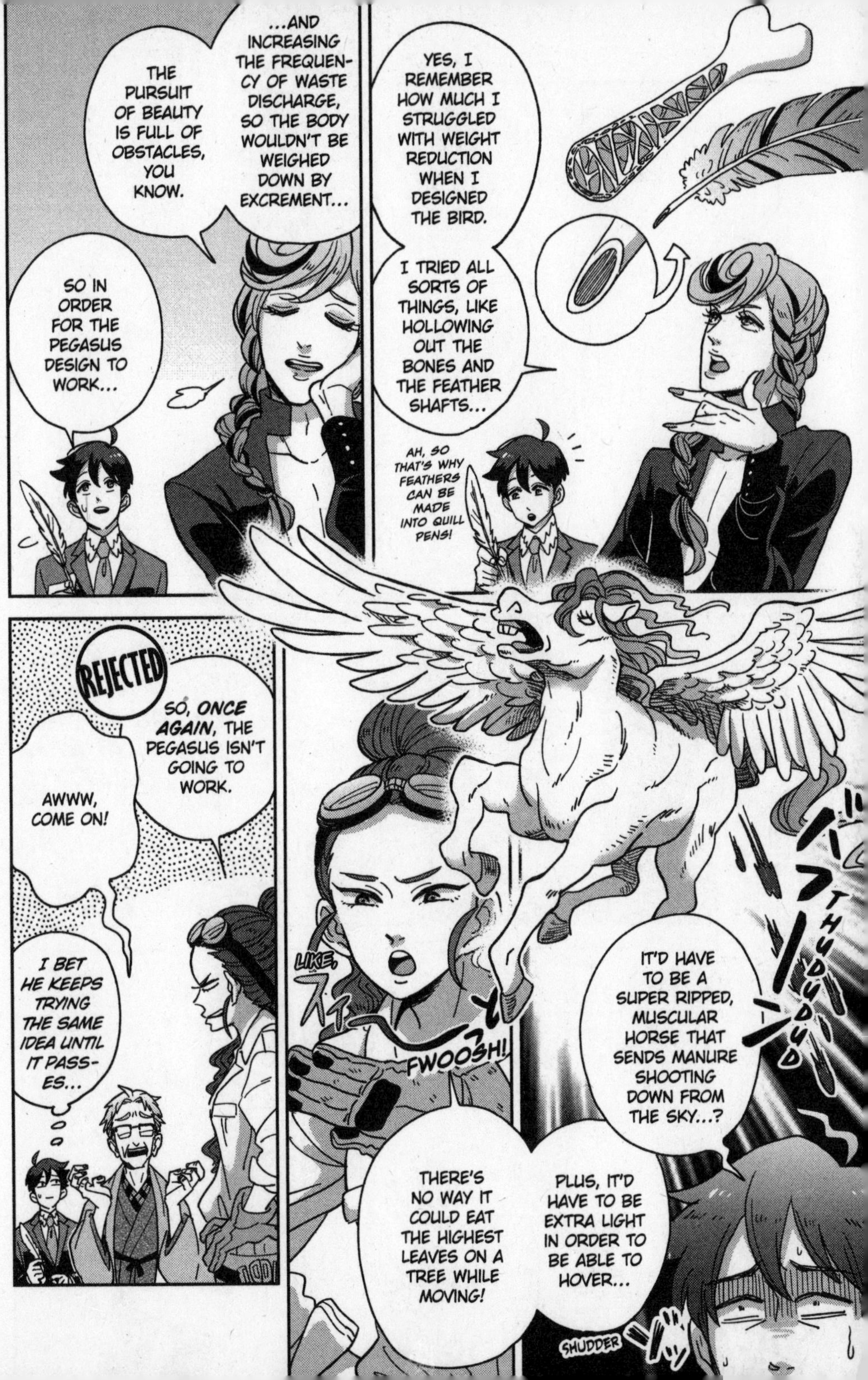

YES, I REMEMBER HOW MUCH I STRUGGLED WITH WEIGHT REDUCTION WHEN I DESIGNED THE BIRD.
I TRIED ALL SORTS OF THINGS, LIKE HOLLOWING OUT THE BONES AND THE FEATHER SHAFTS...
AH, SO THAT'S WHY FEATHERS CAN BE MADE INTO QUILL PENS!
...AND INCREASING THE FREQUENCY OF WASTE DISCHARGE, SO THE BODY WOULDN'T BE WEIGHED DOWN BY EXCREMENT...
THE PURSUIT OF BEAUTY IS FULL OF OBSTACLES, YOU KNOW.
SO IN ORDER FOR THE PEGASUS DESIGN TO WORK...
THUDUDUDUD
IT'D HAVE TO BE A SUPER RIPPED, MUSCULAR HORSE THAT SENDS MANURE SHOOTING DOWN FROM THE SKY...?
PLUS, IT'D HAVE TO BE EXTRA LIGHT IN ORDER TO BE ABLE TO HOVER...
THERE'S NO WAY IT COULD EAT THE HIGHEST LEAVES ON A TREE WHILE MOVING!
LIKE,
FWOOSH!
SHUDDER
REJECTED
SO, *ONCE AGAIN*, THE PEGASUS ISN'T GOING TO WORK.
AWWW, COME ON!
I BET HE KEEPS TRYING THE SAME IDEA UNTIL IT PASSES...

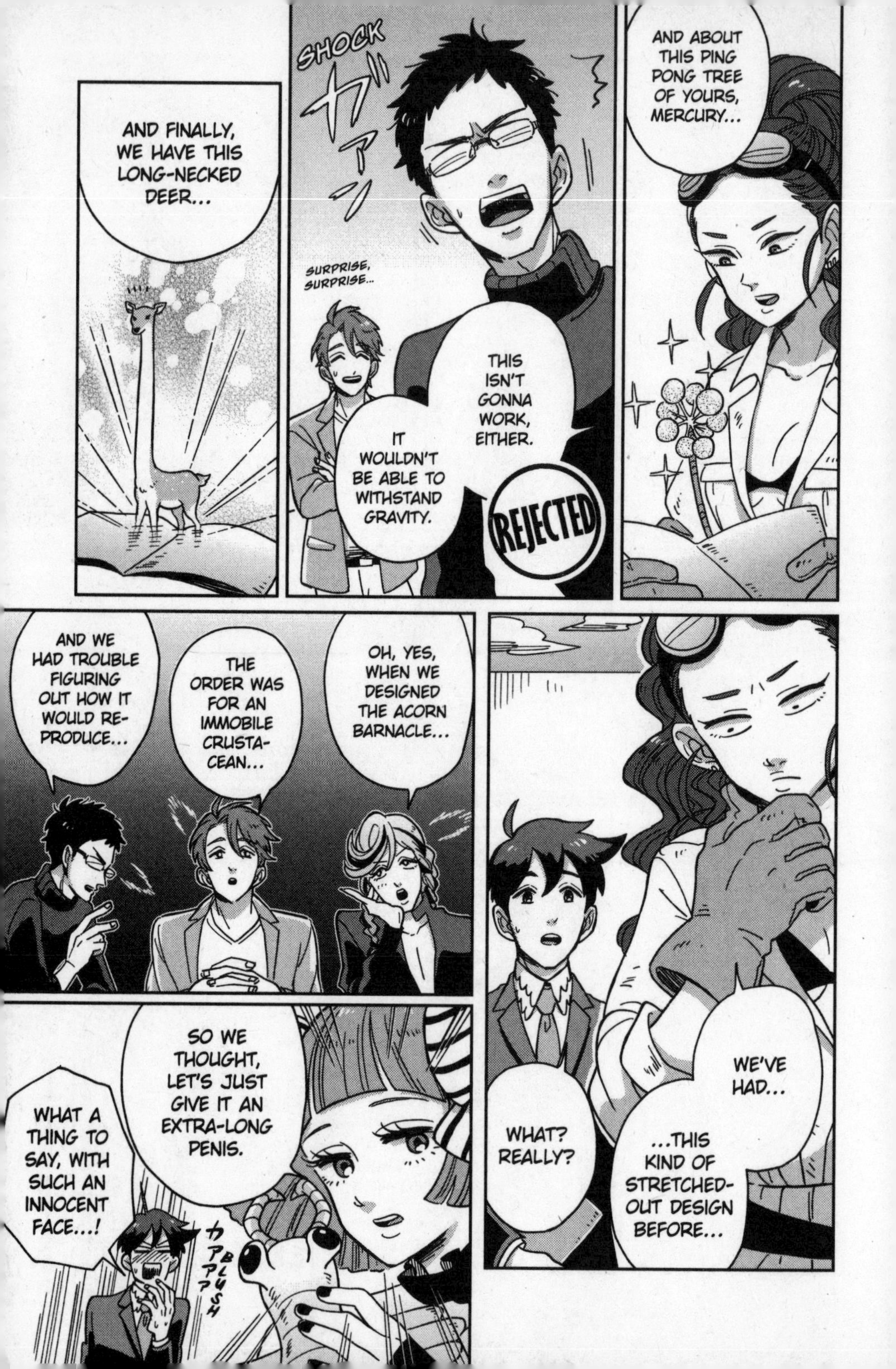
AND ABOUT THIS PING PONG TREE OF YOURS, MERCURY...
SHOCK
THIS ISN'T GONNA WORK, EITHER.
IT WOULDN'T BE ABLE TO WITHSTAND GRAVITY.
REJECTED
SURPRISE, SURPRISE...
AND FINALLY, WE HAVE THIS LONG-NECKED DEER...
WE'VE HAD...
...THIS KIND OF STRETCHED-OUT DESIGN BEFORE...
WHAT? REALLY?
OH, YES, WHEN WE DESIGNED THE ACORN BARNACLE...
THE ORDER WAS FOR AN IMMOBILE CRUSTACEAN...
AND WE HAD TROUBLE FIGURING OUT HOW IT WOULD REPRODUCE...
SO WE THOUGHT, LET'S JUST GIVE IT AN EXTRA-LONG PENIS.
WHAT A THING TO SAY, WITH SUCH AN INNOCENT FACE...!
BLUSH

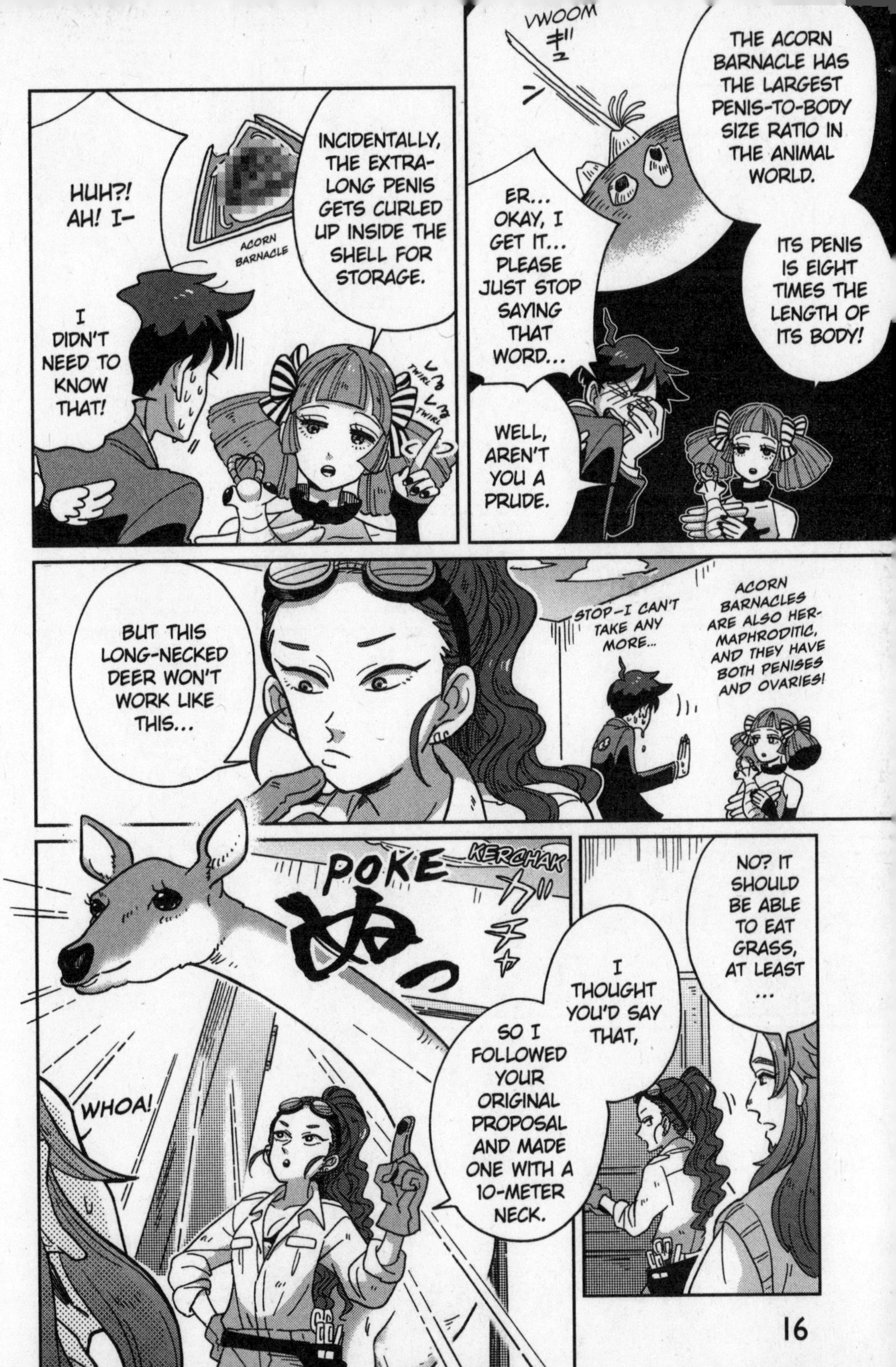
THE ACORN BARNACLE HAS THE LARGEST PENIS-TO-BODY SIZE RATIO IN THE ANIMAL WORLD.
VWOOM
ITS PENIS IS EIGHT TIMES THE LENGTH OF ITS BODY!
ER... OKAY, I GET IT... PLEASE JUST STOP SAYING THAT WORD...
WELL, AREN'T YOU A PRUDE.
INCIDENTALLY, THE EXTRA-LONG PENIS GETS CURLED UP INSIDE THE SHELL FOR STORAGE.
ACORN BARNACLE
HUH?! AH! I–
TWIRL TWIRL
I DIDN'T NEED TO KNOW THAT!
ACORN BARNACLES ARE ALSO HERMAPHRODITIC, AND THEY HAVE BOTH PENISES AND OVARIES!
STOP—I CAN'T TAKE ANY MORE...
BUT THIS LONG-NECKED DEER WON'T WORK LIKE THIS...
NO? IT SHOULD BE ABLE TO EAT GRASS, AT LEAST...
I THOUGHT YOU'D SAY THAT,
SO I FOLLOWED YOUR ORIGINAL PROPOSAL AND MADE ONE WITH A 10-METER NECK.
KERCHAK
POKE
WHOA!

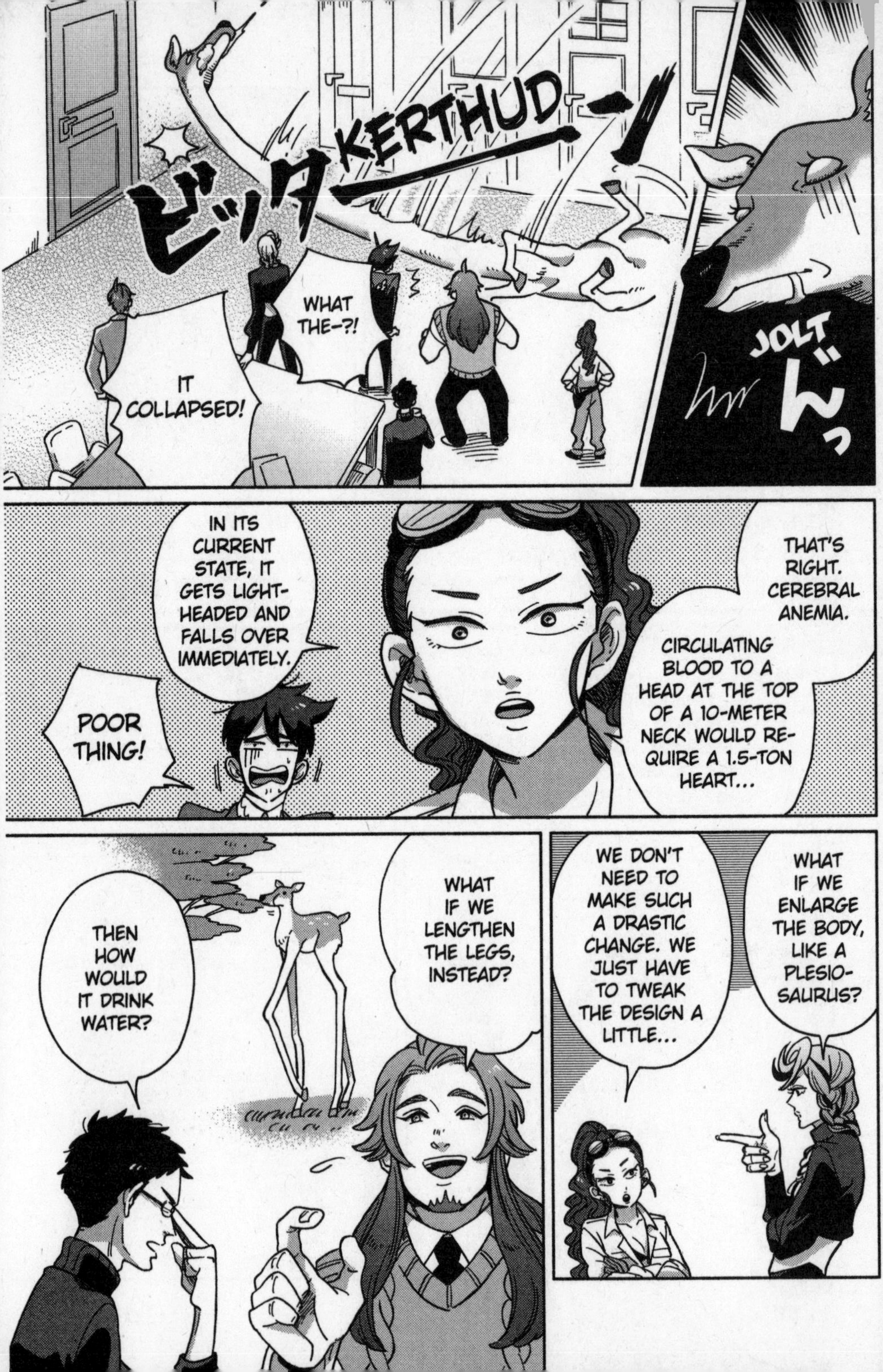
JOLT
ん゛っ
KERTHUD
ビッタ
WHAT THE-?!
IT COLLAPSED!
THAT'S RIGHT. CEREBRAL ANEMIA.
CIRCULATING BLOOD TO A HEAD AT THE TOP OF A 10-METER NECK WOULD RE-QUIRE A 1.5-TON HEART...
IN ITS CURRENT STATE, IT GETS LIGHT-HEADED AND FALLS OVER IMMEDIATELY.
POOR THING!
WHAT IF WE ENLARGE THE BODY, LIKE A PLESIO-SAURUS?
WE DON'T NEED TO MAKE SUCH A DRASTIC CHANGE. WE JUST HAVE TO TWEAK THE DESIGN A LITTLE...
WHAT IF WE LENGTHEN THE LEGS, INSTEAD?
THEN HOW WOULD IT DRINK WATER?

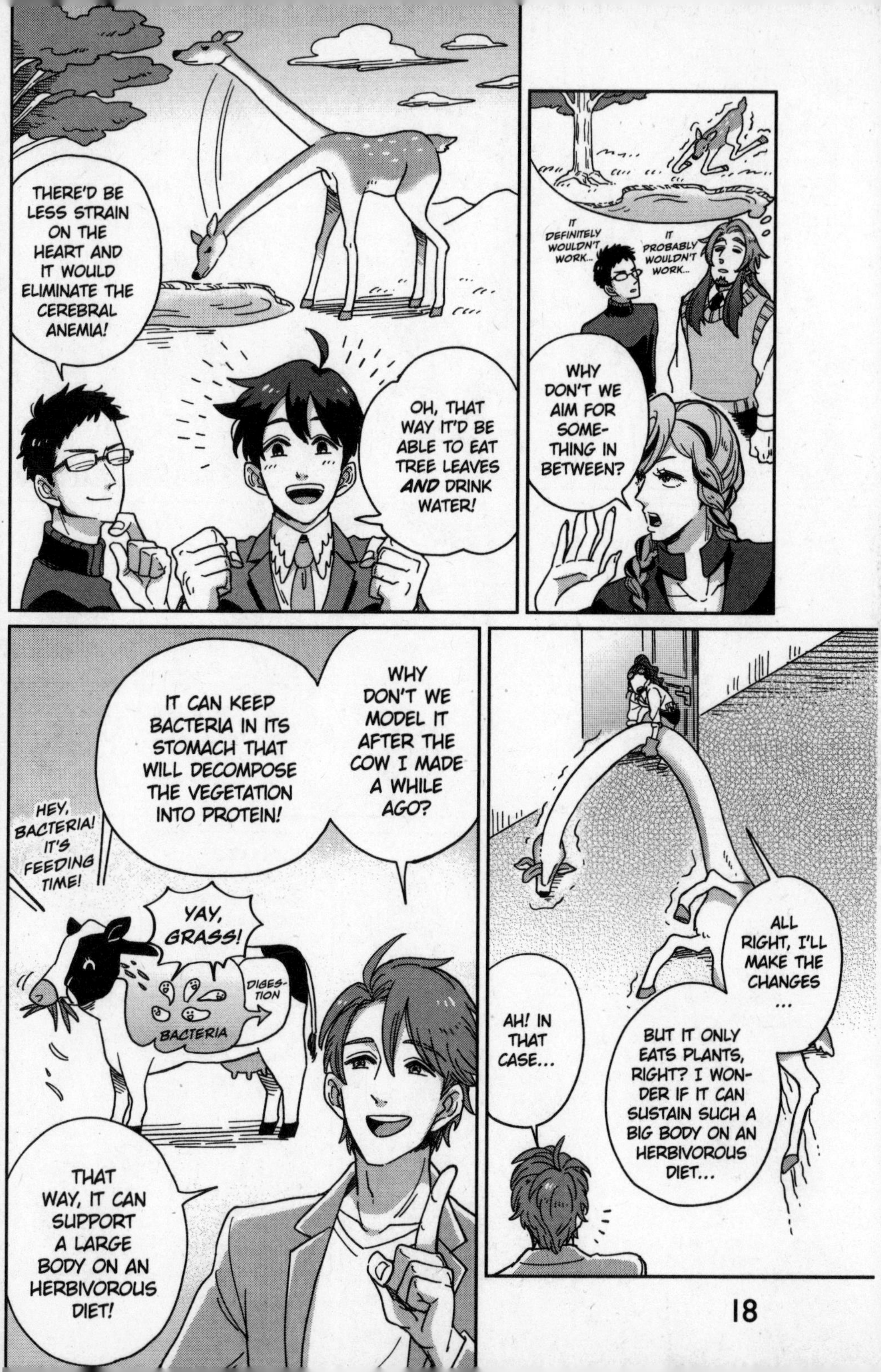
IT PROBABLY WOULDN'T WORK...
IT DEFINITELY WOULDN'T WORK...
WHY DON'T WE AIM FOR SOME-THING IN BETWEEN?
THERE'D BE LESS STRAIN ON THE HEART AND IT WOULD ELIMINATE THE CEREBRAL ANEMIA!
OH, THAT WAY IT'D BE ABLE TO EAT TREE LEAVES **AND** DRINK WATER!
ALL RIGHT, I'LL MAKE THE CHANGES ...
BUT IT ONLY EATS PLANTS, RIGHT? I WON-DER IF IT CAN SUSTAIN SUCH A BIG BODY ON AN HERBIVOROUS DIET...
AH! IN THAT CASE...
WHY DON'T WE MODEL IT AFTER THE COW I MADE A WHILE AGO?
IT CAN KEEP BACTERIA IN ITS STOMACH THAT WILL DECOMPOSE THE VEGETATION INTO PROTEIN!
HEY, BACTERIA! IT'S FEEDING TIME!
YAY, GRASS!
DIGES-TION
BACTERIA
THAT WAY, IT CAN SUPPORT A LARGE BODY ON AN HERBIVOROUS DIET!

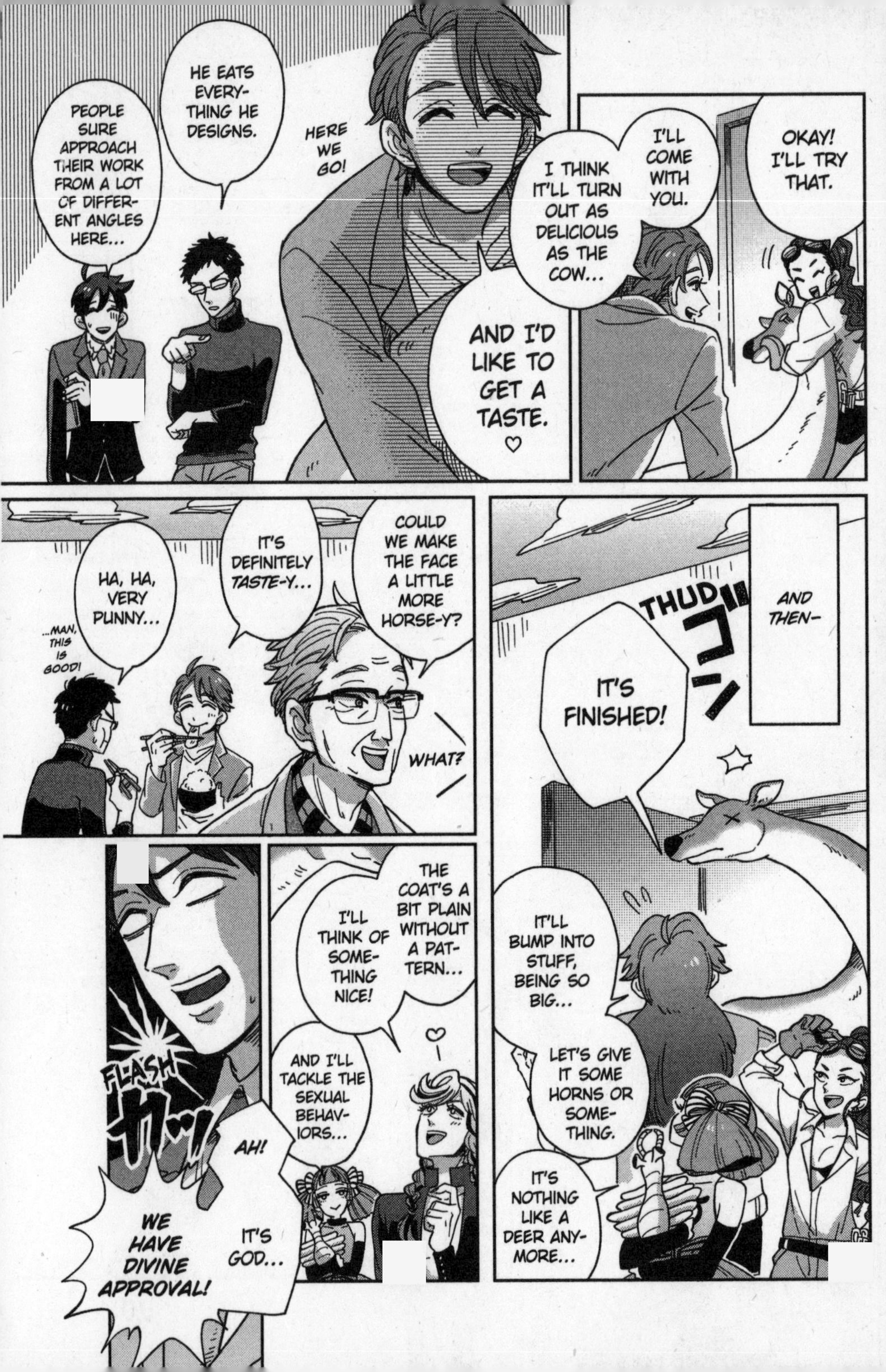
OKAY! I'LL TRY THAT.
I'LL COME WITH YOU.
I THINK IT'LL TURN OUT AS DELICIOUS AS THE COW...
AND I'D LIKE TO GET A TASTE. ♡
HERE WE GO!
HE EATS EVERY-THING HE DESIGNS.
PEOPLE SURE APPROACH THEIR WORK FROM A LOT OF DIFFER-ENT ANGLES HERE...
AND THEN—
THUD
IT'S FINISHED!
IT'LL BUMP INTO STUFF, BEING SO BIG...
LET'S GIVE IT SOME HORNS OR SOME-THING.
IT'S NOTHING LIKE A DEER ANY-MORE...
COULD WE MAKE THE FACE A LITTLE MORE HORSE-Y?
IT'S DEFINITELY *TASTE-Y*...
HA, HA, VERY PUNNY...
...MAN, THIS IS GOOD!
WHAT?
THE COAT'S A BIT PLAIN WITHOUT A PAT-TERN...
I'LL THINK OF SOME-THING NICE!
AND I'LL TACKLE THE SEXUAL BEHAV-IORS...
AH!
IT'S GOD...
FLASH
WE HAVE DIVINE APPROVAL!

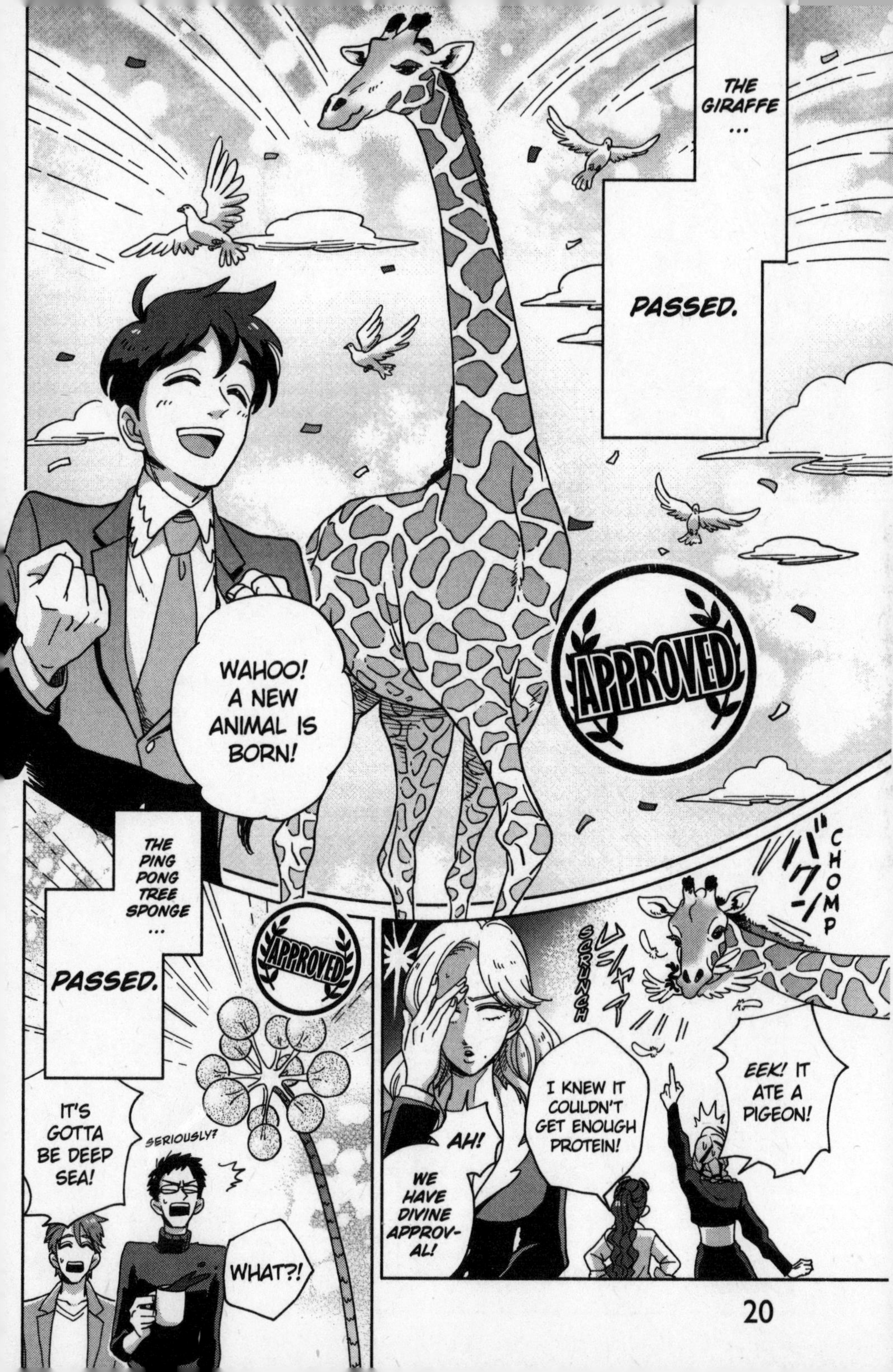
THE GIRAFFE ...
PASSED.
WAHOO! A NEW ANIMAL IS BORN!
APPROVED
CHOMP
SCRUNCH
EEK! IT ATE A PIGEON!
I KNEW IT COULDN'T GET ENOUGH PROTEIN!
AH!
WE HAVE DIVINE APPROV-AL!
THE PING PONG TREE SPONGE ...
PASSED.
APPROVED
IT'S GOTTA BE DEEP SEA!
SERIOUSLY?
WHAT?!

THE ENCYCLOPEDIA OF REAL ANIMALS 01

ANIMAL ENCYCLOPEDIA

ANIMAL 01 | GIRAFFE

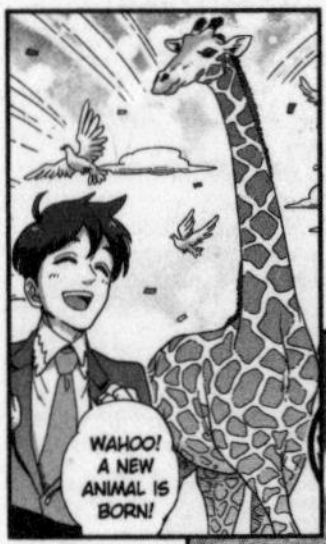
WAHOO! A NEW ANIMAL IS BORN!

THE REAL THING

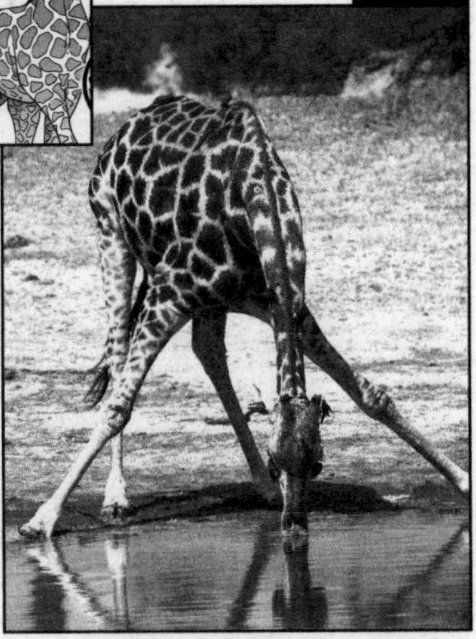

When drinking, a giraffe spreads its front legs to lower its head to the water.
Photo: SIME/Aflo

[Type species] *Giraffa camelopardalis*
[Classification] Class: Mammalia
Order: Artiodactyla
Family: Giraffidae
Genus: *Giraffa*
[Habitat] Savannah
[Height] 4.5-5.5 m (15-18 ft)

Though the giraffe's neck is exceptionally long, it is made up of seven bones, just like a human's. The exact role of the five horn-like structures on the giraffe's head is unknown, though one theory says they prevent the animal from bumping into objects. A study in Tanzania showed that 17 of the 18 courting rituals they observed were between two male giraffes, who often engage in combat by hitting one another with their necks before copulating with each other.

The giraffe has an extremely high blood pressure of 260 mm Hg, which allows blood to circulate to its brain. Valves in the jugular veins that keep blood from flowing backward and specialized capillaries at the back of the head prevent the animal from fainting when lowering or raising its head.

When their herbivorous diet doesn't provide enough protein to sustain their large bodies, giraffes are sometimes known to eat small animals. At the Tama Zoological Park in Tokyo, they have been observed to prey on pigeons.

ANIMAL 02 ACORN BARNACLE

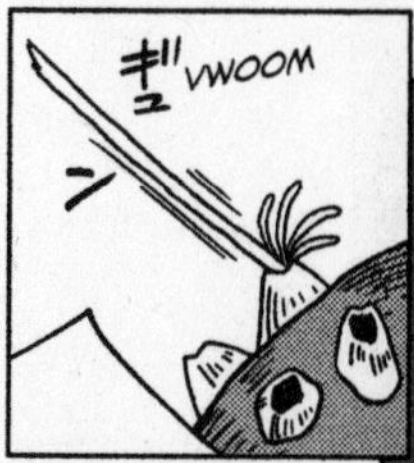
VWOOM

An acorn barnacle extends its legs from its shell to prey on plankton.

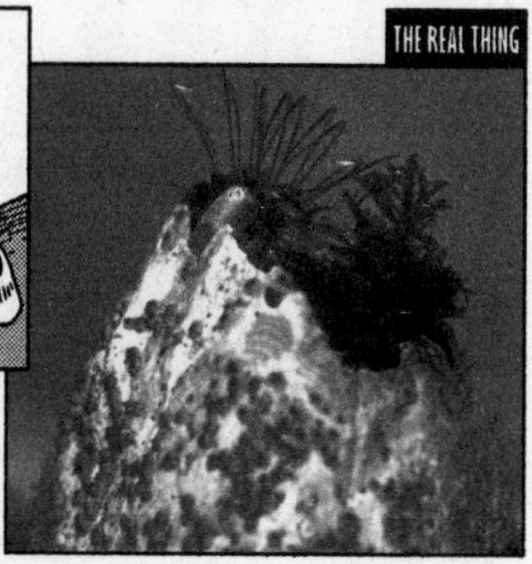
THE REAL THING

Gakken/Aflo

[Name] Acorn barnacle
[Classification] Phylum: Arthropoda
Class: Maxillopoda
Order: Sessilia
Suborder: Balanomorpha
[Habitat] Oceans around the world (They are exclusively marine.)
[Size] Several millimeters to several centimeters

Often mistaken for a type of shellfish, the acorn barnacle is in fact a sessile crustacean and therefore related to shrimp and crabs. They are hermaphroditic but engage in sexual reproduction. These gutsy creatures conquered the drawbacks of mating while immobile by ingeniously extending their penises to reach their partners. It's said that the acorn barnacle's penis can reach as long as eight to 30 times the height of its body, giving it the largest penis-to-body size ratio in the world. There is a length limit, however, and acorn barnacles grow in colonies.

ANIMAL 03 PING PONG TREE SPONGE

Interestingly, this species of sea sponge is carnivorous, and feeds on polychaetes and crustaceans. It attracts prey with the glowing, blue-white globules growing off the top of its trunk-like stem. The surface of these globules has a Velcro-like texture, and the sponge begins digestion once its prey is stuck and unable to move. Because it was discovered relatively recently, few images of this creature exist. On a side note: it is unable to grow or shrink at will.

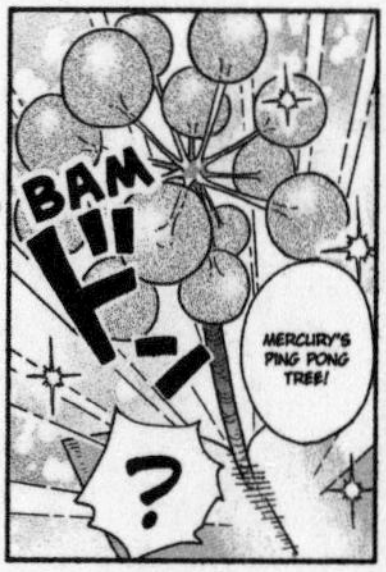
BAM
MERCURY'S PING PONG TREE!
?

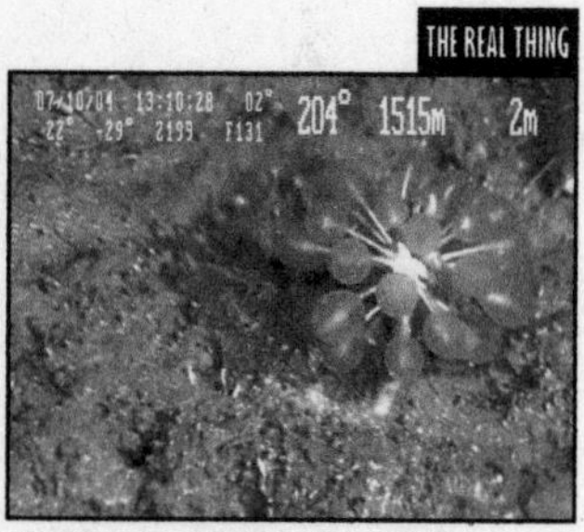
THE REAL THING
204° 1515m 2m

An image taken from video footage shot in October 2007.
Provided by the Japan Agency for Marine-Earth Science and Technology

[Type genus] *Cladorhizidae*
[Classification] Class: Demospongiae
Order: Poecilosclerida
Family: Cladorhizidae
[Habitat] Oceans at depths of 2,600-3,000 m (8,500-9,800 ft)
[Height] 50 cm (20 in)

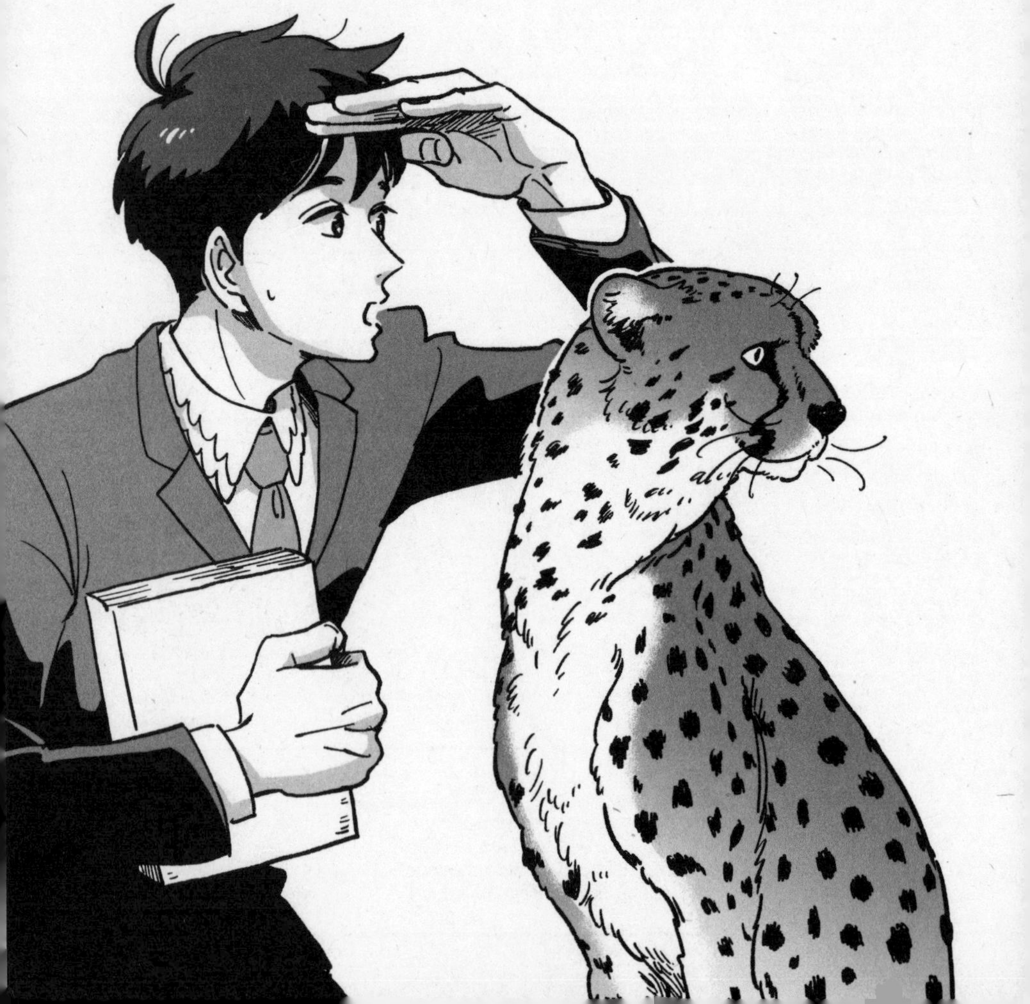

HEAVEN'S
DESIGN TEAM

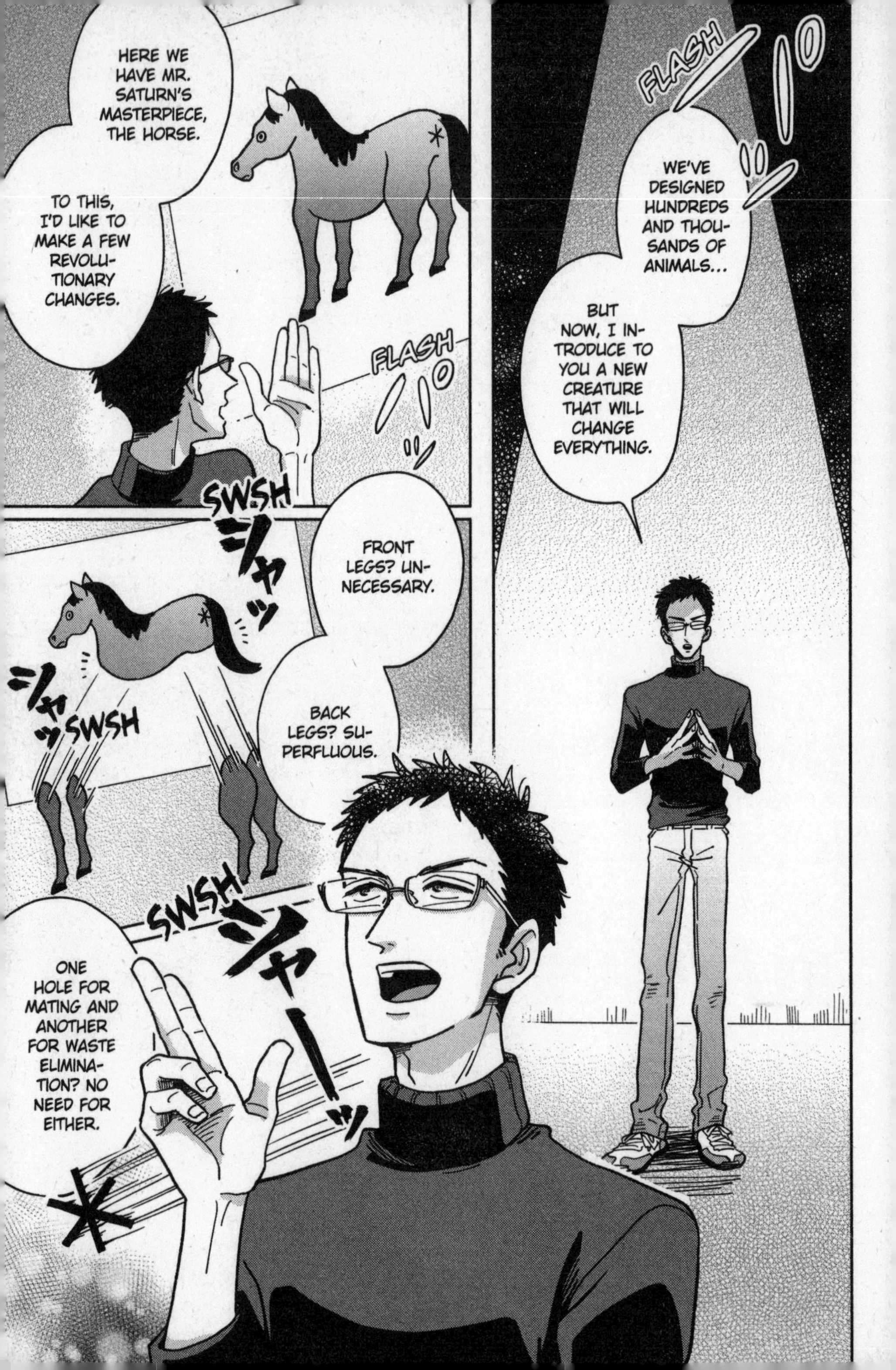
FLASH
WE'VE DESIGNED HUNDREDS AND THOUSANDS OF ANIMALS...
BUT NOW, I INTRODUCE TO YOU A NEW CREATURE THAT WILL CHANGE EVERYTHING.
HERE WE HAVE MR. SATURN'S MASTERPIECE, THE HORSE.
TO THIS, I'D LIKE TO MAKE A FEW REVOLUTIONARY CHANGES.
FLASH
SWSH
シャッ
FRONT LEGS? UNNECESSARY.
シャッ
SWSH
BACK LEGS? SUPERFLUOUS.
SWSH
シャーッ
ONE HOLE FOR MATING AND ANOTHER FOR WASTE ELIMINATION? NO NEED FOR EITHER.

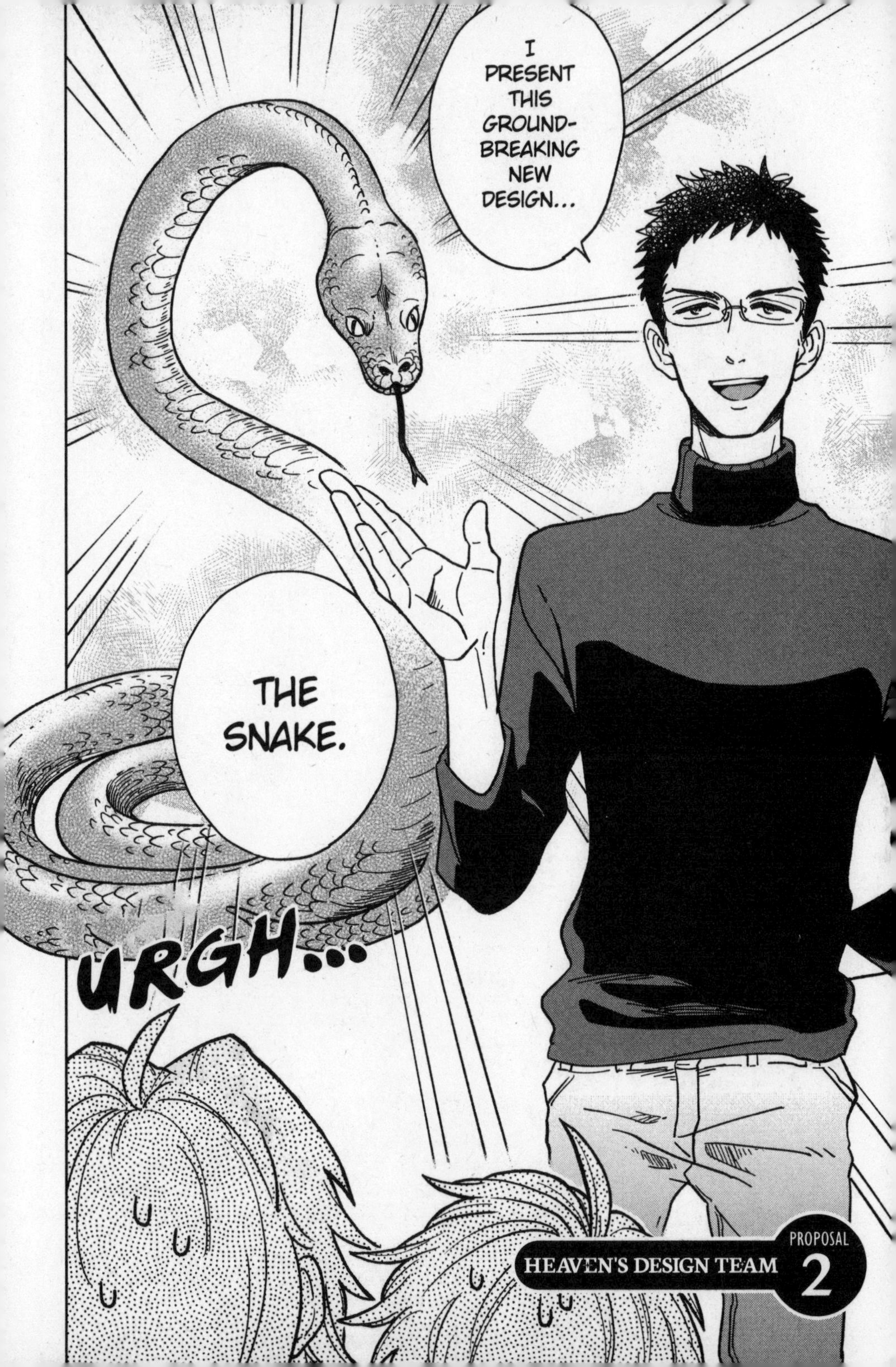
I PRESENT THIS GROUND-BREAKING NEW DESIGN...
THE SNAKE.
URGH...
PROPOSAL 2
HEAVEN'S DESIGN TEAM

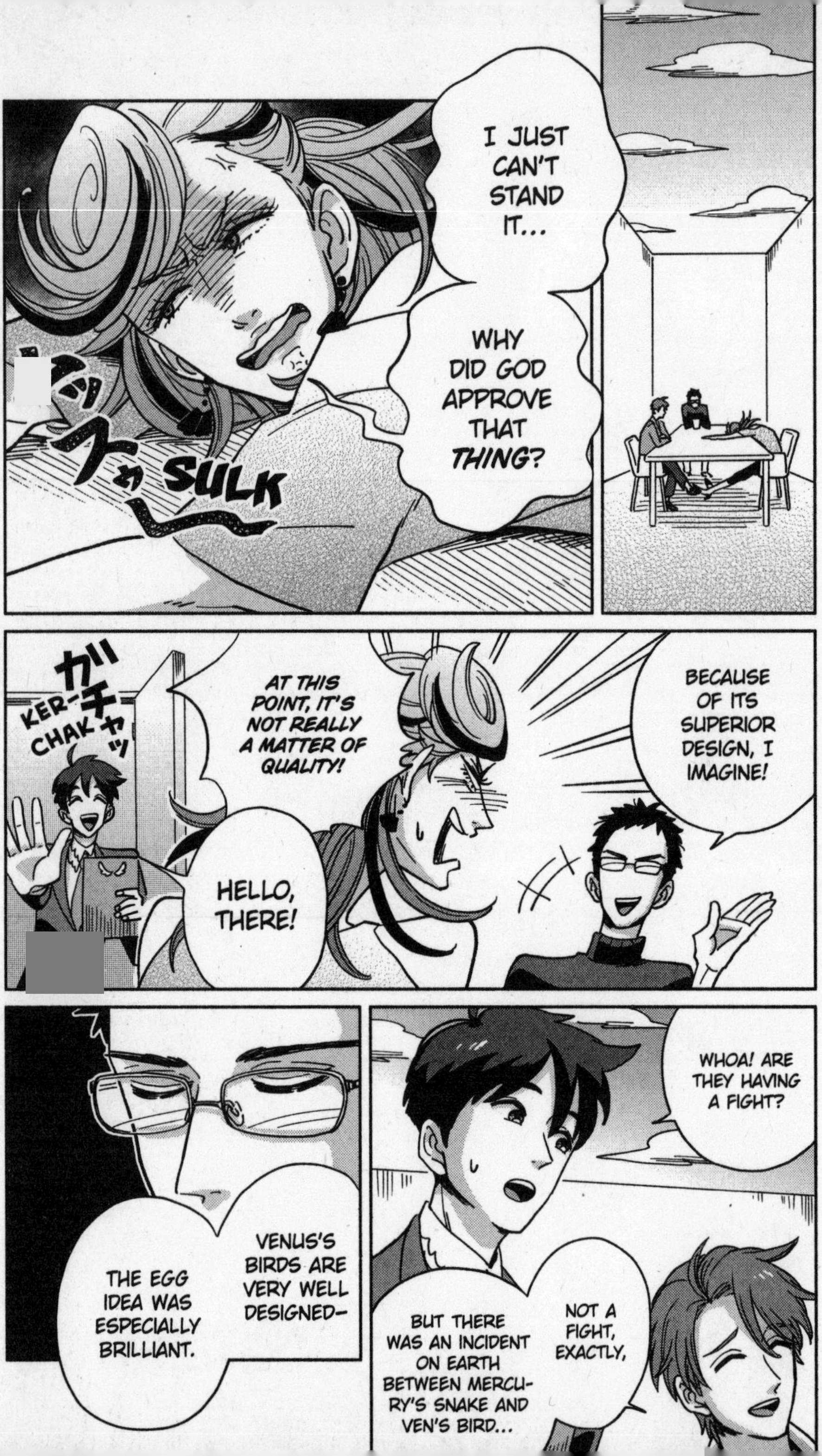
I JUST CAN'T STAND IT...
WHY DID GOD APPROVE THAT *THING*?
SULK
BECAUSE OF ITS SUPERIOR DESIGN, I IMAGINE!
AT THIS POINT, IT'S NOT REALLY A MATTER OF QUALITY!
ガチャッ
KER-CHAK
HELLO, THERE!
WHOA! ARE THEY HAVING A FIGHT?
NOT A FIGHT, EXACTLY,
BUT THERE WAS AN INCIDENT ON EARTH BETWEEN MERCURY'S SNAKE AND VEN'S BIRD...
VENUS'S BIRDS ARE VERY WELL DESIGNED—
THE EGG IDEA WAS ESPECIALLY BRILLIANT.

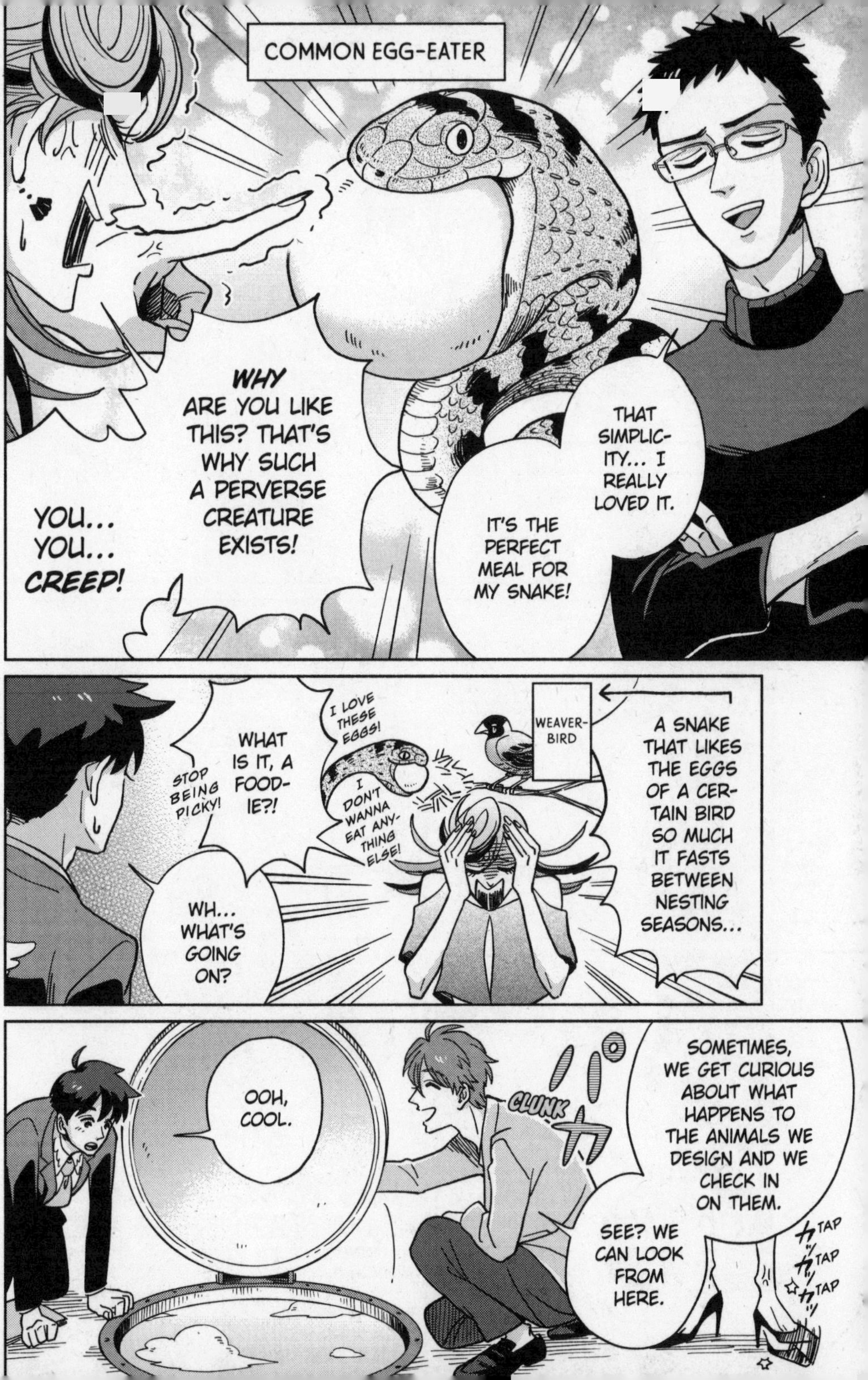
COMMON EGG-EATER
THAT SIMPLICITY... I REALLY LOVED IT.
IT'S THE PERFECT MEAL FOR MY SNAKE!
WHY ARE YOU LIKE THIS? THAT'S WHY SUCH A PERVERSE CREATURE EXISTS!
YOU... YOU... CREEP!
A SNAKE THAT LIKES THE EGGS OF A CERTAIN BIRD SO MUCH IT FASTS BETWEEN NESTING SEASONS...
WEAVER-BIRD
I LOVE THESE EGGS!
I DON'T WANNA EAT ANYTHING ELSE!
WHAT IS IT, A FOODIE?!
STOP BEING PICKY!
WH... WHAT'S GOING ON?
SOMETIMES, WE GET CURIOUS ABOUT WHAT HAPPENS TO THE ANIMALS WE DESIGN AND WE CHECK IN ON THEM.
SEE? WE CAN LOOK FROM HERE.
TAP TAP TAP
CLUNK
OOH, COOL.

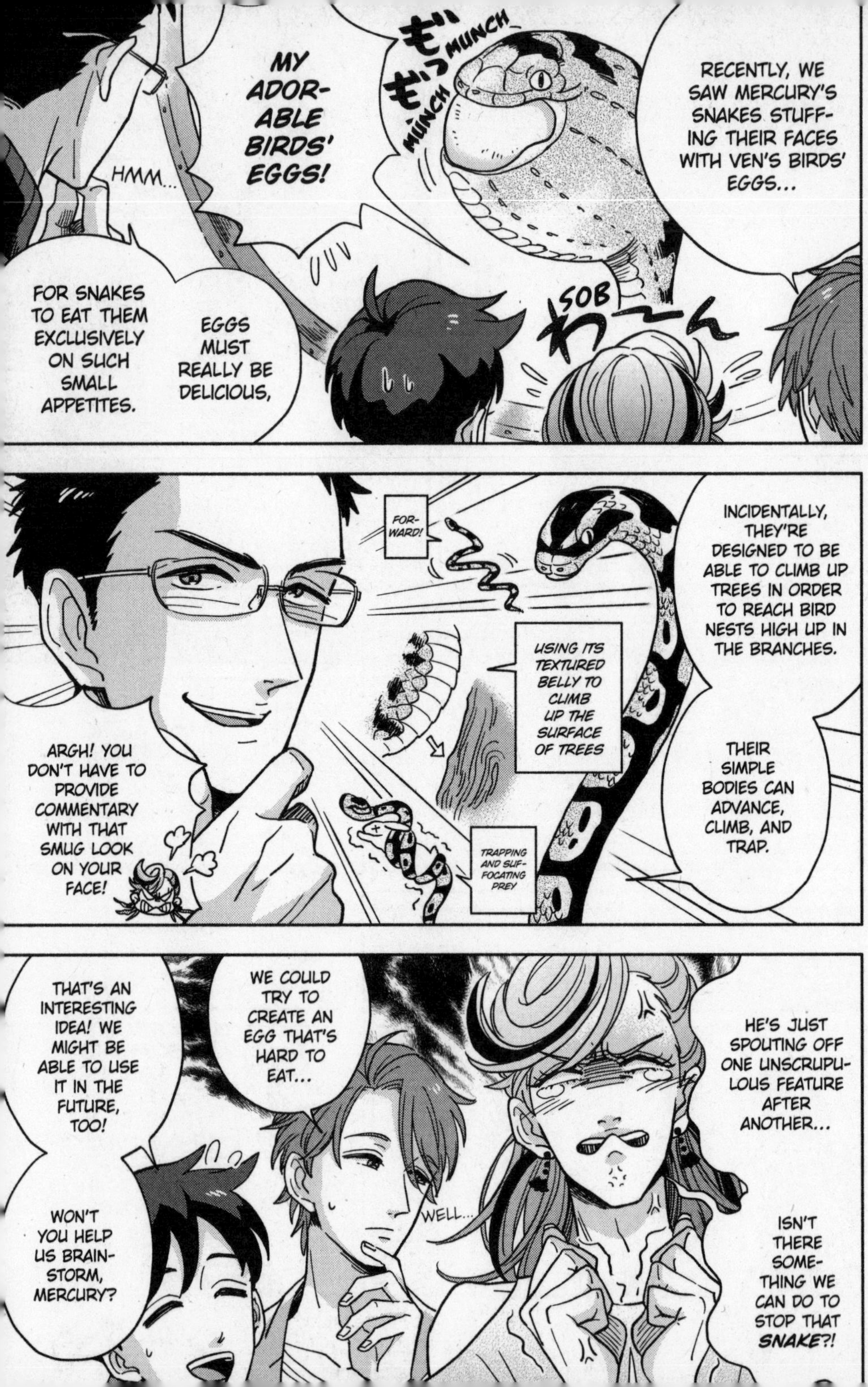
RECENTLY, WE SAW MERCURY'S SNAKES STUFFING THEIR FACES WITH VEN'S BIRDS' EGGS...
MUNCH MUNCH
MY ADORABLE BIRDS' EGGS!
SOB
HMM...
EGGS MUST REALLY BE DELICIOUS,
FOR SNAKES TO EAT THEM EXCLUSIVELY ON SUCH SMALL APPETITES.
INCIDENTALLY, THEY'RE DESIGNED TO BE ABLE TO CLIMB UP TREES IN ORDER TO REACH BIRD NESTS HIGH UP IN THE BRANCHES.
THEIR SIMPLE BODIES CAN ADVANCE, CLIMB, AND TRAP.
FORWARD!
USING ITS TEXTURED BELLY TO CLIMB UP THE SURFACE OF TREES
TRAPPING AND SUFFOCATING PREY
ARGH! YOU DON'T HAVE TO PROVIDE COMMENTARY WITH THAT SMUG LOOK ON YOUR FACE!
HE'S JUST SPOUTING OFF ONE UNSCRUPULOUS FEATURE AFTER ANOTHER...
ISN'T THERE SOMETHING WE CAN DO TO STOP THAT SNAKE?!
WE COULD TRY TO CREATE AN EGG THAT'S HARD TO EAT...
THAT'S AN INTERESTING IDEA! WE MIGHT BE ABLE TO USE IT IN THE FUTURE, TOO!
WELL...
WON'T YOU HELP US BRAINSTORM, MERCURY?

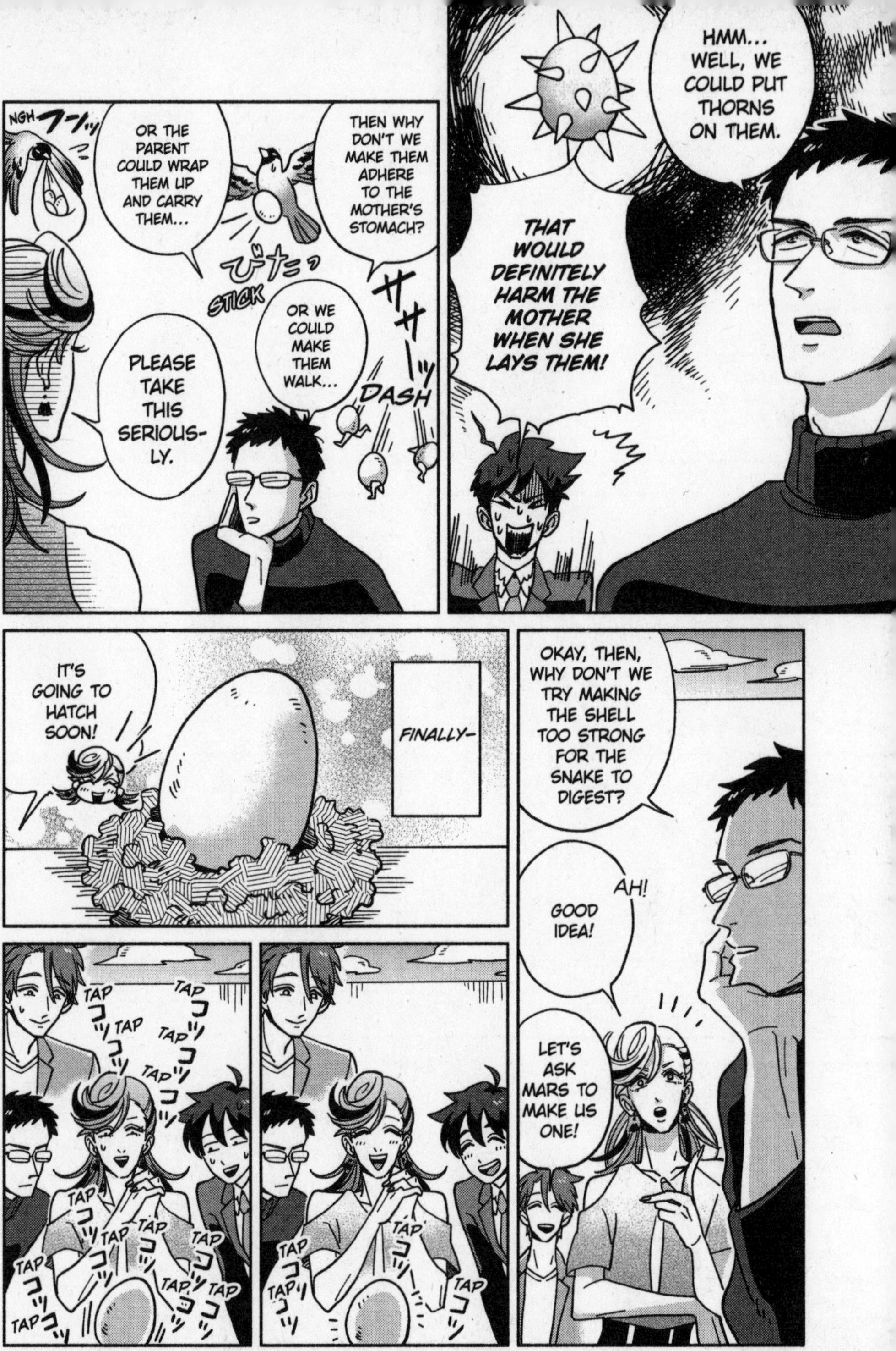
HMM... WELL, WE COULD PUT THORNS ON THEM.
THAT WOULD DEFINITELY HARM THE MOTHER WHEN SHE LAYS THEM!
THEN WHY DON'T WE MAKE THEM ADHERE TO THE MOTHER'S STOMACH?
ぴたっ
STICK
OR THE PARENT COULD WRAP THEM UP AND CARRY THEM...
フーッ
NGH
OR WE COULD MAKE THEM WALK...
ササーッ
DASH
PLEASE TAKE THIS SERIOUS-LY.
OKAY, THEN, WHY DON'T WE TRY MAKING THE SHELL TOO STRONG FOR THE SNAKE TO DIGEST?
AH!
GOOD IDEA!
LET'S ASK MARS TO MAKE US ONE!
FINALLY-
IT'S GOING TO HATCH SOON!
TAP TAP TAP TAP TAP TAP TAP TAP TAP TAP TAP TAP
TAP TAP TAP TAP

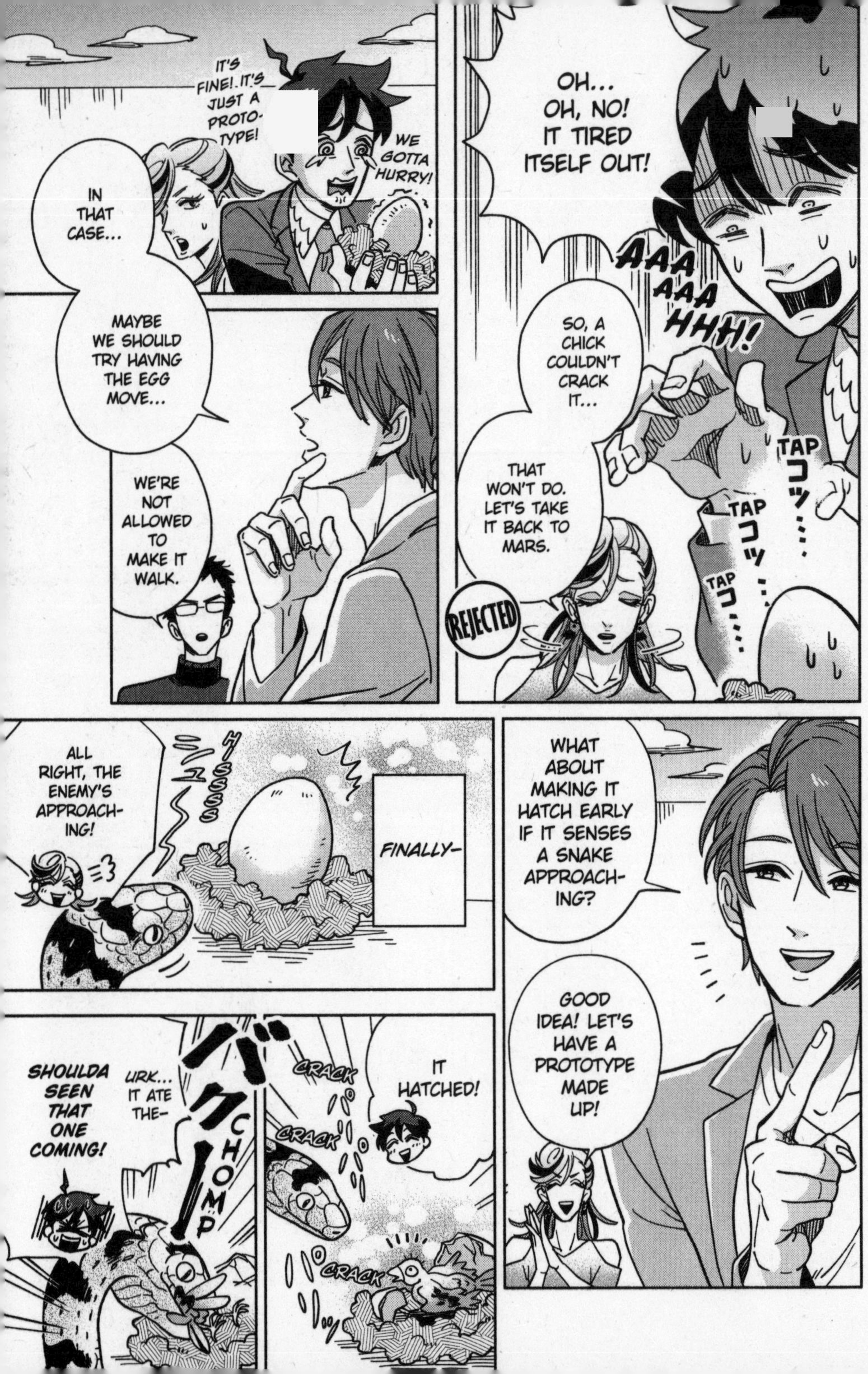

OH... OH, NO! IT TIRED ITSELF OUT!
AAAAAAHHH!
SO, A CHICK COULDN'T CRACK IT...
THAT WON'T DO. LET'S TAKE IT BACK TO MARS.
REJECTED
TAP コッ...
TAP コッ...
TAP コ...
IT'S FINE! IT'S JUST A PROTO-TYPE!
WE GOTTA HURRY!
IN THAT CASE...
MAYBE WE SHOULD TRY HAVING THE EGG MOVE...
WE'RE NOT ALLOWED TO MAKE IT WALK.
WHAT ABOUT MAKING IT HATCH EARLY IF IT SENSES A SNAKE APPROACHING?
GOOD IDEA! LET'S HAVE A PROTOTYPE MADE UP!
FINALLY-
HISSSS
ALL RIGHT, THE ENEMY'S APPROACHING!
CRACK
CRACK
IT HATCHED!
CRACK
CHOMP
URK... IT ATE THE-
SHOULDA SEEN THAT ONE COMING!

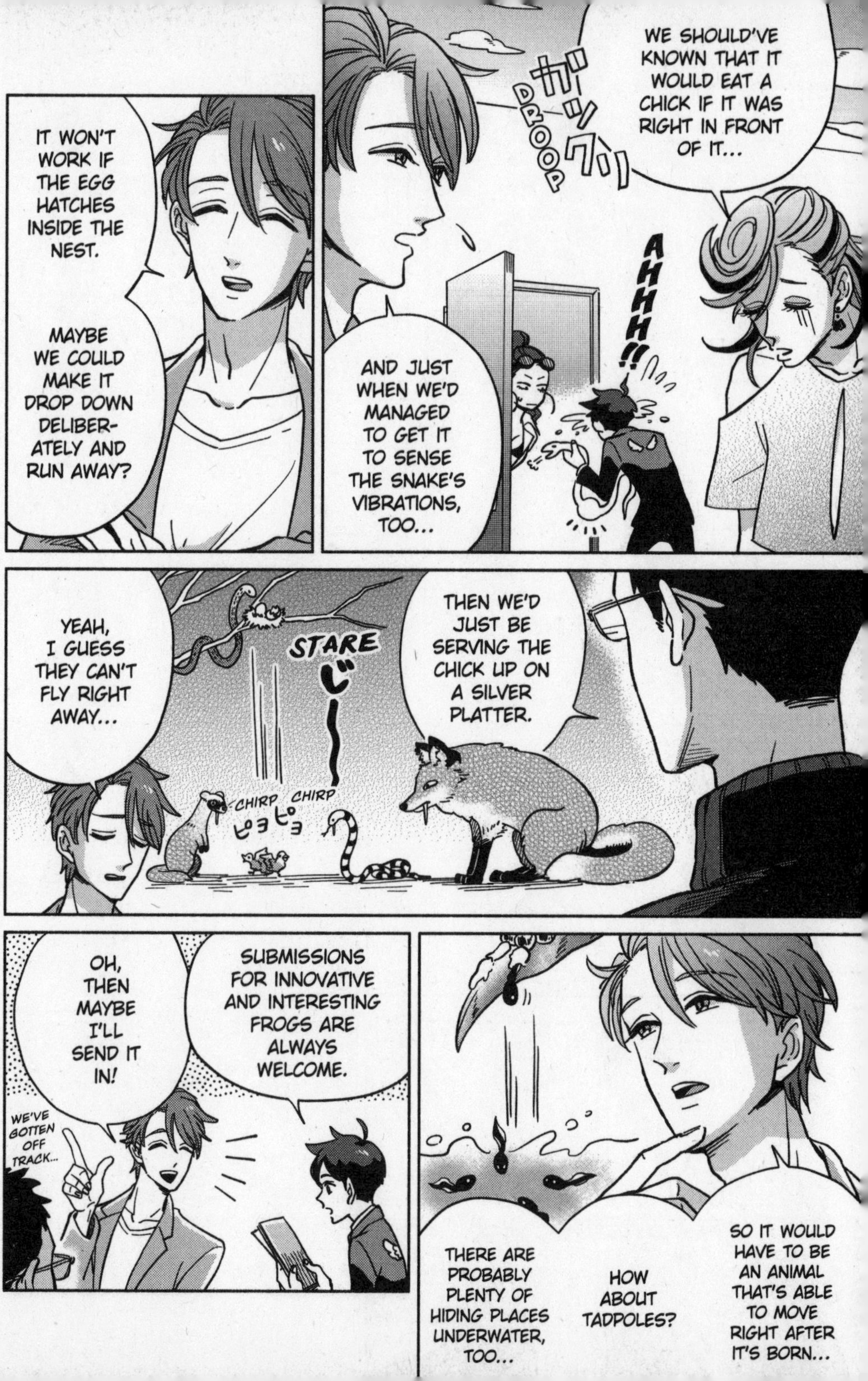
WE SHOULD'VE KNOWN THAT IT WOULD EAT A CHICK IF IT WAS RIGHT IN FRONT OF IT...
ガックリ
DROOP
AHHHH!!
AND JUST WHEN WE'D MANAGED TO GET IT TO SENSE THE SNAKE'S VIBRATIONS, TOO...
IT WON'T WORK IF THE EGG HATCHES INSIDE THE NEST.
MAYBE WE COULD MAKE IT DROP DOWN DELIBERATELY AND RUN AWAY?
THEN WE'D JUST BE SERVING THE CHICK UP ON A SILVER PLATTER.
STARE
じー
CHIRP CHIRP
ピヨピヨ
YEAH, I GUESS THEY CAN'T FLY RIGHT AWAY...
SO IT WOULD HAVE TO BE AN ANIMAL THAT'S ABLE TO MOVE RIGHT AFTER IT'S BORN...
HOW ABOUT TADPOLES?
THERE ARE PROBABLY PLENTY OF HIDING PLACES UNDERWATER, TOO...
SUBMISSIONS FOR INNOVATIVE AND INTERESTING FROGS ARE ALWAYS WELCOME.
OH, THEN MAYBE I'LL SEND IT IN!
WE'VE GOTTEN OFF TRACK...

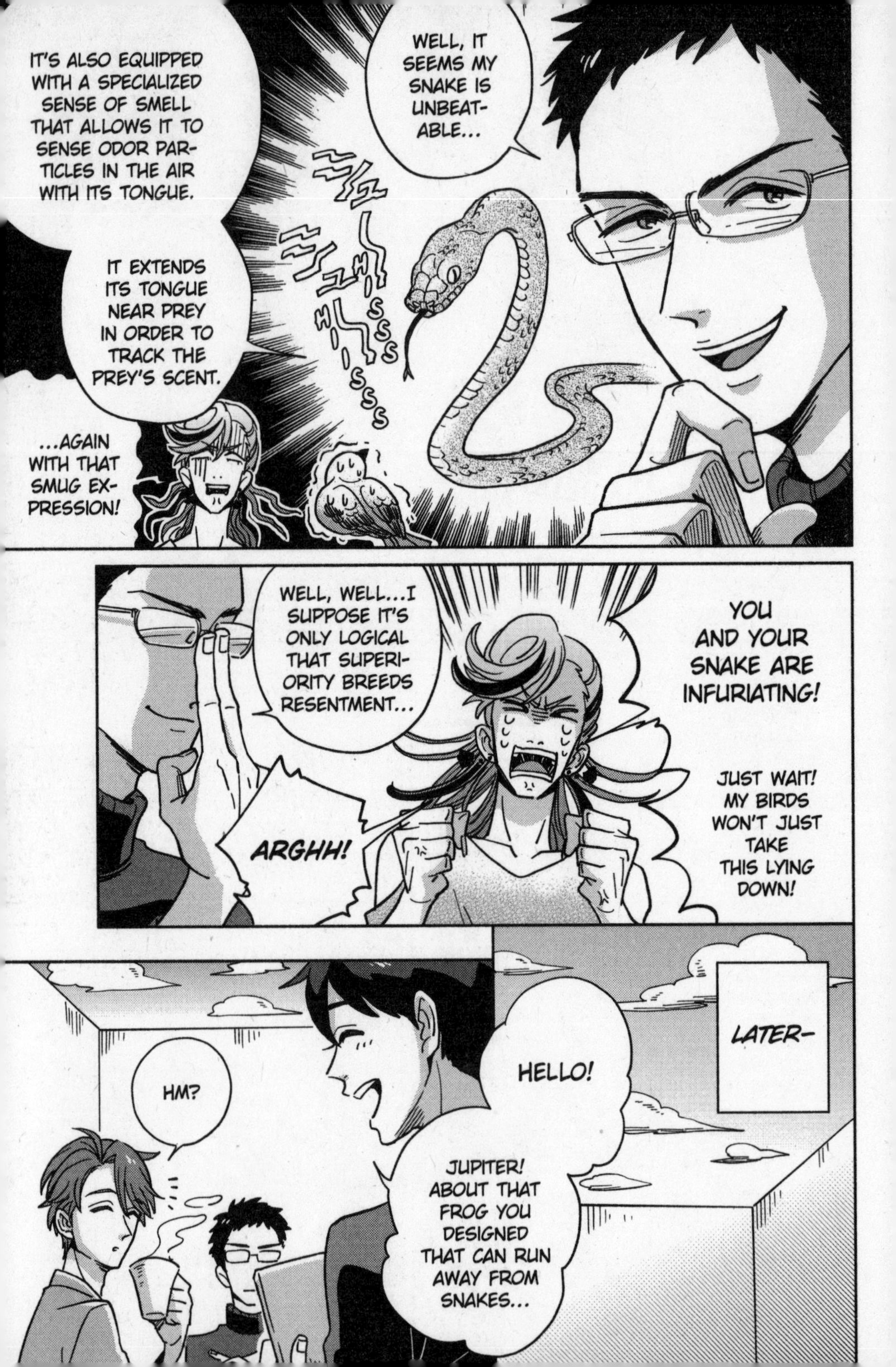
WELL, IT SEEMS MY SNAKE IS UNBEAT-ABLE...
IT'S ALSO EQUIPPED WITH A SPECIALIZED SENSE OF SMELL THAT ALLOWS IT TO SENSE ODOR PAR-TICLES IN THE AIR WITH ITS TONGUE.
IT EXTENDS ITS TONGUE NEAR PREY IN ORDER TO TRACK THE PREY'S SCENT.
HISSS HISSS
...AGAIN WITH THAT SMUG EX-PRESSION!
YOU AND YOUR SNAKE ARE INFURIATING!
JUST WAIT! MY BIRDS WON'T JUST TAKE THIS LYING DOWN!
ARGHH!
WELL, WELL...I SUPPOSE IT'S ONLY LOGICAL THAT SUPERI-ORITY BREEDS RESENTMENT...
LATER-
HELLO!
JUPITER! ABOUT THAT FROG YOU DESIGNED THAT CAN RUN AWAY FROM SNAKES...
HM?

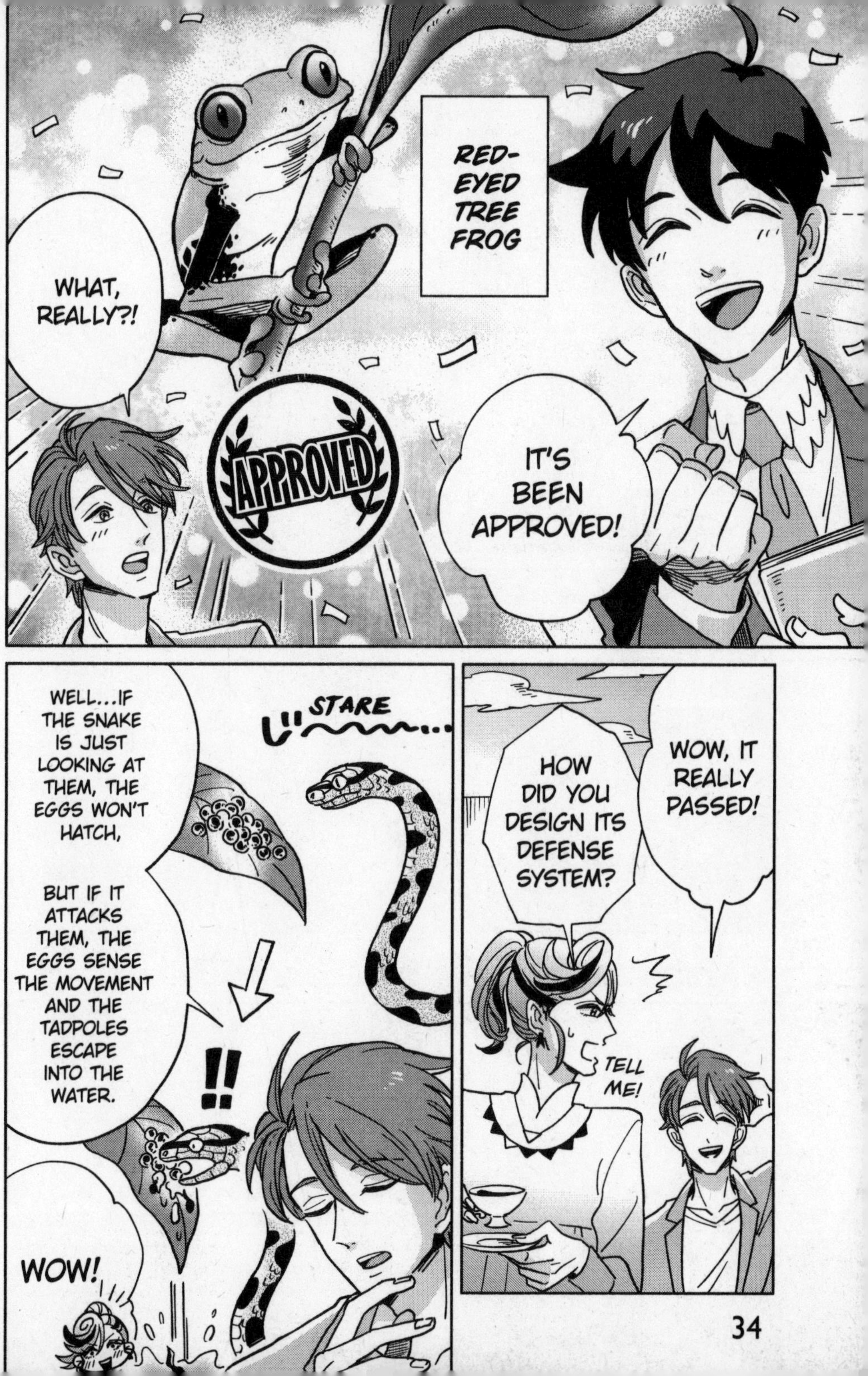
RED-EYED TREE FROG
IT'S BEEN APPROVED!
APPROVED
WHAT, REALLY?!
WOW, IT REALLY PASSED!
HOW DID YOU DESIGN ITS DEFENSE SYSTEM?
TELL ME!
STARE
WELL...IF THE SNAKE IS JUST LOOKING AT THEM, THE EGGS WON'T HATCH,
BUT IF IT ATTACKS THEM, THE EGGS SENSE THE MOVEMENT AND THE TADPOLES ESCAPE INTO THE WATER.
!!
WOW!

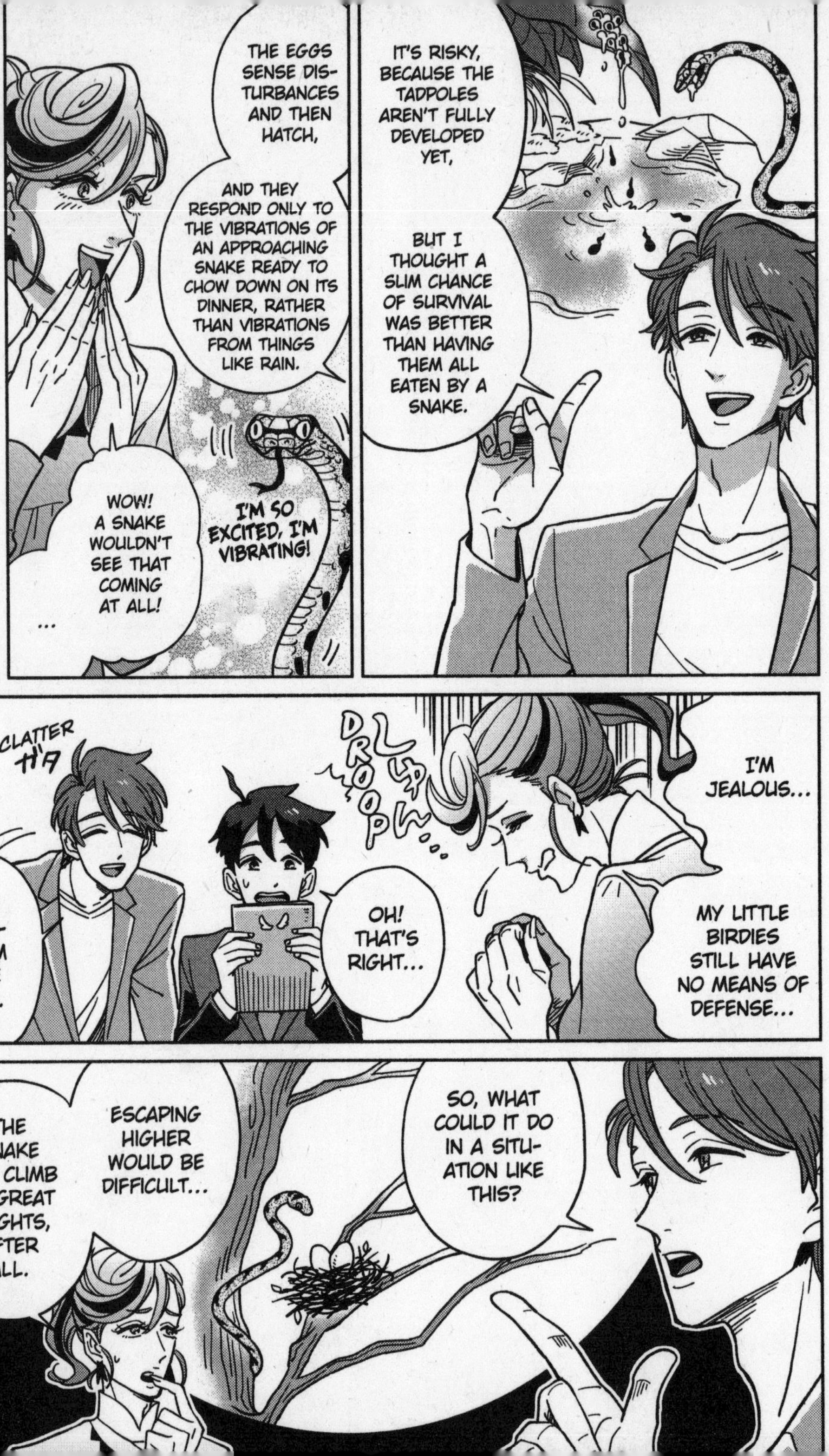
IT'S RISKY, BECAUSE THE TADPOLES AREN'T FULLY DEVELOPED YET,
BUT I THOUGHT A SLIM CHANCE OF SURVIVAL WAS BETTER THAN HAVING THEM ALL EATEN BY A SNAKE.
THE EGGS SENSE DISTURBANCES AND THEN HATCH,
AND THEY RESPOND ONLY TO THE VIBRATIONS OF AN APPROACHING SNAKE READY TO CHOW DOWN ON ITS DINNER, RATHER THAN VIBRATIONS FROM THINGS LIKE RAIN.
I'M SO EXCITED, I'M VIBRATING!
WOW! A SNAKE WOULDN'T SEE THAT COMING AT ALL!
...
I'M JEALOUS...
MY LITTLE BIRDIES STILL HAVE NO MEANS OF DEFENSE...
DROOP
しゅん
OH! THAT'S RIGHT...
CLATTER
ガタ
LET'S BRAINSTORM SOME MORE.
SO, WHAT COULD IT DO IN A SITUATION LIKE THIS?
ESCAPING HIGHER WOULD BE DIFFICULT...
THE SNAKE CAN CLIMB TO GREAT HEIGHTS, AFTER ALL.

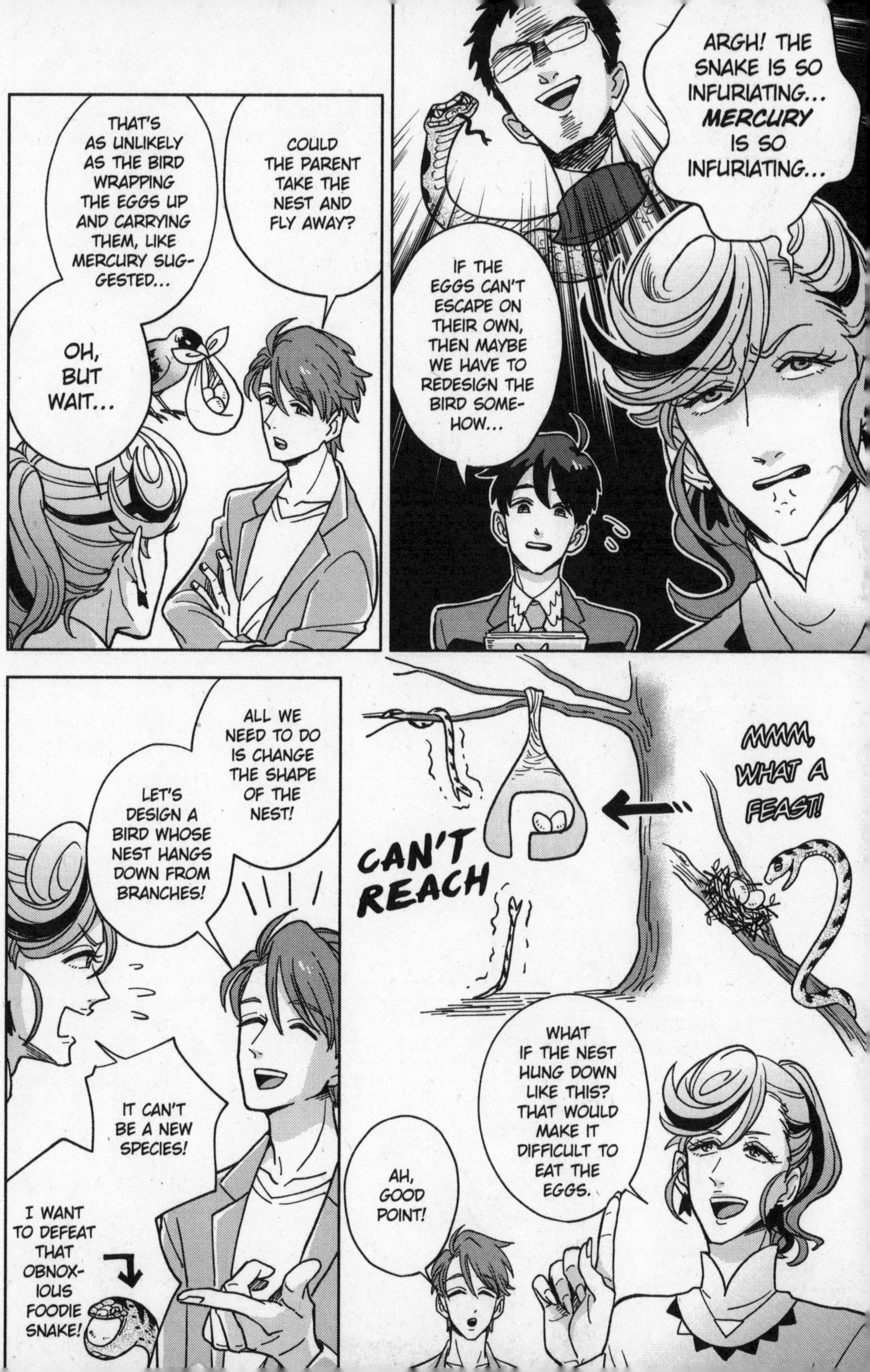
ARGH! THE SNAKE IS SO INFURIATING... **MERCURY** IS SO INFURIATING...
IF THE EGGS CAN'T ESCAPE ON THEIR OWN, THEN MAYBE WE HAVE TO REDESIGN THE BIRD SOMEHOW...
COULD THE PARENT TAKE THE NEST AND FLY AWAY?
THAT'S AS UNLIKELY AS THE BIRD WRAPPING THE EGGS UP AND CARRYING THEM, LIKE MERCURY SUGGESTED...
OH, BUT WAIT...
MMM, WHAT A FEAST!
CAN'T REACH
WHAT IF THE NEST HUNG DOWN LIKE THIS? THAT WOULD MAKE IT DIFFICULT TO EAT THE EGGS.
AH, GOOD POINT!
ALL WE NEED TO DO IS CHANGE THE SHAPE OF THE NEST!
LET'S DESIGN A BIRD WHOSE NEST HANGS DOWN FROM BRANCHES!
IT CAN'T BE A NEW SPECIES!
I WANT TO DEFEAT THAT OBNOXIOUS FOODIE SNAKE!

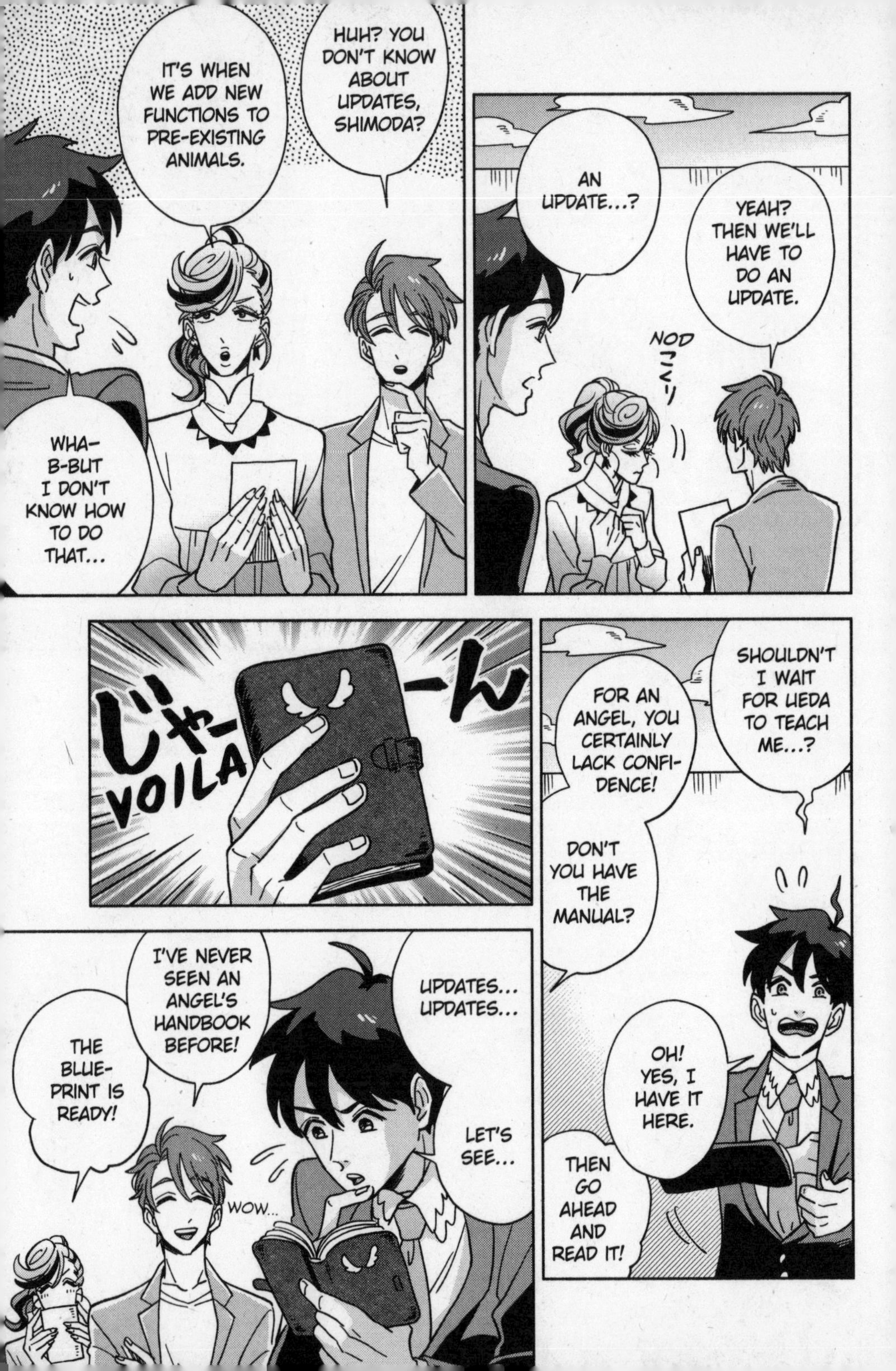
AN UPDATE...?
YEAH? THEN WE'LL HAVE TO DO AN UPDATE.
NOD
コクッ
HUH? YOU DON'T KNOW ABOUT UPDATES, SHIMODA?
IT'S WHEN WE ADD NEW FUNCTIONS TO PRE-EXISTING ANIMALS.
WHA- B-BUT I DON'T KNOW HOW TO DO THAT...
SHOULDN'T I WAIT FOR UEDA TO TEACH ME...?
FOR AN ANGEL, YOU CERTAINLY LACK CONFI-DENCE!
DON'T YOU HAVE THE MANUAL?
OH! YES, I HAVE IT HERE.
THEN GO AHEAD AND READ IT!
じゃーん
VOILA
UPDATES... UPDATES...
I'VE NEVER SEEN AN ANGEL'S HANDBOOK BEFORE!
THE BLUE-PRINT IS READY!
LET'S SEE...
WOW...

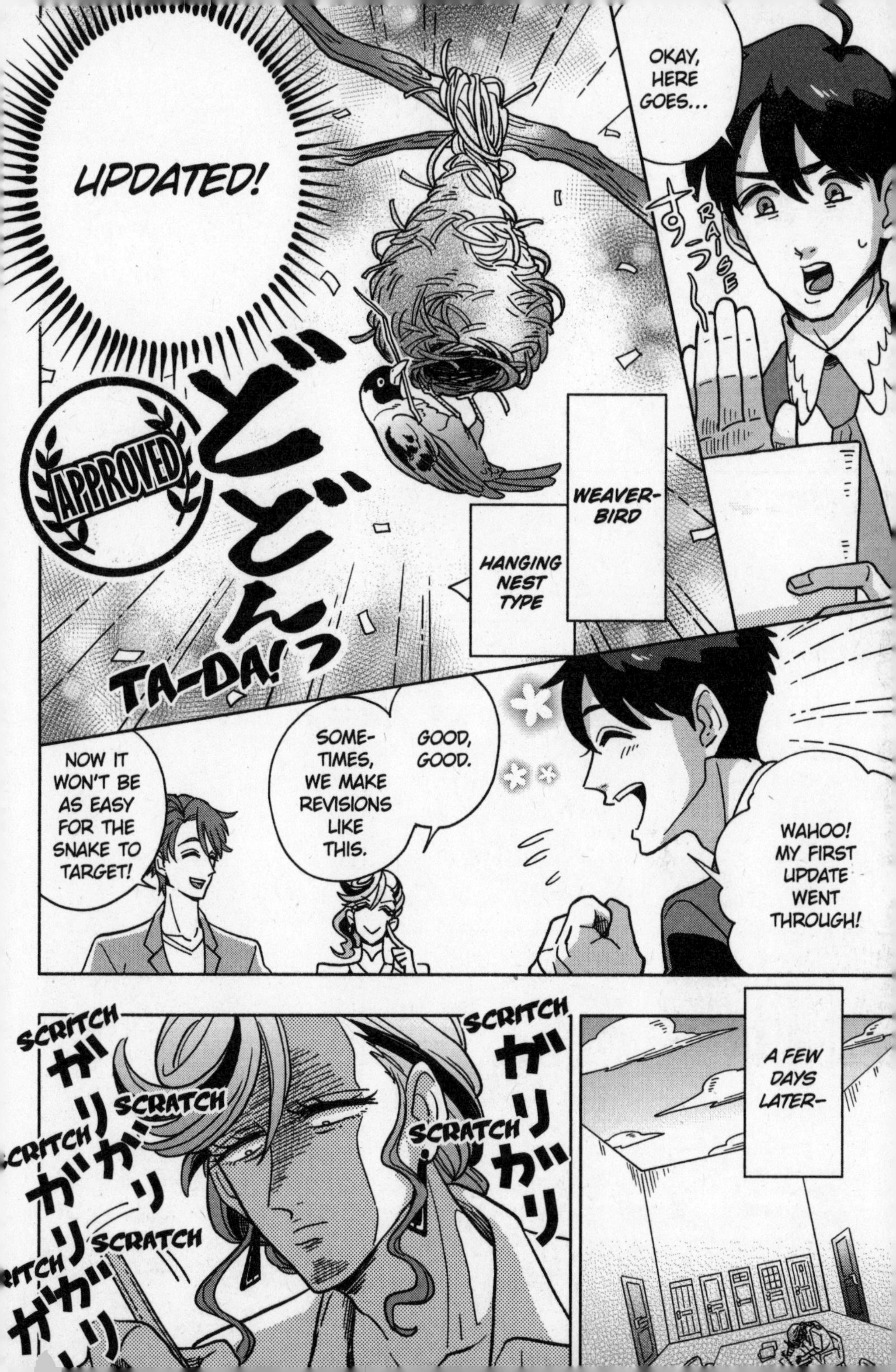
OKAY, HERE GOES...
RAISE
UPDATED!
WEAVER-BIRD
HANGING NEST TYPE
APPROVED
どどんっ
TA-DA!
WAHOO! MY FIRST UPDATE WENT THROUGH!
GOOD, GOOD.
SOME-TIMES, WE MAKE REVISIONS LIKE THIS.
NOW IT WON'T BE AS EASY FOR THE SNAKE TO TARGET!
A FEW DAYS LATER–
SCRITCH
ガリガリ
SCRATCH
SCRITCH
SCRATCH
SCRITCH
SCRATCH
SCRITCH

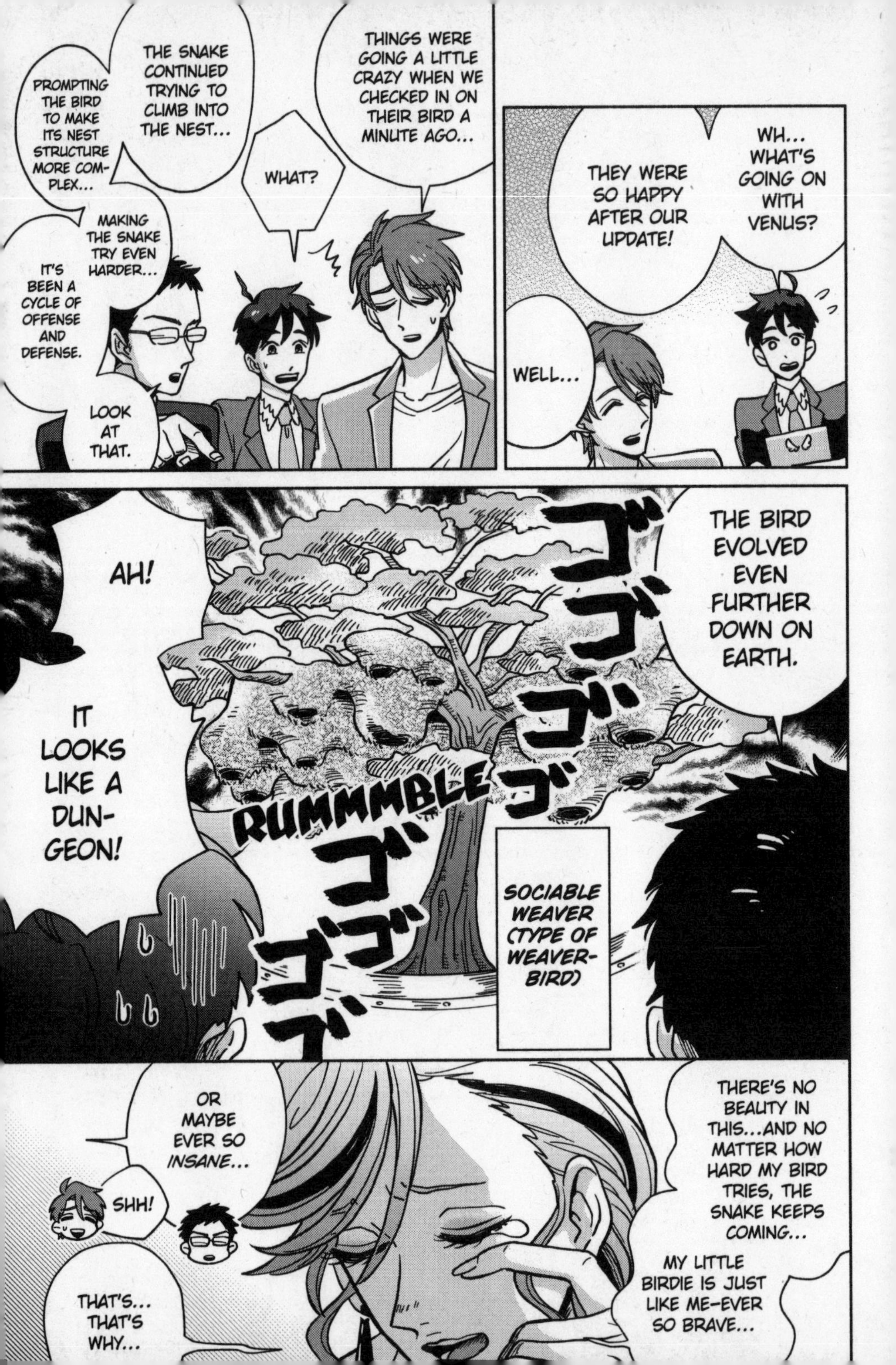
WH... WHAT'S GOING ON WITH VENUS?
THEY WERE SO HAPPY AFTER OUR UPDATE!
WELL...
THINGS WERE GOING A LITTLE CRAZY WHEN WE CHECKED IN ON THEIR BIRD A MINUTE AGO...
WHAT?
THE SNAKE CONTINUED TRYING TO CLIMB INTO THE NEST...
PROMPTING THE BIRD TO MAKE ITS NEST STRUCTURE MORE COM-PLEX...
MAKING THE SNAKE TRY EVEN HARDER...
IT'S BEEN A CYCLE OF OFFENSE AND DEFENSE.
LOOK AT THAT.
THE BIRD EVOLVED EVEN FURTHER DOWN ON EARTH.
ゴゴゴゴ
RUMMMBLE
ゴゴゴゴ
SOCIABLE WEAVER (TYPE OF WEAVER-BIRD)
AH!
IT LOOKS LIKE A DUN-GEON!
THERE'S NO BEAUTY IN THIS...AND NO MATTER HOW HARD MY BIRD TRIES, THE SNAKE KEEPS COMING...
MY LITTLE BIRDIE IS JUST LIKE ME—EVER SO BRAVE...
OR MAYBE EVER SO INSANE...
SHH!
THAT'S... THAT'S WHY...

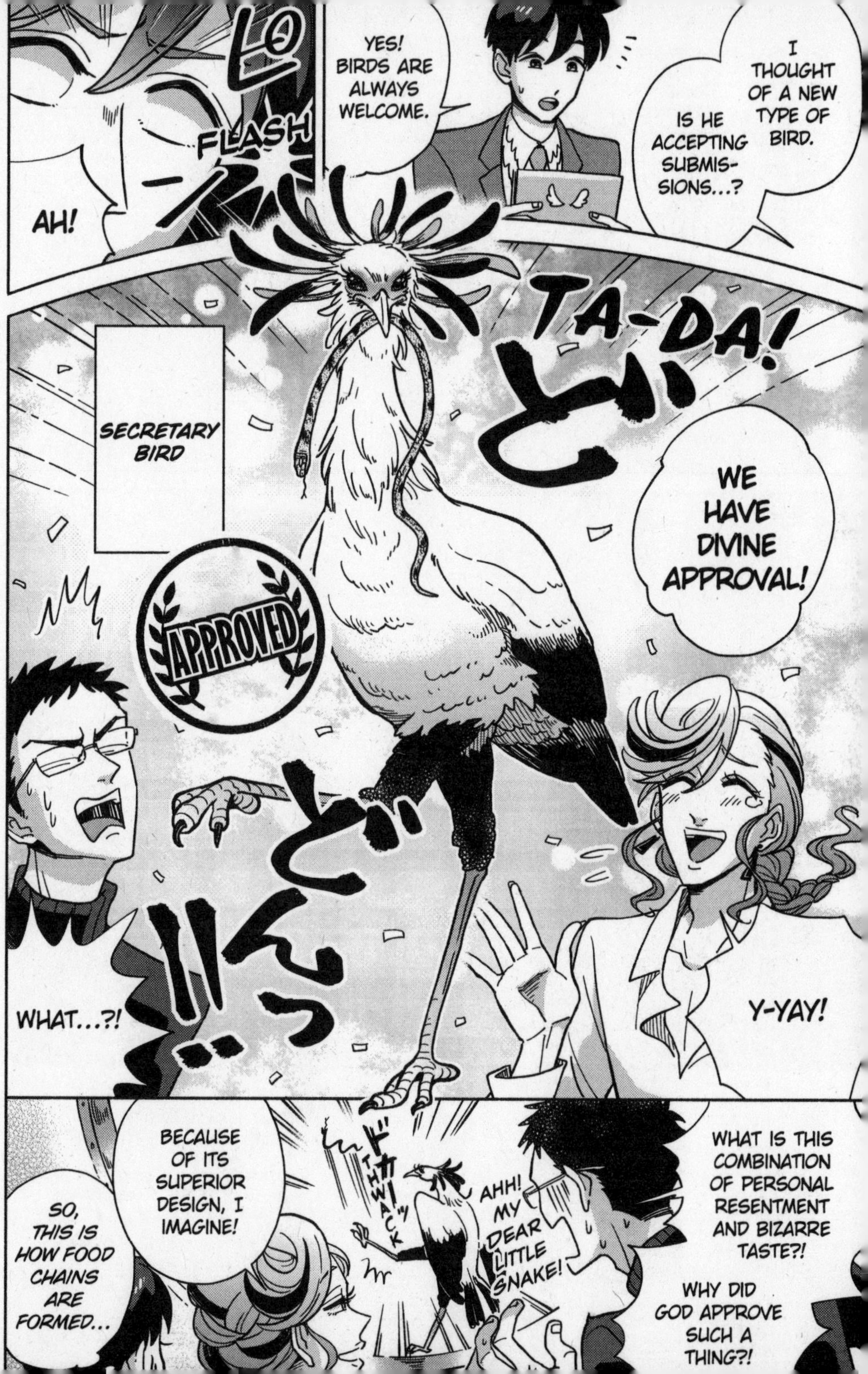

I THOUGHT OF A NEW TYPE OF BIRD.
IS HE ACCEPTING SUBMISSIONS...?
YES! BIRDS ARE ALWAYS WELCOME.
FLASH
AH!
TA-DA!
WE HAVE DIVINE APPROVAL!
SECRETARY BIRD
APPROVED
Y-YAY!
WHAT...?!
WHAT IS THIS COMBINATION OF PERSONAL RESENTMENT AND BIZARRE TASTE?!
WHY DID GOD APPROVE SUCH A THING?!
AHH! MY DEAR LITTLE SNAKE!
THWACK
BECAUSE OF ITS SUPERIOR DESIGN, I IMAGINE!
SO, THIS IS HOW FOOD CHAINS ARE FORMED...

THE ENCYCLOPEDIA OF REAL ANIMALS 02

ANIMAL ENCYCLOPEDIA

ANIMAL 04 | RED-EYED TREE FROG

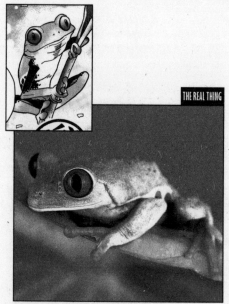

THE REAL THING

The bright-red eyes for which it is named have vertically-narrowed pupils.

Photo: Blickwinkel/Aflo

[Type species] *Agalychnis callidryas*
[Classification] Class: Amphibia
Order: Anura
Family: Hylidae
Genus: *Agalychnis*
[Range] Central America
[Length] 5-7.5 cm (2-3 in)

Characterized by vibrant red eyes set against its green body, the red-eyed tree frog lays its gelatin-covered eggs on leaves positioned above pools of water. Normally, tadpoles hatch after about a week, then drop into the water below to begin their lives. However, if a snake attacks, the tadpoles hatch prematurely within seconds and try to escape into the water. The underdeveloped tadpoles make easy prey, but they choose to be born early rather than passively allow themselves to be eaten. Research led by Boston University's Karen Warkentin showed that the eggs are able to detect the specific vibrations created by an attacking snake, which cue emergency hatching. They also sense other threats, such as pathogenic fungi, floods, and dehydration, and can escape them via premature hatching. They are true masters of risk management!

ANIMAL 05 | COMMON EGG-EATER

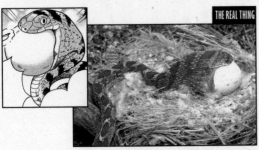

THE REAL THING

The common egg-eater can swallow eggs much larger than the size of its own head.
Photo: Photoshot/Aflo

[Type species] *Dasypeltis scabra*
[Classification] Class: Reptilia
Order: Squamata
Family: Colubridae
Genus: *Dasypeltis*
[Range] Southern Africa
[Length] 70-100 cm (28-40 in)

The common egg-eater is the ultimate picky eater, feeding exclusively on birds' eggs and fasting outside of the nesting season. Because it eats only eggs, its teeth have degenerated and disappeared, and in their place are specialized protrusions that pierce the eggs' shells in the esophagus. It is particularly fond of weaverbird eggs, and it's said that the reason weaverbird nests are so complex is because of the neverending battle waged between the two species.

ANIMAL 06 | WEAVERBIRD

Named for the complex nests it weaves, the weaverbird became a master home builder in response to repeated stalking by the common egg-eater. The southern masked weaver builds a circular, hanging nest with the entrance situated underneath to keep snakes from entering. The sociable weaver, on the other hand, creates giant, labyrinthine communal nests.

A southern masked weaver and its nest made of leaves and twigs. Photo: AGE FOTOSTOCK/Aflo

THE REAL THING

[Name] Weaverbird
[Classification] Class: Aves
Order: Passeriformes
Family: Ploceidae
[Range] Southern Africa, South Asia, Southeast Asia
[Height] Around 15 cm (6in) (Sociable weaver)

HEAVEN'S
DESIGN TEAM

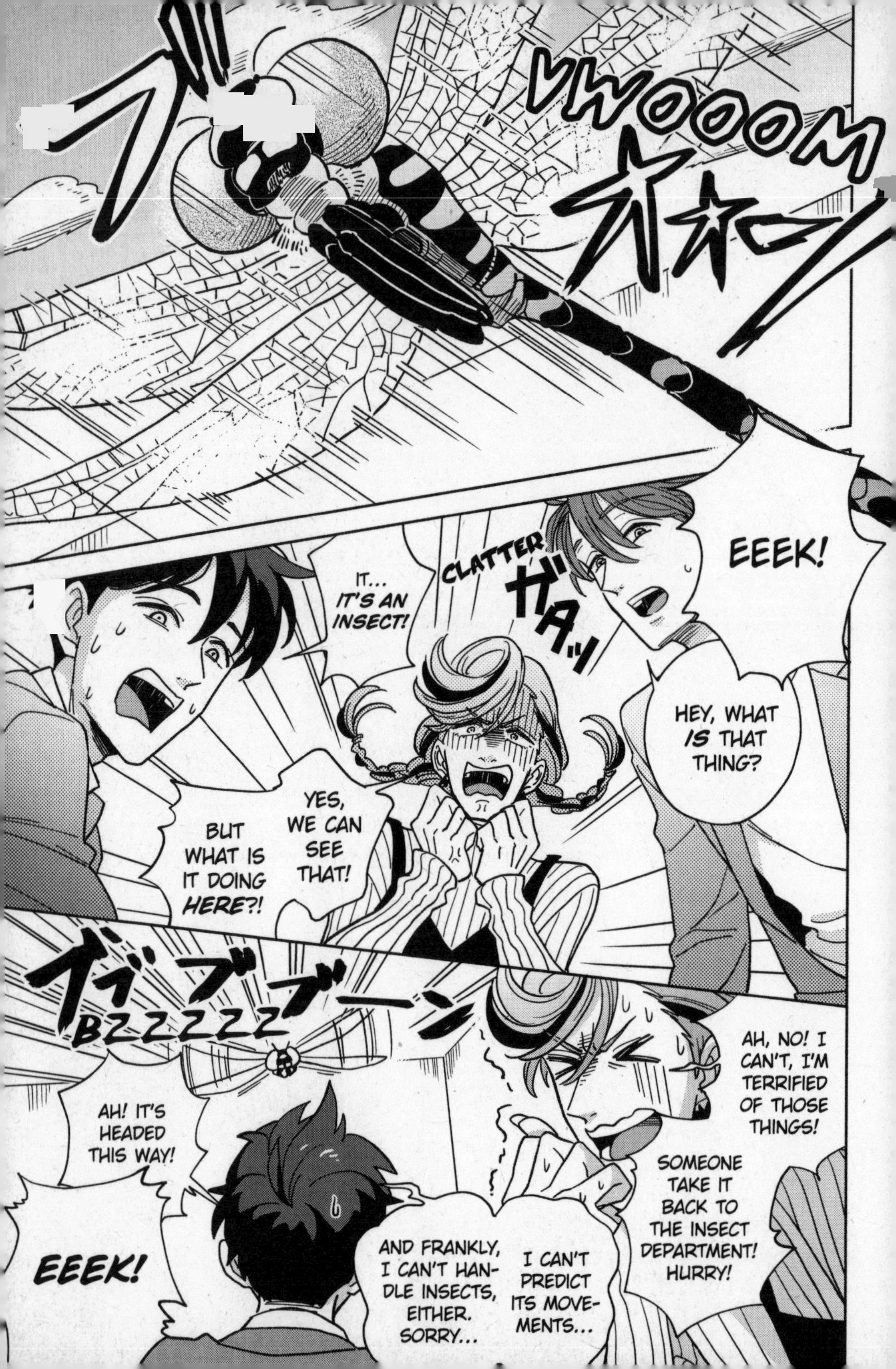
VWOOOM
EEEK!
HEY, WHAT *IS* THAT THING?
CLATTER
IT... *IT'S AN INSECT!*
YES, WE CAN SEE THAT!
BUT WHAT IS IT DOING *HERE*?!
BZZZZZZ
AH, NO! I CAN'T, I'M TERRIFIED OF THOSE THINGS!
SOMEONE TAKE IT BACK TO THE INSECT DEPARTMENT! HURRY!
I CAN'T PREDICT ITS MOVE-MENTS...
AND FRANKLY, I CAN'T HAN-DLE INSECTS, EITHER. SORRY...
AH! IT'S HEADED THIS WAY!
EEEK!

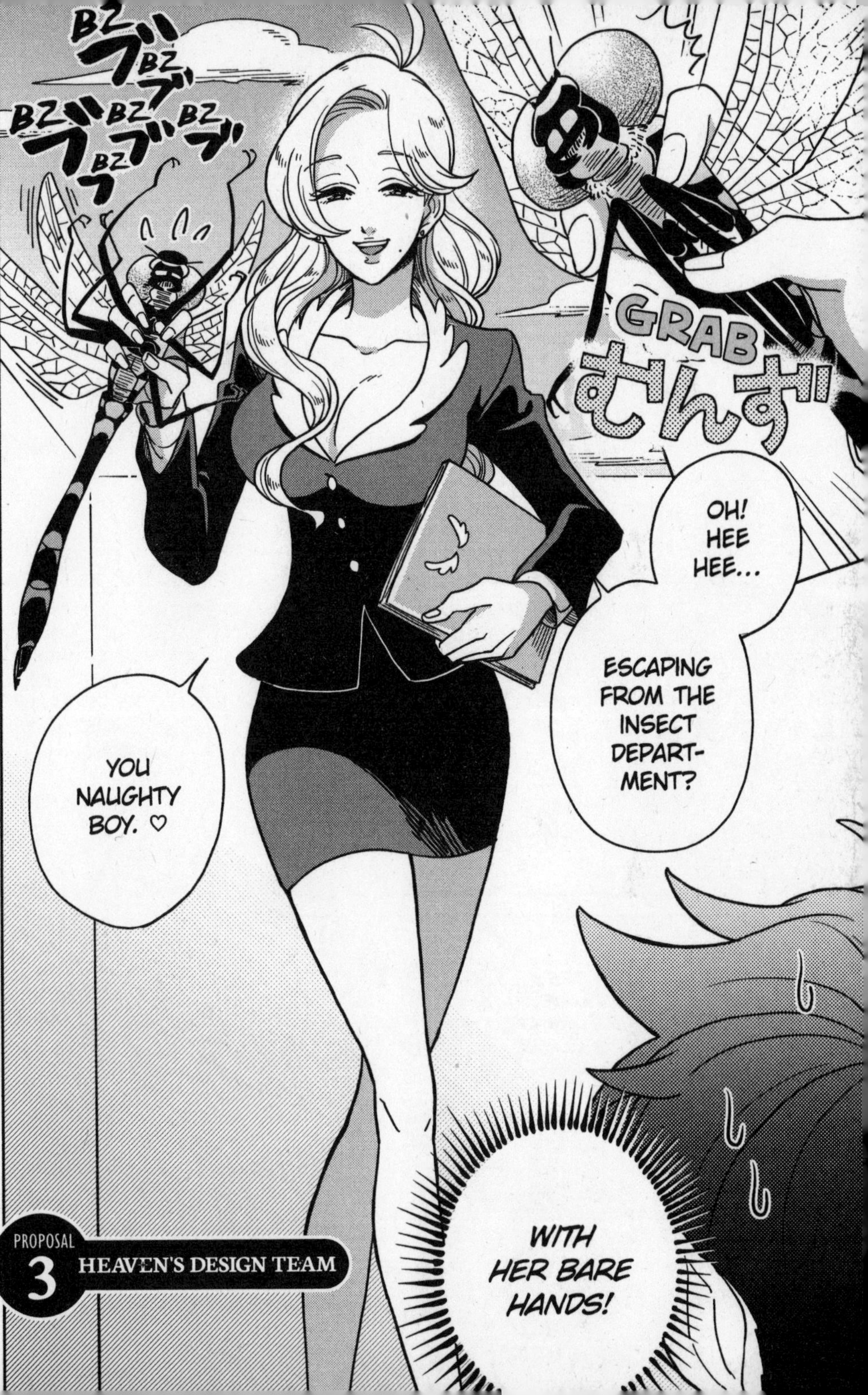
GRAB むんず
BZ ブ BZ ブ BZ ブ BZ ブ BZ ブ BZ ブ
OH! HEE HEE...
ESCAPING FROM THE INSECT DEPART-MENT?
YOU NAUGHTY BOY. ♡
WITH HER BARE HANDS!

PROPOSAL 3 HEAVEN'S DESIGN TEAM

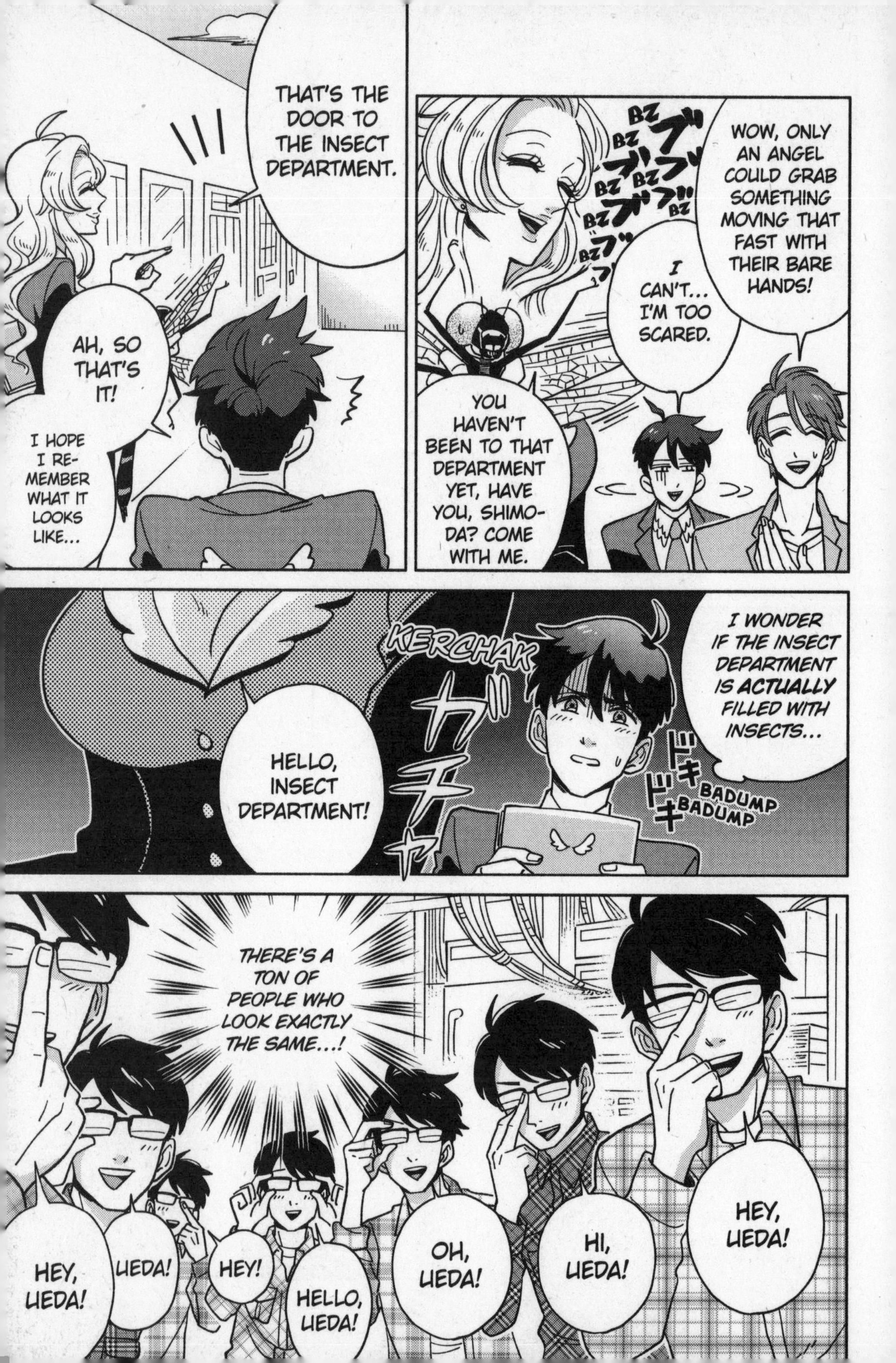
WOW, ONLY AN ANGEL COULD GRAB SOMETHING MOVING THAT FAST WITH THEIR BARE HANDS!
BZ BZ BZ BZ BZ BZ BZ
I CAN'T... I'M TOO SCARED.
YOU HAVEN'T BEEN TO THAT DEPARTMENT YET, HAVE YOU, SHIMODA? COME WITH ME.
THAT'S THE DOOR TO THE INSECT DEPARTMENT.
AH, SO THAT'S IT!
I HOPE I RE-MEMBER WHAT IT LOOKS LIKE...
I WONDER IF THE INSECT DEPARTMENT IS ACTUALLY FILLED WITH INSECTS...
BADUMP BADUMP
KERCHAK
HELLO, INSECT DEPARTMENT!
THERE'S A TON OF PEOPLE WHO LOOK EXACTLY THE SAME...!
HEY, UEDA!
HI, UEDA!
OH, UEDA!
HELLO, UEDA!
HEY!
UEDA!
HEY, UEDA!

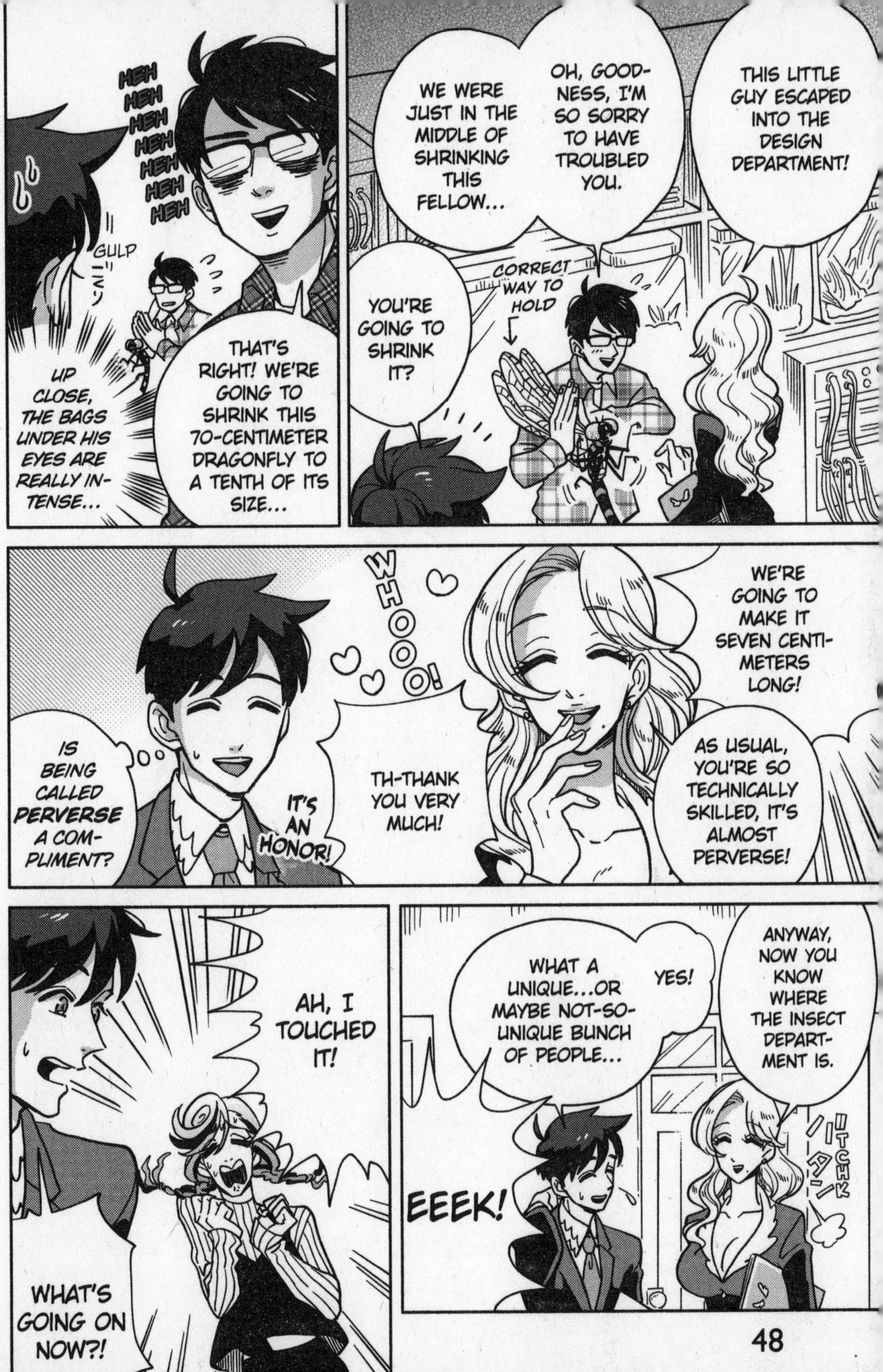
THIS LITTLE GUY ESCAPED INTO THE DESIGN DEPARTMENT!
OH, GOODNESS, I'M SO SORRY TO HAVE TROUBLED YOU.
WE WERE JUST IN THE MIDDLE OF SHRINKING THIS FELLOW...
CORRECT WAY TO HOLD
YOU'RE GOING TO SHRINK IT?
HEH HEH HEH HEH HEH HEH HEH
THAT'S RIGHT! WE'RE GOING TO SHRINK THIS 70-CENTIMETER DRAGONFLY TO A TENTH OF ITS SIZE...
GULP
UP CLOSE, THE BAGS UNDER HIS EYES ARE REALLY INTENSE...
WE'RE GOING TO MAKE IT SEVEN CENTIMETERS LONG!
AS USUAL, YOU'RE SO TECHNICALLY SKILLED, IT'S ALMOST PERVERSE!
WHOOOO!
TH-THANK YOU VERY MUCH!
IT'S AN HONOR!
IS BEING CALLED PERVERSE A COMPLIMENT?
ANYWAY, NOW YOU KNOW WHERE THE INSECT DEPARTMENT IS.
YES!
WHAT A UNIQUE...OR MAYBE NOT-SO-UNIQUE BUNCH OF PEOPLE...
ITCHK
EEEK!
AH, I TOUCHED IT!
WHAT'S GOING ON NOW?!

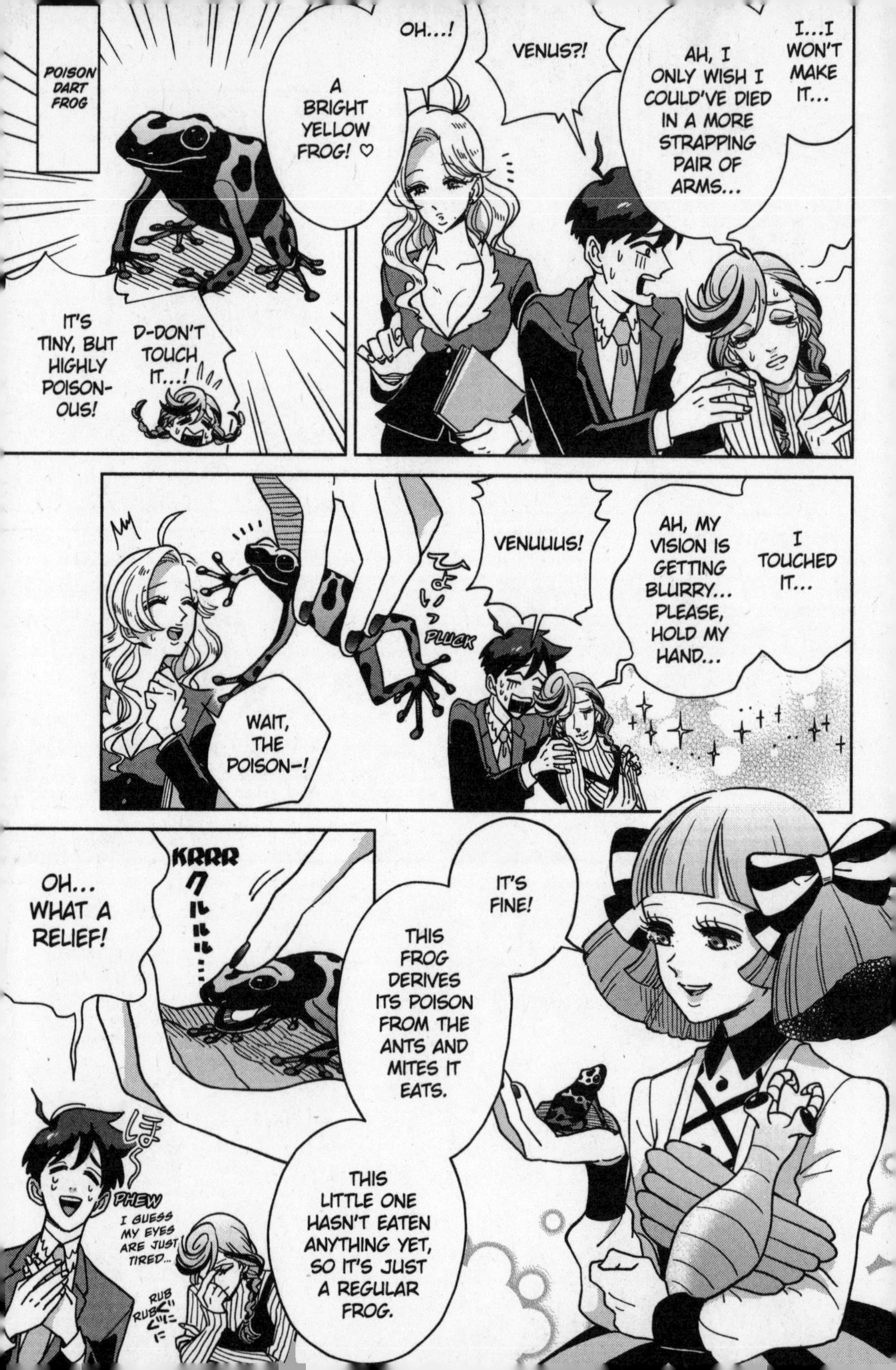

I...I WON'T MAKE IT...
AH, I ONLY WISH I COULD'VE DIED IN A MORE STRAPPING PAIR OF ARMS...
VENUS?!
OH...!
A BRIGHT YELLOW FROG! ♡
POISON DART FROG
D-DON'T TOUCH IT...!
IT'S TINY, BUT HIGHLY POISON-OUS!
I TOUCHED IT...
AH, MY VISION IS GETTING BLURRY... PLEASE, HOLD MY HAND...
VENUUUS!
PLUCK
WAIT, THE POISON—!
IT'S FINE!
THIS FROG DERIVES ITS POISON FROM THE ANTS AND MITES IT EATS.
THIS LITTLE ONE HASN'T EATEN ANYTHING YET, SO IT'S JUST A REGULAR FROG.
KRRR
OH... WHAT A RELIEF!
PHEW
I GUESS MY EYES ARE JUST TIRED...
RUB RUB

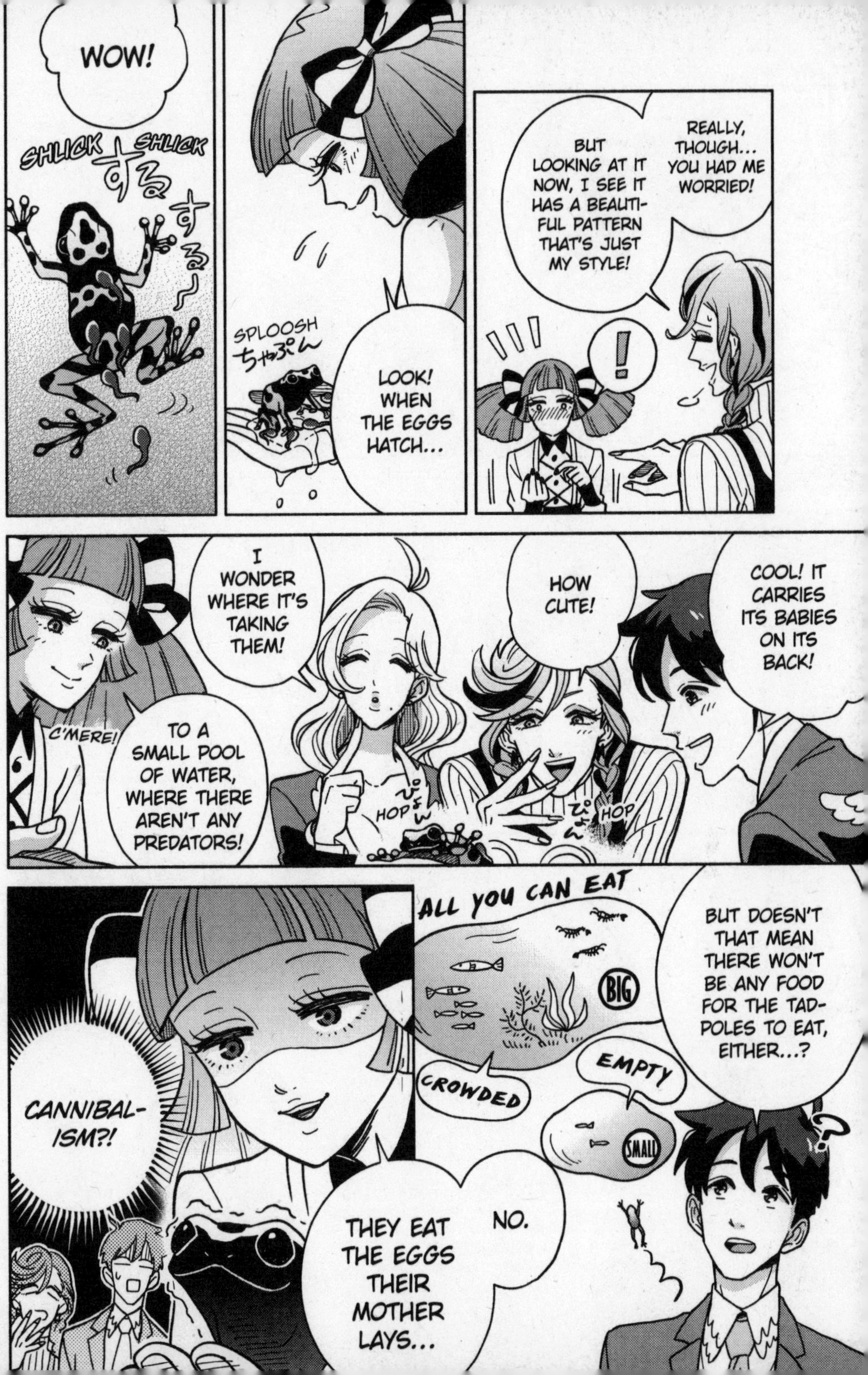

REALLY, THOUGH... YOU HAD ME WORRIED!
BUT LOOKING AT IT NOW, I SEE IT HAS A BEAUTI-FUL PATTERN THAT'S JUST MY STYLE!
!
LOOK! WHEN THE EGGS HATCH...
SPLOOSH ちゃぷん
WOW!
SHLICK する SHLICK するる〜
COOL! IT CARRIES ITS BABIES ON ITS BACK!
HOW CUTE!
I WONDER WHERE IT'S TAKING THEM!
HOP ぴょん
HOP ぴょん
C'MERE!
TO A SMALL POOL OF WATER, WHERE THERE AREN'T ANY PREDATORS!
BUT DOESN'T THAT MEAN THERE WON'T BE ANY FOOD FOR THE TAD-POLES TO EAT, EITHER...?
ALL YOU CAN EAT
BIG
CROWDED
EMPTY
SMALL
NO.
THEY EAT THE EGGS THEIR MOTHER LAYS...
CANNIBAL-ISM?!

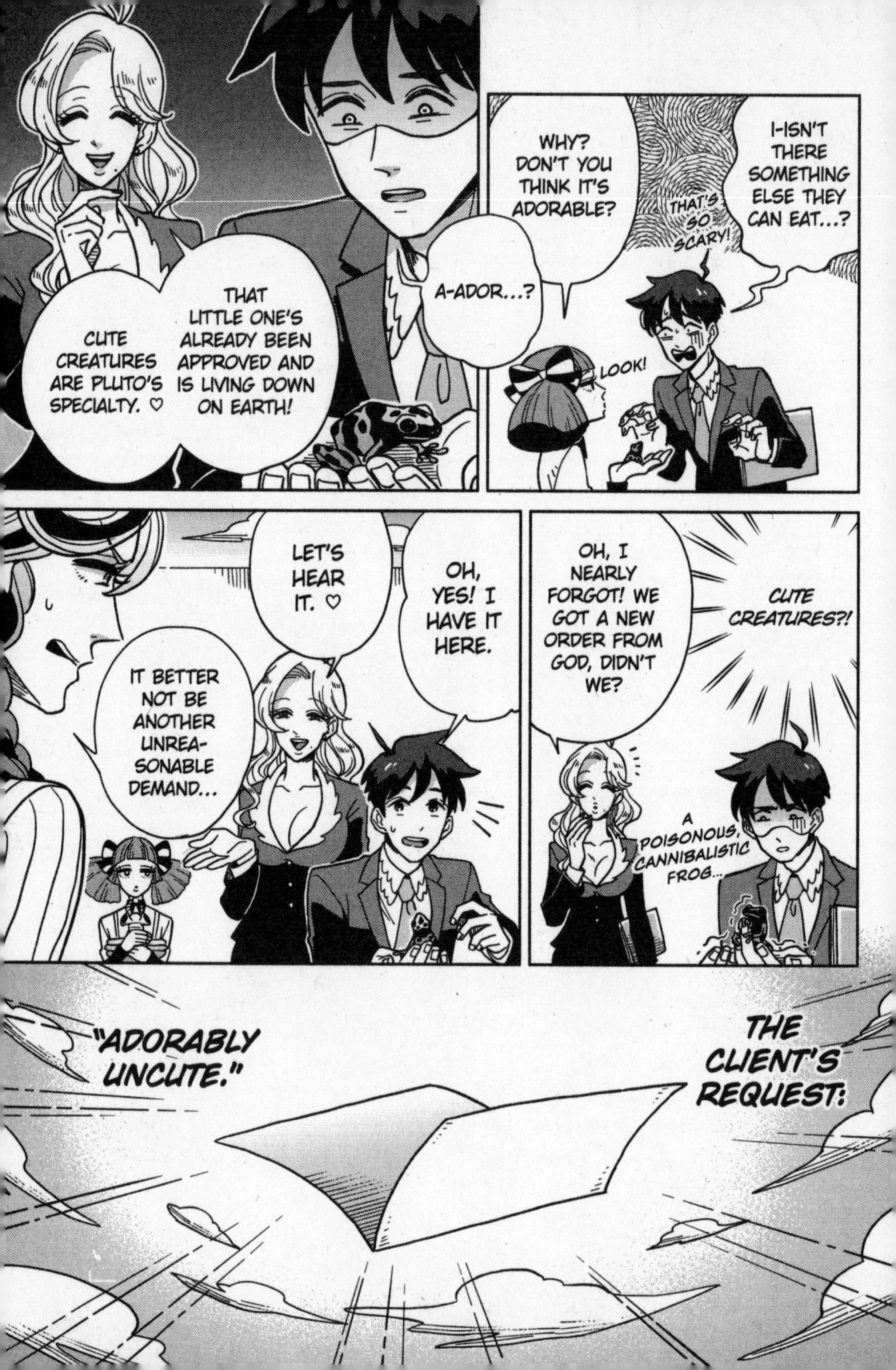
I-ISN'T THERE SOMETHING ELSE THEY CAN EAT...?
THAT'S SO SCARY!
WHY? DON'T YOU THINK IT'S ADORABLE?
LOOK!
A-ADOR...?
THAT LITTLE ONE'S ALREADY BEEN APPROVED AND IS LIVING DOWN ON EARTH!
CUTE CREATURES ARE PLUTO'S SPECIALTY. ♡
CUTE CREATURES?!
OH, I NEARLY FORGOT! WE GOT A NEW ORDER FROM GOD, DIDN'T WE?
A POISONOUS, CANNIBALISTIC FROG...
OH, YES! I HAVE IT HERE.
LET'S HEAR IT. ♡
IT BETTER NOT BE ANOTHER UNREA-SONABLE DEMAND...
THE CLIENT'S REQUEST:
"ADORABLY UNCUTE."

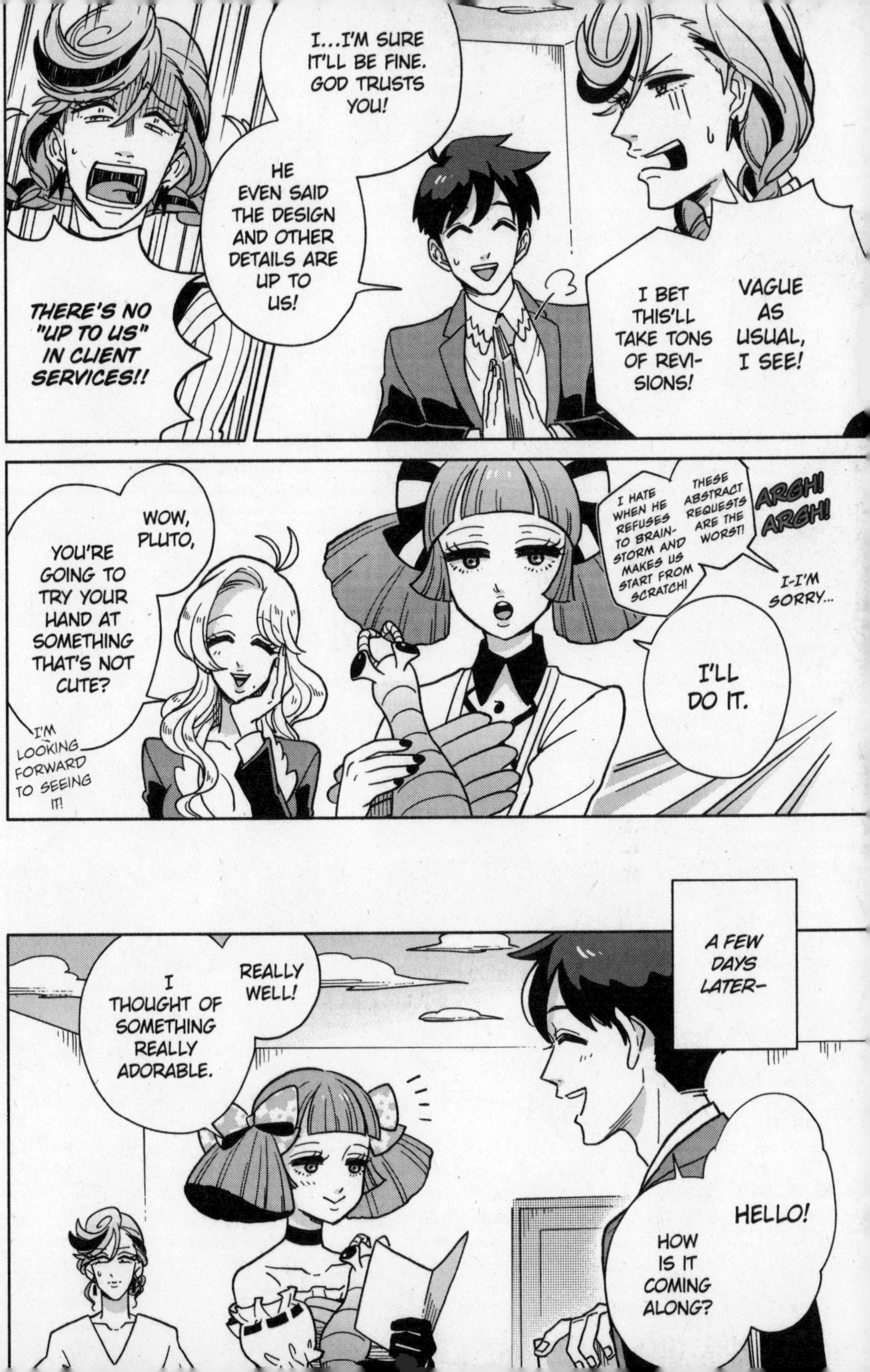

VAGUE AS USUAL, I SEE!
I BET THIS'LL TAKE TONS OF REVI-SIONS!
I...I'M SURE IT'LL BE FINE. GOD TRUSTS YOU!
HE EVEN SAID THE DESIGN AND OTHER DETAILS ARE UP TO US!
THERE'S NO "UP TO US" IN CLIENT SERVICES!!
ARGH! ARGH!
THESE ABSTRACT REQUESTS ARE THE WORST!
I HATE WHEN HE REFUSES TO BRAIN-STORM AND MAKES US START FROM SCRATCH!
I-I'M SORRY...
I'LL DO IT.
WOW, PLUTO,
YOU'RE GOING TO TRY YOUR HAND AT SOMETHING THAT'S NOT CUTE?
I'M LOOKING FORWARD TO SEEING IT!
A FEW DAYS LATER–
HELLO!
HOW IS IT COMING ALONG?
REALLY WELL!
I THOUGHT OF SOMETHING REALLY ADORABLE.

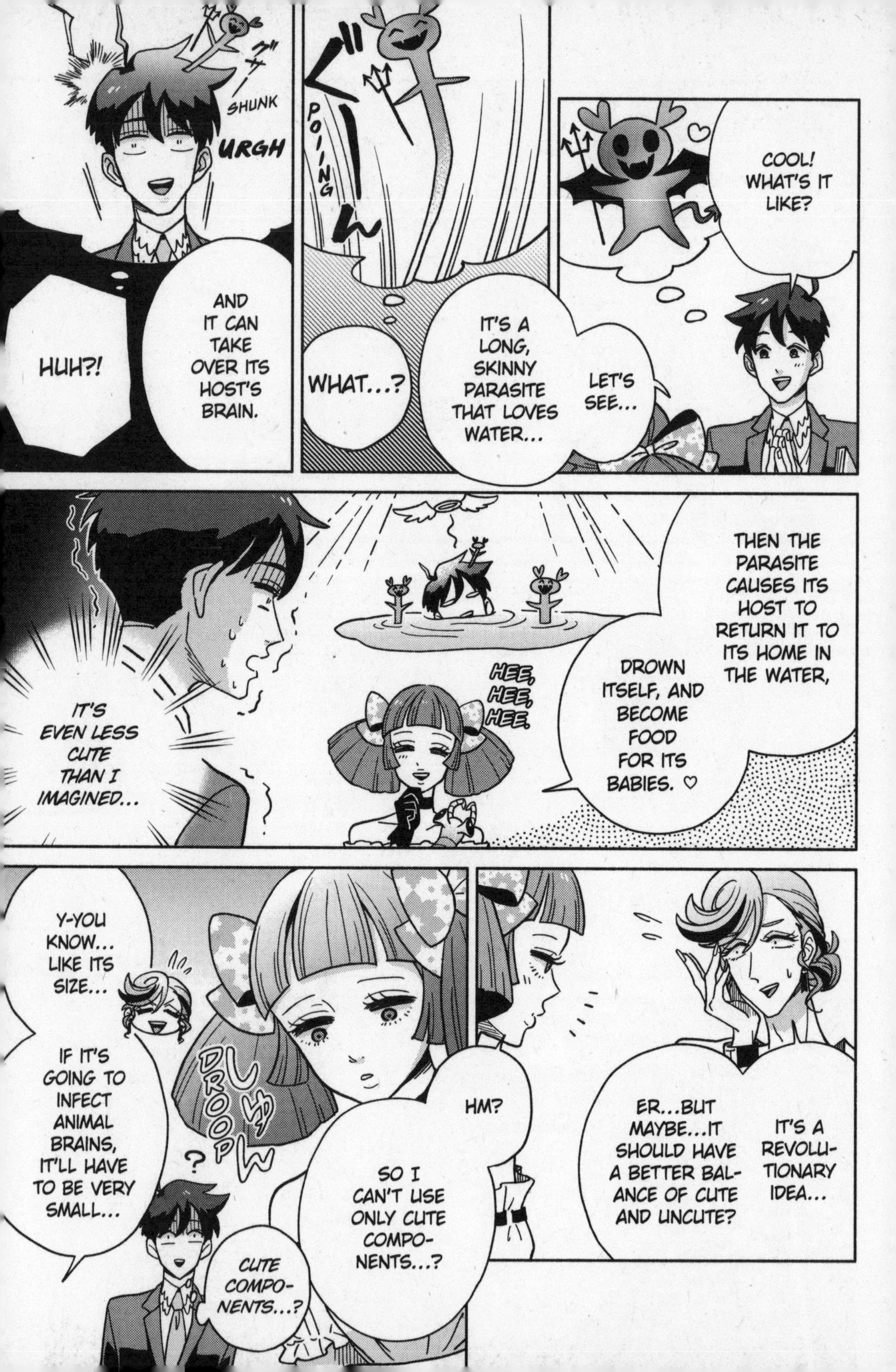
COOL! WHAT'S IT LIKE?
LET'S SEE...
IT'S A LONG, SKINNY PARASITE THAT LOVES WATER...
POIIING
WHAT...?
SHUNK
URGH
AND IT CAN TAKE OVER ITS HOST'S BRAIN.
HUH?!
THEN THE PARASITE CAUSES ITS HOST TO RETURN IT TO ITS HOME IN THE WATER,
DROWN ITSELF, AND BECOME FOOD FOR ITS BABIES. ♡
HEE, HEE, HEE.
IT'S EVEN LESS CUTE THAN I IMAGINED...
IT'S A REVOLUTIONARY IDEA...
ER...BUT MAYBE...IT SHOULD HAVE A BETTER BALANCE OF CUTE AND UNCUTE?
HM?
SO I CAN'T USE ONLY CUTE COMPONENTS...?
DROOP
Y-YOU KNOW... LIKE ITS SIZE...
IF IT'S GOING TO INFECT ANIMAL BRAINS, IT'LL HAVE TO BE VERY SMALL...
?
CUTE COMPONENTS...?

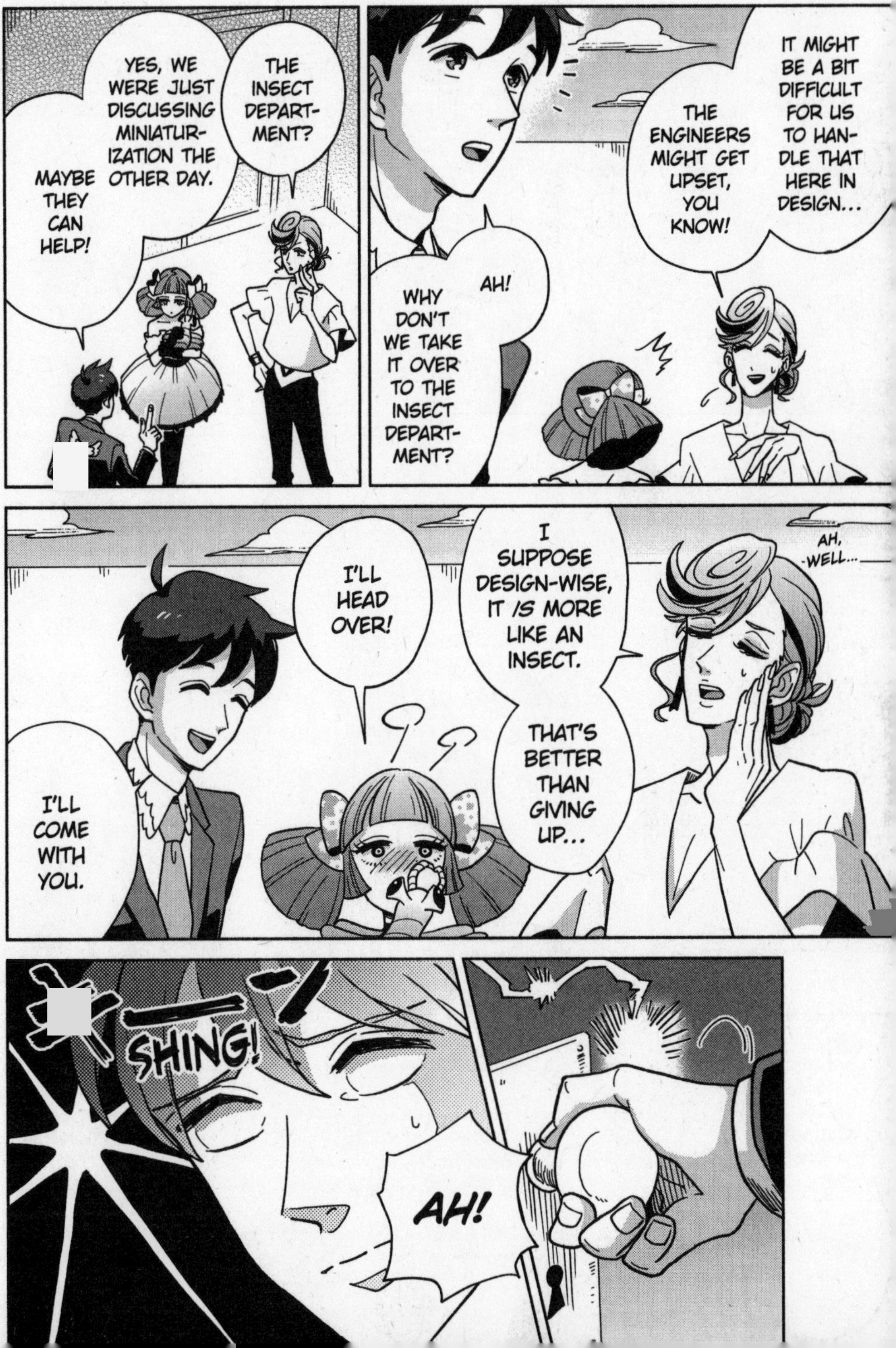
IT MIGHT BE A BIT DIFFICULT FOR US TO HANDLE THAT HERE IN DESIGN...
THE ENGINEERS MIGHT GET UPSET, YOU KNOW!
AH!
WHY DON'T WE TAKE IT OVER TO THE INSECT DEPARTMENT?
THE INSECT DEPARTMENT?
YES, WE WERE JUST DISCUSSING MINIATURIZATION THE OTHER DAY.
MAYBE THEY CAN HELP!
AH, WELL...
I SUPPOSE DESIGN-WISE, IT *IS* MORE LIKE AN INSECT.
THAT'S BETTER THAN GIVING UP...
I'LL HEAD OVER!
I'LL COME WITH YOU.
SHING!
AH!

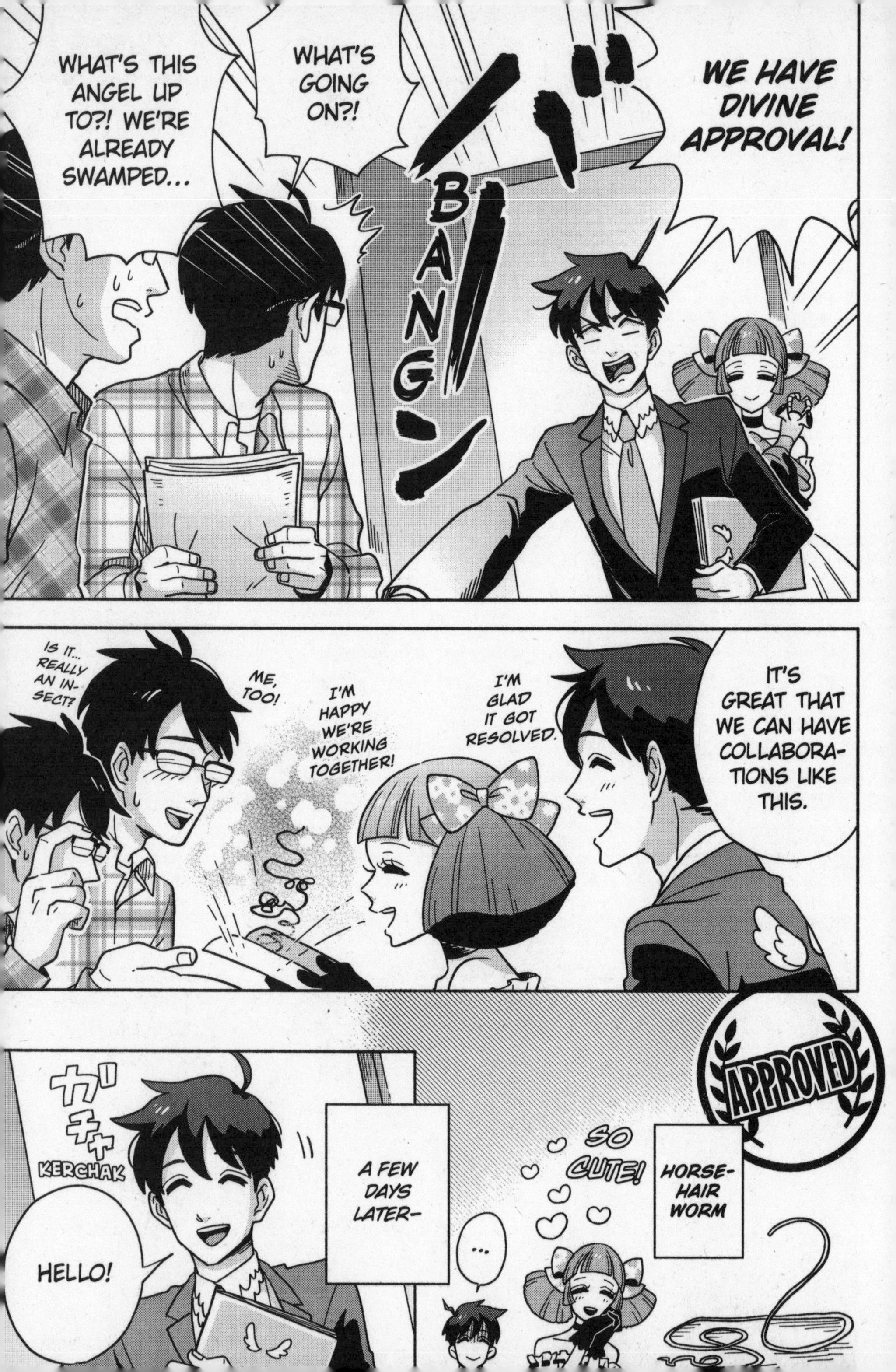
WE HAVE DIVINE APPROVAL!
BANG
WHAT'S GOING ON?!
WHAT'S THIS ANGEL UP TO?! WE'RE ALREADY SWAMPED...
IT'S GREAT THAT WE CAN HAVE COLLABORATIONS LIKE THIS.
I'M GLAD IT GOT RESOLVED.
I'M HAPPY WE'RE WORKING TOGETHER!
ME, TOO!
IS IT... REALLY AN INSECT?
APPROVED
HORSE-HAIR WORM
SO CUTE!
...
A FEW DAYS LATER-
ガチャ
KERCHAK
HELLO!

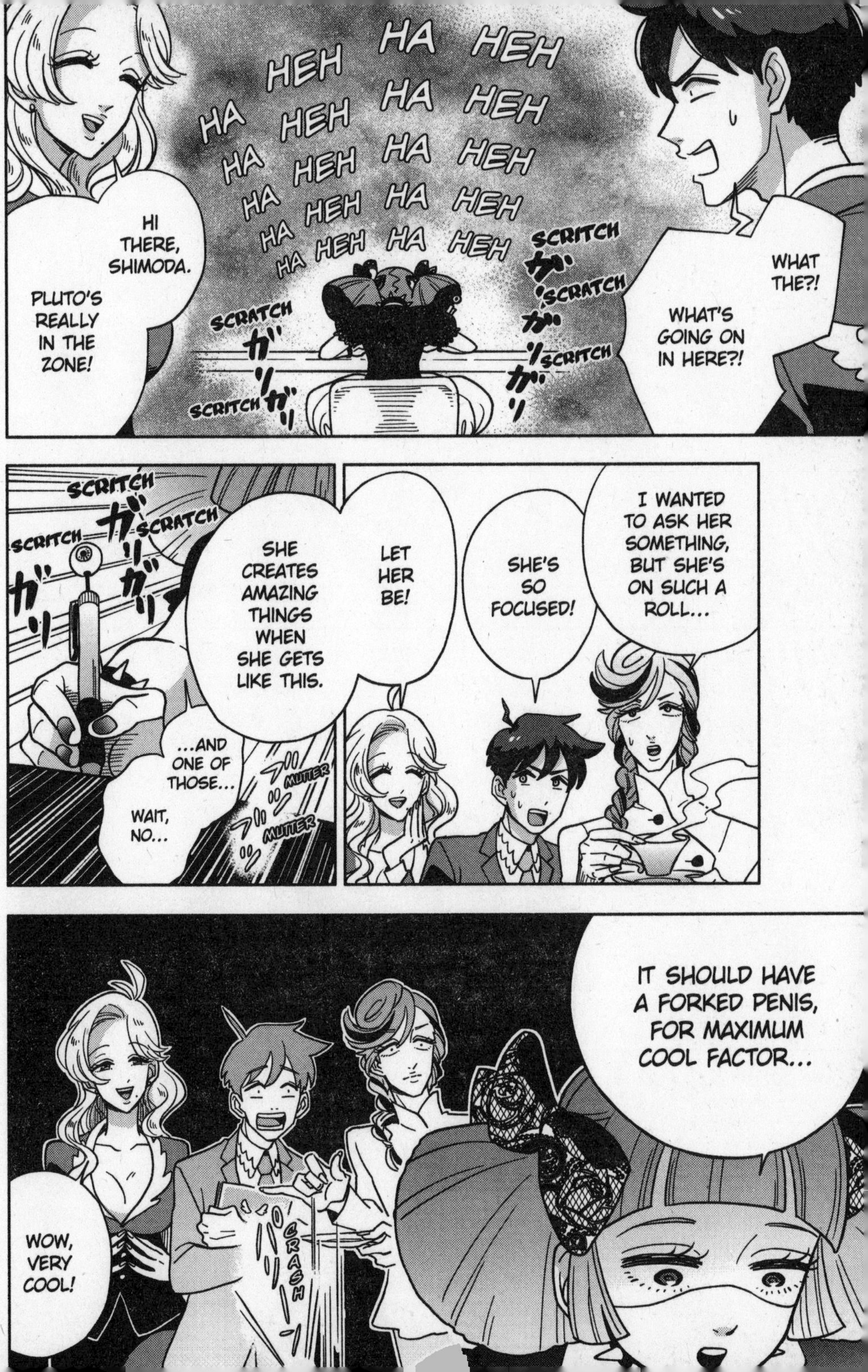
WHAT THE?!
WHAT'S GOING ON IN HERE?!
HA HEH HA HEH HA HEH HA HEH HA HEH HA HEH HA HEH HA HEH HA HEH HA HEH HA HEH HA HEH
HI THERE, SHIMODA.
PLUTO'S REALLY IN THE ZONE!
SCRITCH SCRATCH SCRITCH SCRATCH SCRITCH
I WANTED TO ASK HER SOMETHING, BUT SHE'S ON SUCH A ROLL...
SHE'S SO FOCUSED!
LET HER BE!
SHE CREATES AMAZING THINGS WHEN SHE GETS LIKE THIS.
SCRITCH SCRATCH SCRITCH
...AND ONE OF THOSE...
WAIT, NO...
MUTTER MUTTER
IT SHOULD HAVE A FORKED PENIS, FOR MAXIMUM COOL FACTOR...
CRASH
WOW, VERY COOL!

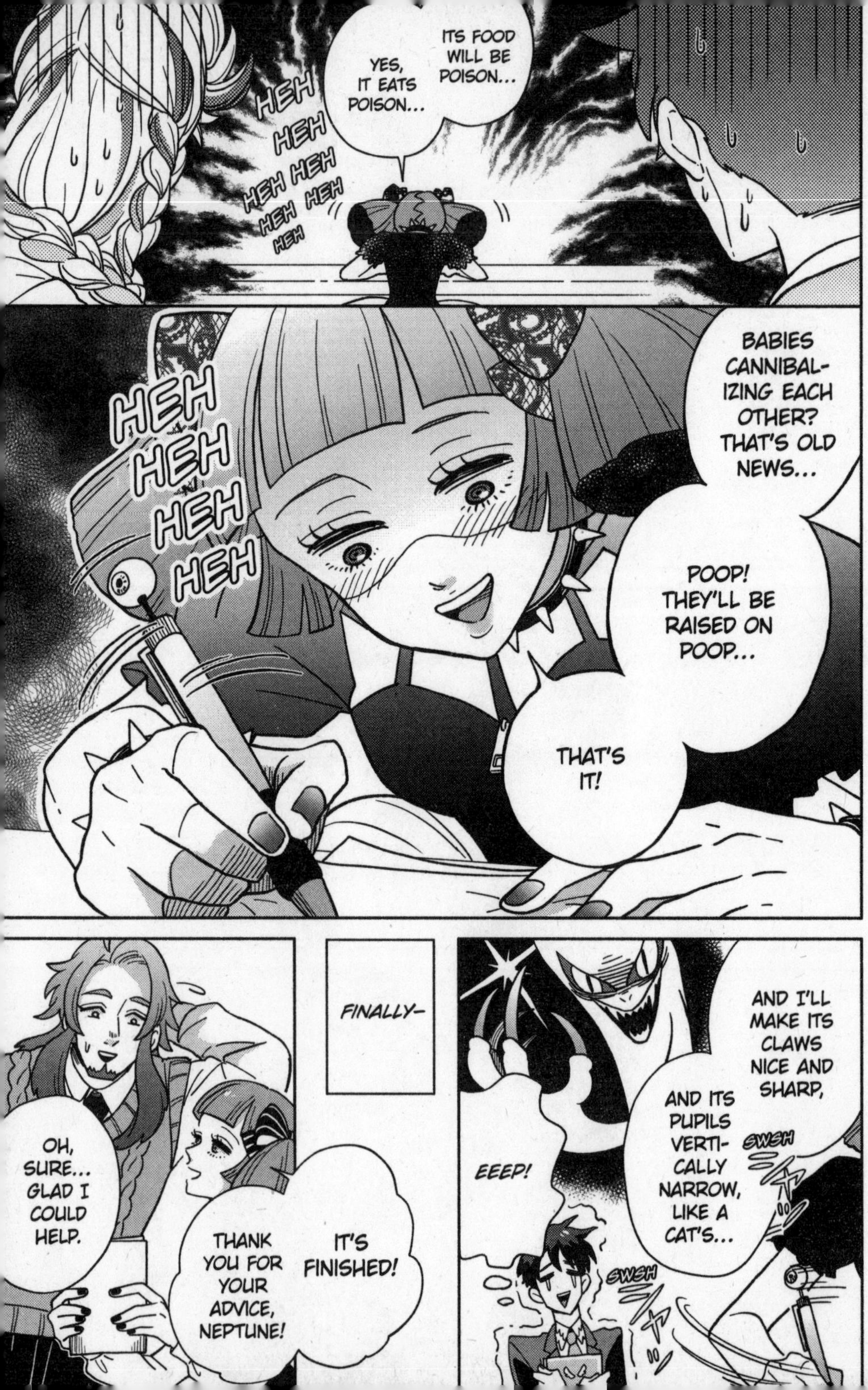
YES, IT EATS POISON... ITS FOOD WILL BE POISON...
HEH HEH HEH HEH HEH HEH HEH
BABIES CANNIBAL-IZING EACH OTHER? THAT'S OLD NEWS...
POOP! THEY'LL BE RAISED ON POOP...
THAT'S IT!
HEH HEH HEH HEH
AND I'LL MAKE ITS CLAWS NICE AND SHARP,
AND ITS PUPILS VERTI-CALLY NARROW, LIKE A CAT'S...
SWSH
SWSH
EEEP!
FINALLY—
IT'S FINISHED!
THANK YOU FOR YOUR ADVICE, NEPTUNE!
OH, SURE... GLAD I COULD HELP.

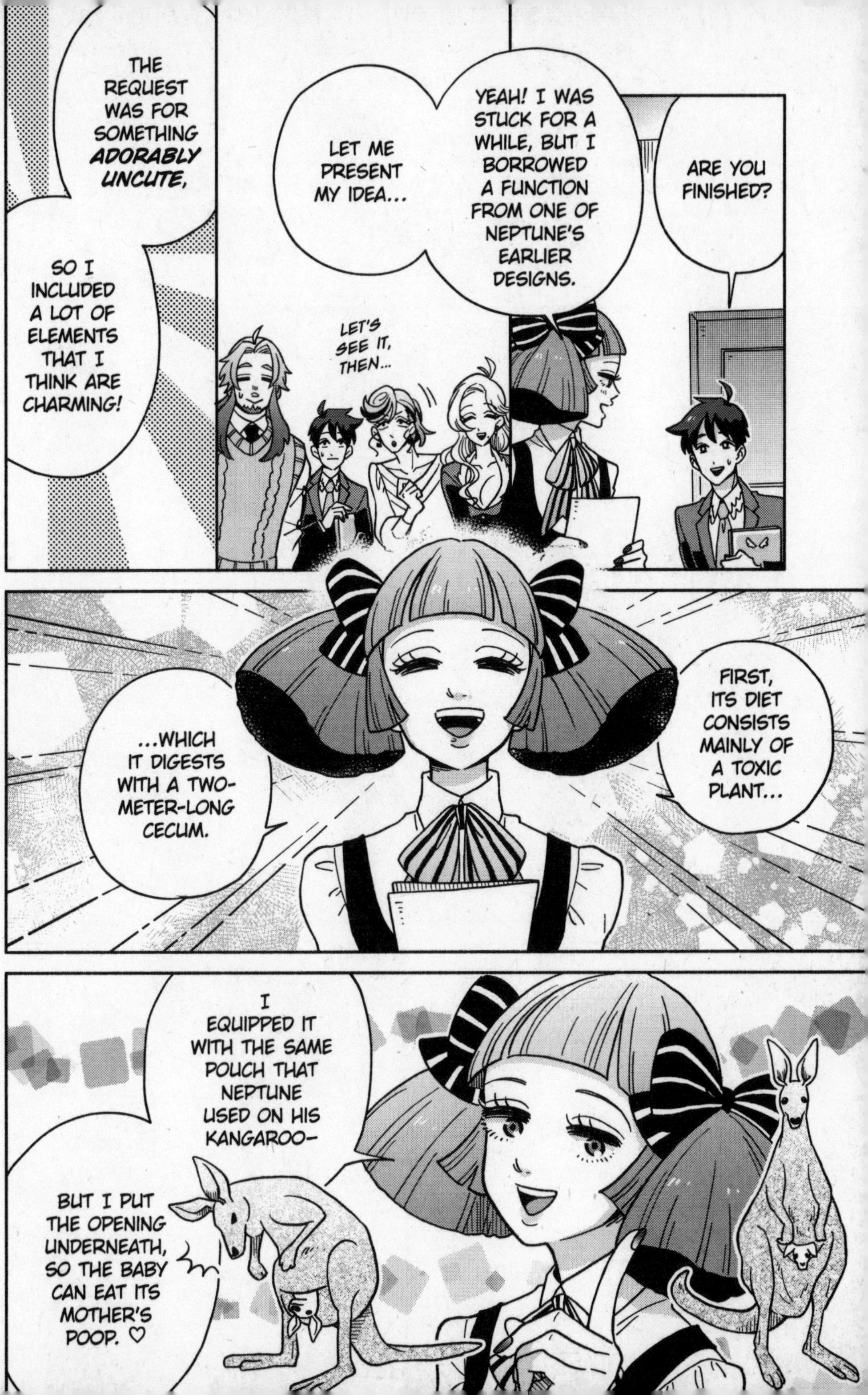
ARE YOU FINISHED?
YEAH! I WAS STUCK FOR A WHILE, BUT I BORROWED A FUNCTION FROM ONE OF NEPTUNE'S EARLIER DESIGNS.
LET ME PRESENT MY IDEA...
LET'S SEE IT, THEN...
THE REQUEST WAS FOR SOMETHING ***ADORABLY UNCUTE***,
SO I INCLUDED A LOT OF ELEMENTS THAT I THINK ARE CHARMING!
FIRST, ITS DIET CONSISTS MAINLY OF A TOXIC PLANT...
...WHICH IT DIGESTS WITH A TWO-METER-LONG CECUM.
I EQUIPPED IT WITH THE SAME POUCH THAT NEPTUNE USED ON HIS KANGAROO-
BUT I PUT THE OPENING UNDERNEATH, SO THE BABY CAN EAT ITS MOTHER'S POOP. ♡

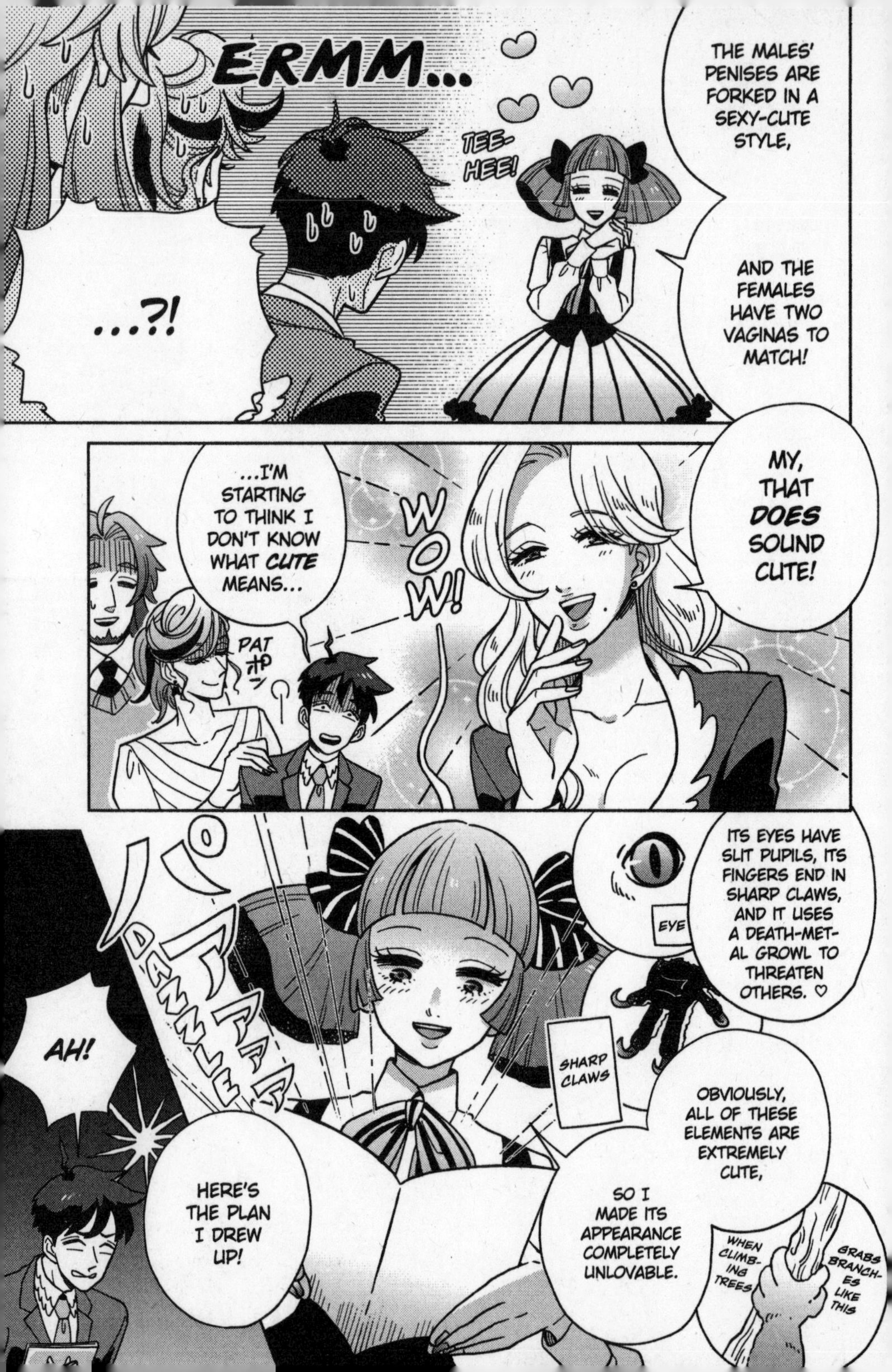
THE MALES' PENISES ARE FORKED IN A SEXY-CUTE STYLE,
AND THE FEMALES HAVE TWO VAGINAS TO MATCH!
TEE-HEE!
ERMM...
...?!
MY, THAT DOES SOUND CUTE!
WOW!
...I'M STARTING TO THINK I DON'T KNOW WHAT CUTE MEANS...
PAT
ITS EYES HAVE SLIT PUPILS, ITS FINGERS END IN SHARP CLAWS, AND IT USES A DEATH-METAL GROWL TO THREATEN OTHERS. ♡
EYE
SHARP CLAWS
DANNLE
AH!
OBVIOUSLY, ALL OF THESE ELEMENTS ARE EXTREMELY CUTE,
SO I MADE ITS APPEARANCE COMPLETELY UNLOVABLE.
GRABS BRANCHES LIKE THIS
WHEN CLIMBING TREES
HERE'S THE PLAN I DREW UP!

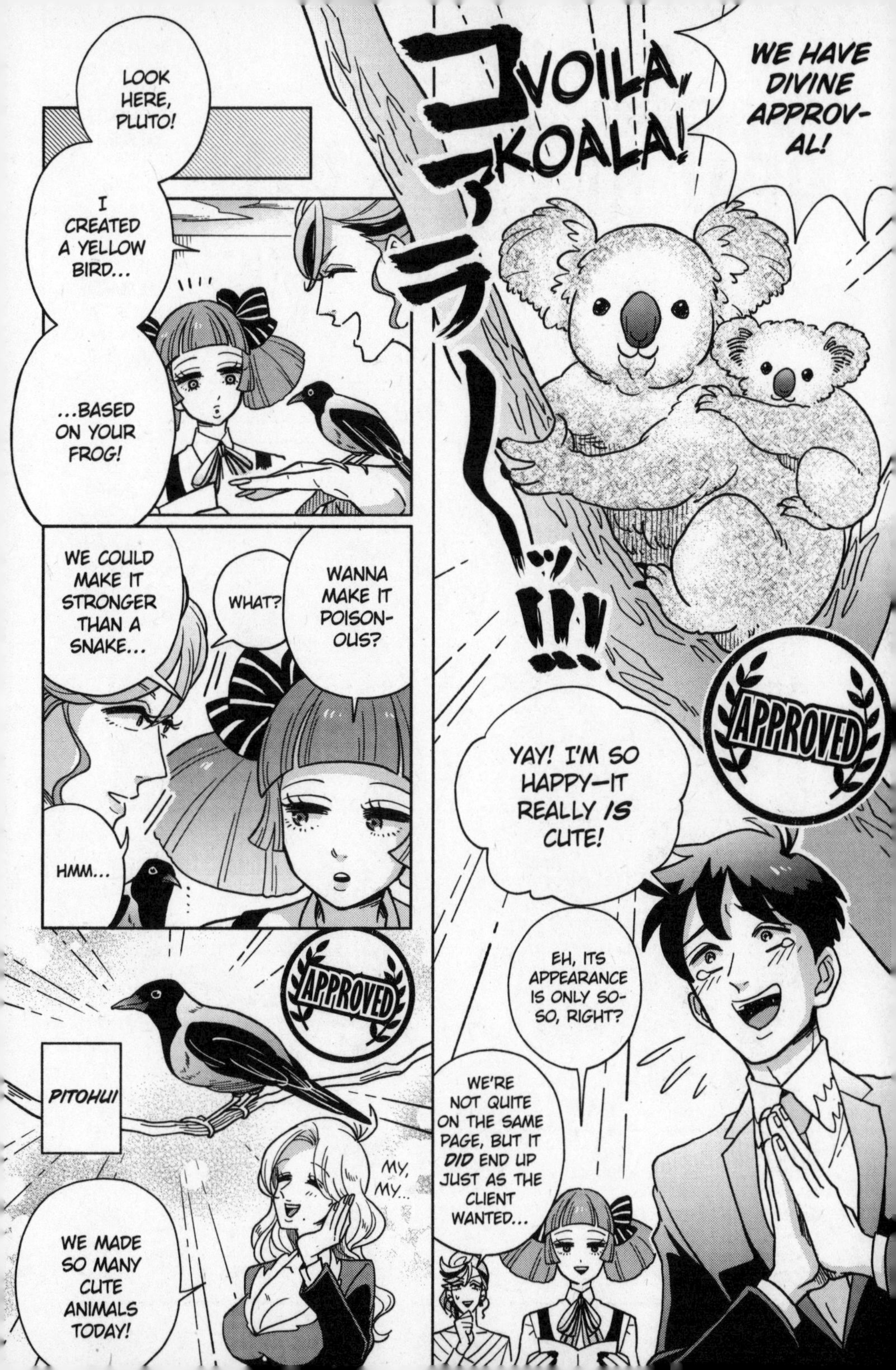
WE HAVE DIVINE APPROV-AL!
VOILA, KOALA!
APPROVED
YAY! I'M SO HAPPY—IT REALLY *IS* CUTE!
EH, ITS APPEARANCE IS ONLY SO-SO, RIGHT?
WE'RE NOT QUITE ON THE SAME PAGE, BUT IT *DID* END UP JUST AS THE CLIENT WANTED...
LOOK HERE, PLUTO!
I CREATED A YELLOW BIRD...
...BASED ON YOUR FROG!
WANNA MAKE IT POISON-OUS?
WHAT?
WE COULD MAKE IT STRONGER THAN A SNAKE...
HMM...
APPROVED
PITOHUI
MY, MY...
WE MADE SO MANY CUTE ANIMALS TODAY!

THE ENCYCLOPEDIA OF REAL ANIMALS 03

ANIMAL ENCYCLOPEDIA

ANIMAL 07 | KOALA

THE REAL THING

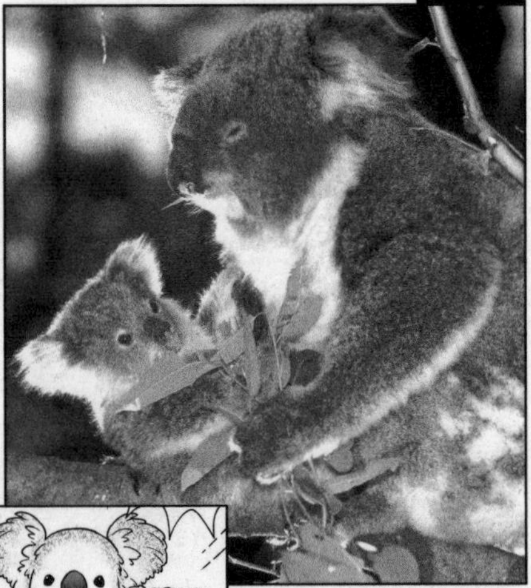

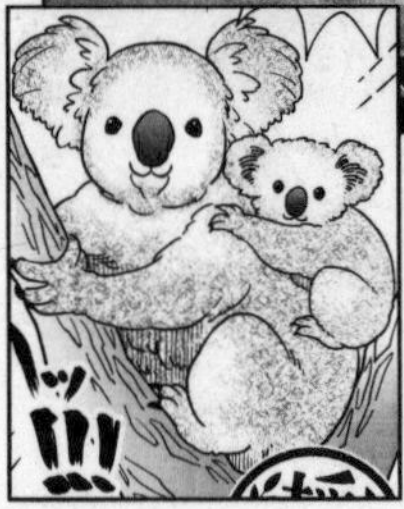

The koala spends 18-20 hours per day resting or sleeping.
Photo: Ardea/Aflo

[Type species] *Phascolarctos cinereus*
[Classification] Class: Mammalia
Order: Diprotodontia
Family: Phascolarctidae
Genus: *Phascolarctos*
[Range] Australia
[Height] 65-80 cm (2-2.5 ft)

The only extant member of the koala (phascolarctidae) family, the real-life koala exhibits all of the characteristics introduced during the Design Department's development session. It actively chooses to eat the leaves of the eucalyptus, a plant that essentially advertises itself as unappetizing by being tough, nutrient-poor, and difficult to digest. The koala's cecum is two meters (six-and-a-half feet) long, and it uses a variety of intestinal bacteria to digest its food. The mother koala produces a predigested, feces-like substance called pap, which it feeds to the joey as a transitional food during weaning to pass along the bacteria necessary to digest eucalyptus. In order to conserve its hard-won energy, the male koala generally engages in vocal assaults rather than physical ones. It's speculated that this is one reason the male's bellow developed into a threatening, death-metal growl.

ANIMAL 08 | HORSEHAIR WORM

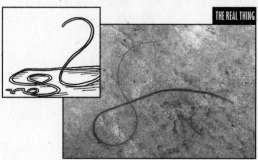

THE REAL THING

Photo: AGE FOTOSTOCK/Aflo

The horsehair worm is prevalent around the world, and, as of 2014, over 300 species of this water-dweller have been discovered. The larva, once consumed, lives as a parasite in its host (often an insect). Once it matures, the worm infects its host's brain, forcing it to dive into a body of water suitable for mating and drown itself. It's believed that it controls the host's movements by injecting a specialized protein into the host's brain, but this is still being studied.

[Name] Gordiacea
[Classification] Phylum: Nematomorpha
Class: Gordioidea
[Habitat] Aquatic environments and inside hosts
[Length] From several centimeters to several dozens of centimeters

ANIMAL 09 | PITOHUI

Endemic to New Guinea, the pitohui is a genus of poisonous bird characterized by its bright coloration, which serves as a warning to predators. The birds' tissue and feathers contain homobatrachotoxin, the same neurotoxin found in poison dart frogs. Simply holding a feather in the mouth can cause numbness. Pitohuis do not produce the batrachotoxin themselves, but rather accumulate it from the beetles they eat. In theory, just one milligram of the highly toxic compound could kill more than 10 adult men.

THE REAL THING

APPROVED

The hooded pitohui is one variation of this bird.
Photo: picture alliance/Aflo

[Name] Pitohui
[Classification] Class: Aves
Order: Passeriformes
[Range] New Guinea
[Length] Around 20 cm (8 in)

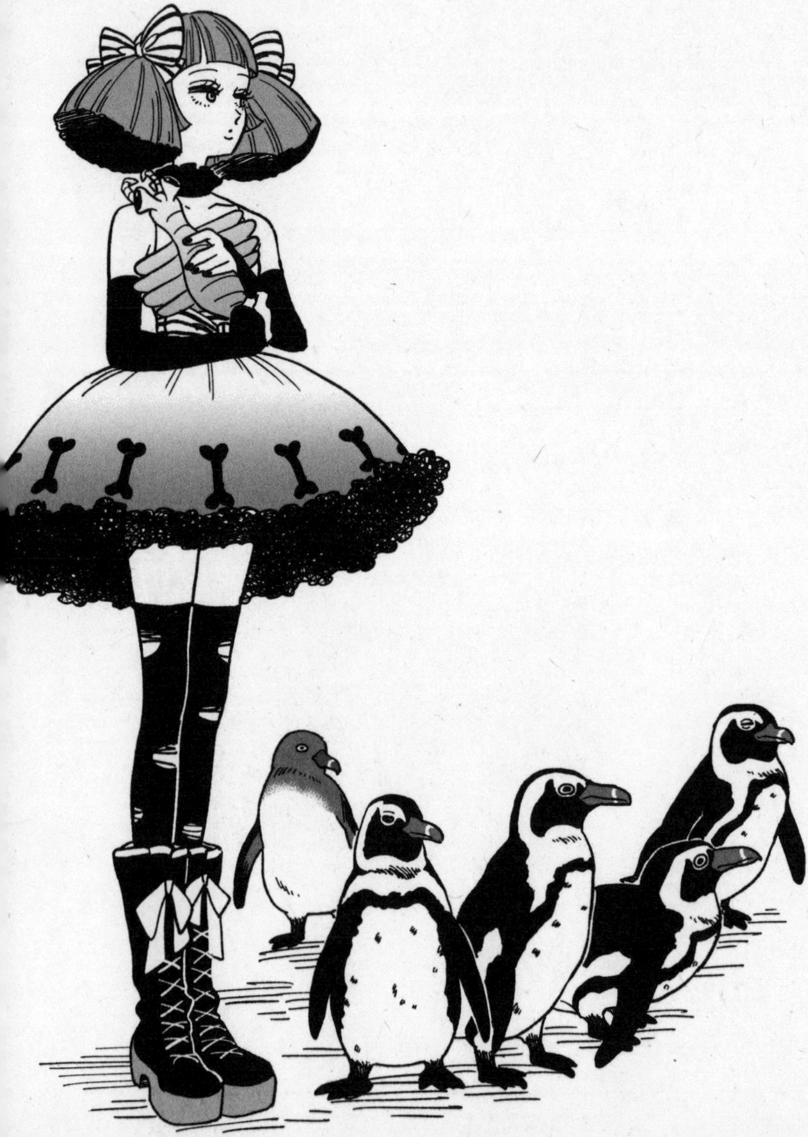

HEAVEN'S DESIGN TEAM

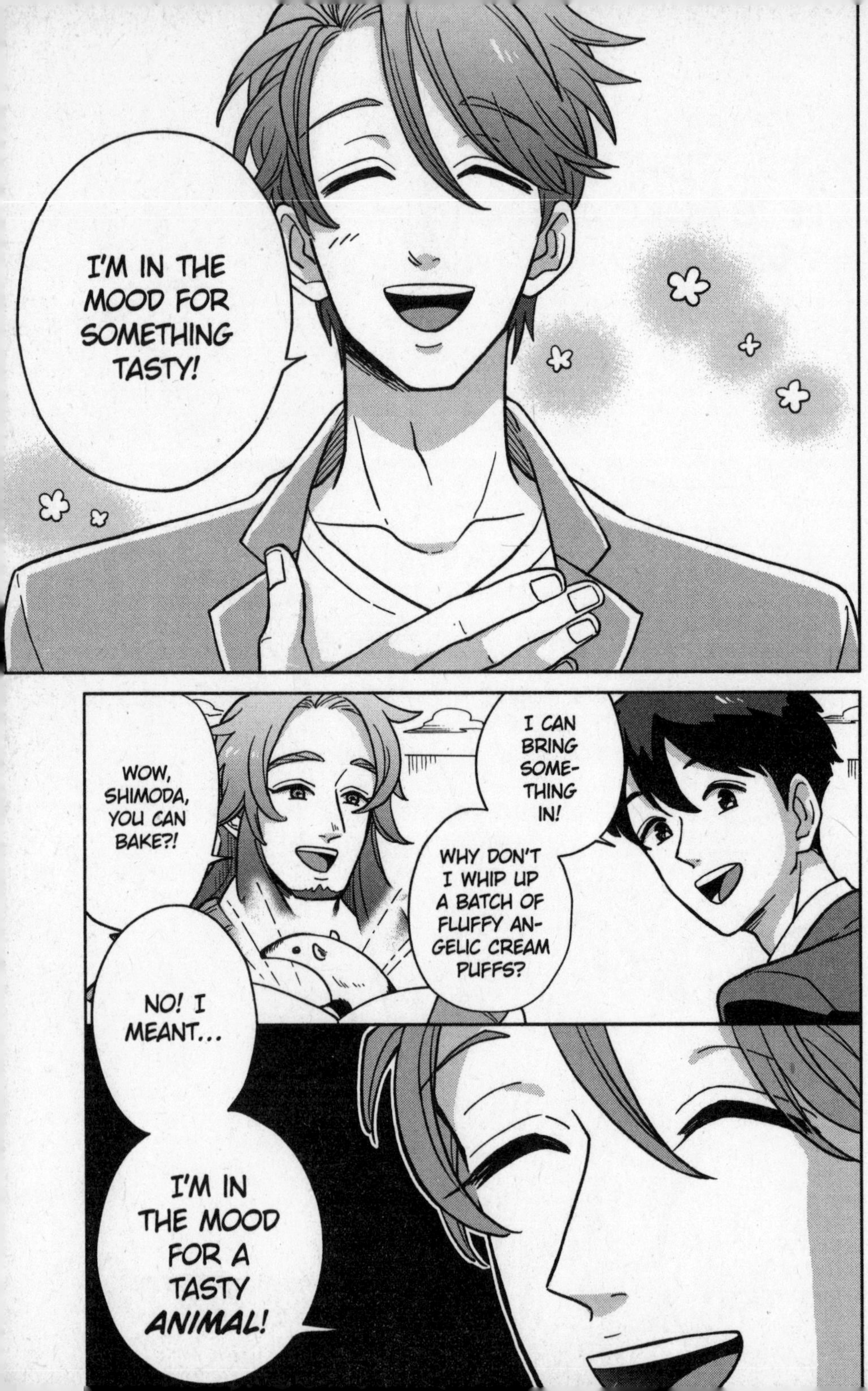
I'M IN THE MOOD FOR SOMETHING TASTY!
I CAN BRING SOME-THING IN!
WHY DON'T I WHIP UP A BATCH OF FLUFFY AN-GELIC CREAM PUFFS?
WOW, SHIMODA, YOU CAN BAKE?!
NO! I MEANT...
I'M IN THE MOOD FOR A TASTY ANIMAL!

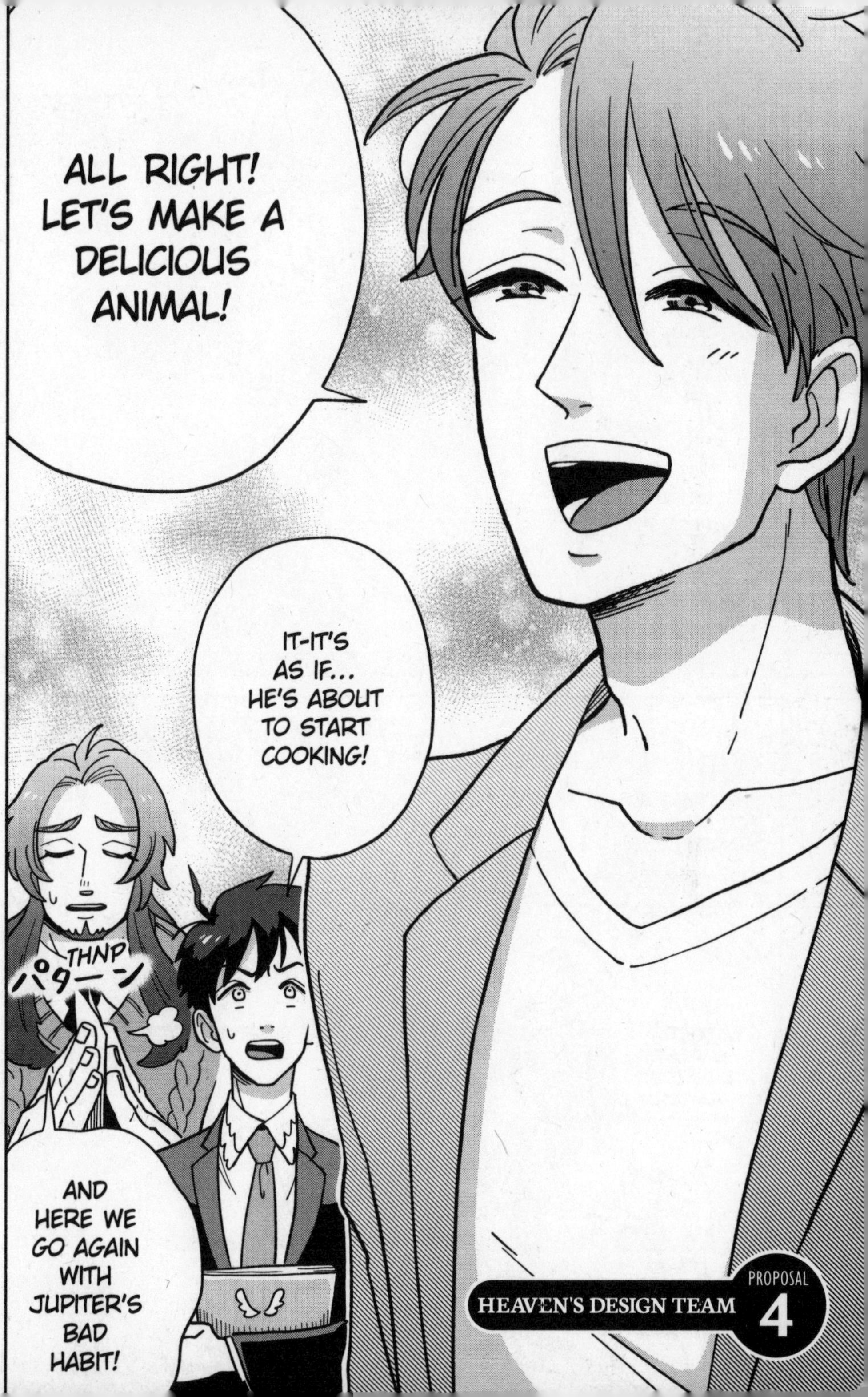
ALL RIGHT! LET'S MAKE A DELICIOUS ANIMAL!
IT-IT'S AS IF... HE'S ABOUT TO START COOKING!
THNP
パターン
AND HERE WE GO AGAIN WITH JUPITER'S BAD HABIT!
HEAVEN'S DESIGN TEAM
PROPOSAL
4

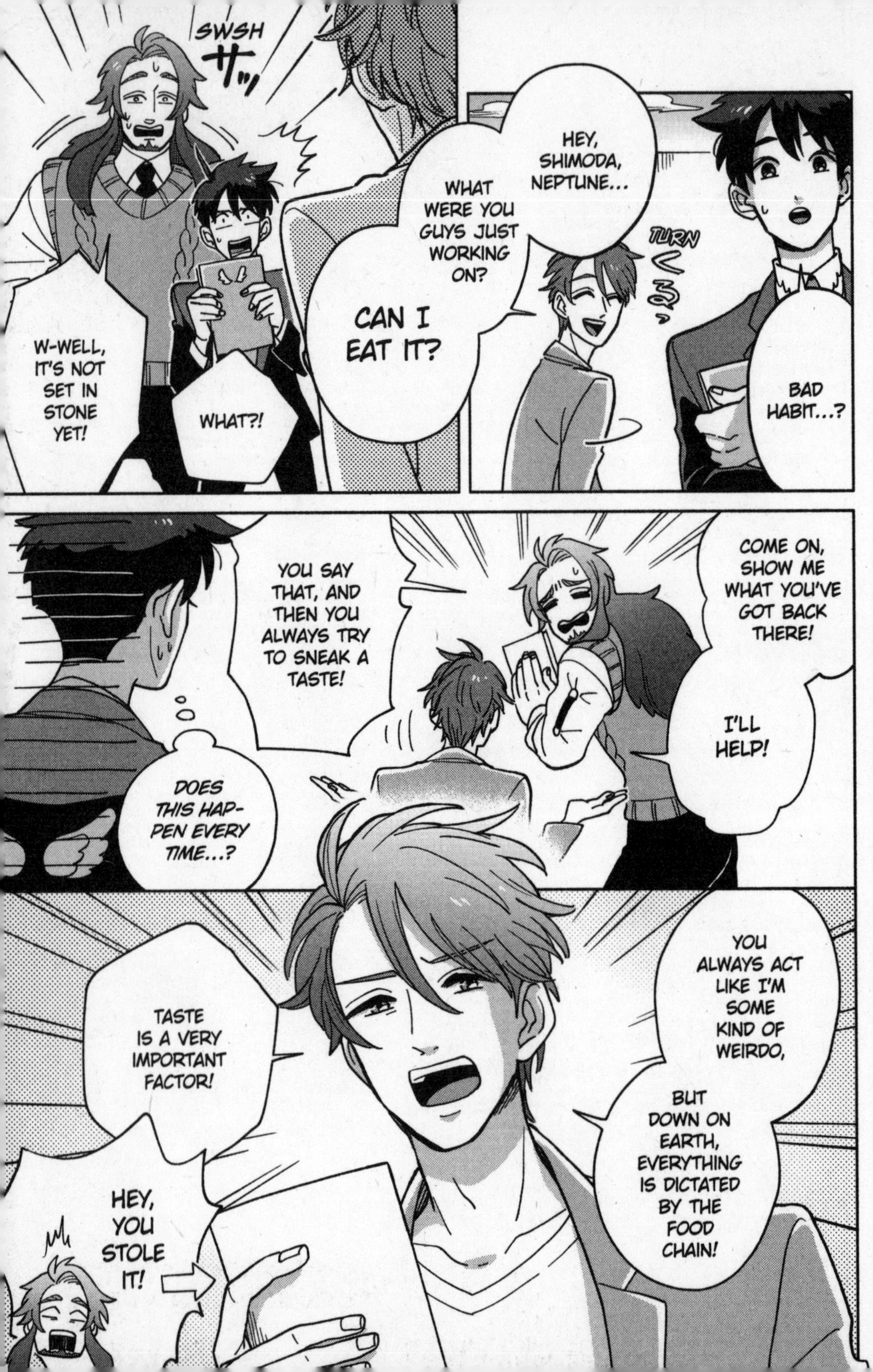
HEY, SHIMODA, NEPTUNE... WHAT WERE YOU GUYS JUST WORKING ON?
TURN くる
CAN I EAT IT?
BAD HABIT...?
SWSH サッ
W-WELL, IT'S NOT SET IN STONE YET!
WHAT?!
COME ON, SHOW ME WHAT YOU'VE GOT BACK THERE!
I'LL HELP!
YOU SAY THAT, AND THEN YOU ALWAYS TRY TO SNEAK A TASTE!
DOES THIS HAP-PEN EVERY TIME...?
YOU ALWAYS ACT LIKE I'M SOME KIND OF WEIRDO,
BUT DOWN ON EARTH, EVERYTHING IS DICTATED BY THE FOOD CHAIN!
TASTE IS A VERY IMPORTANT FACTOR!
HEY, YOU STOLE IT!

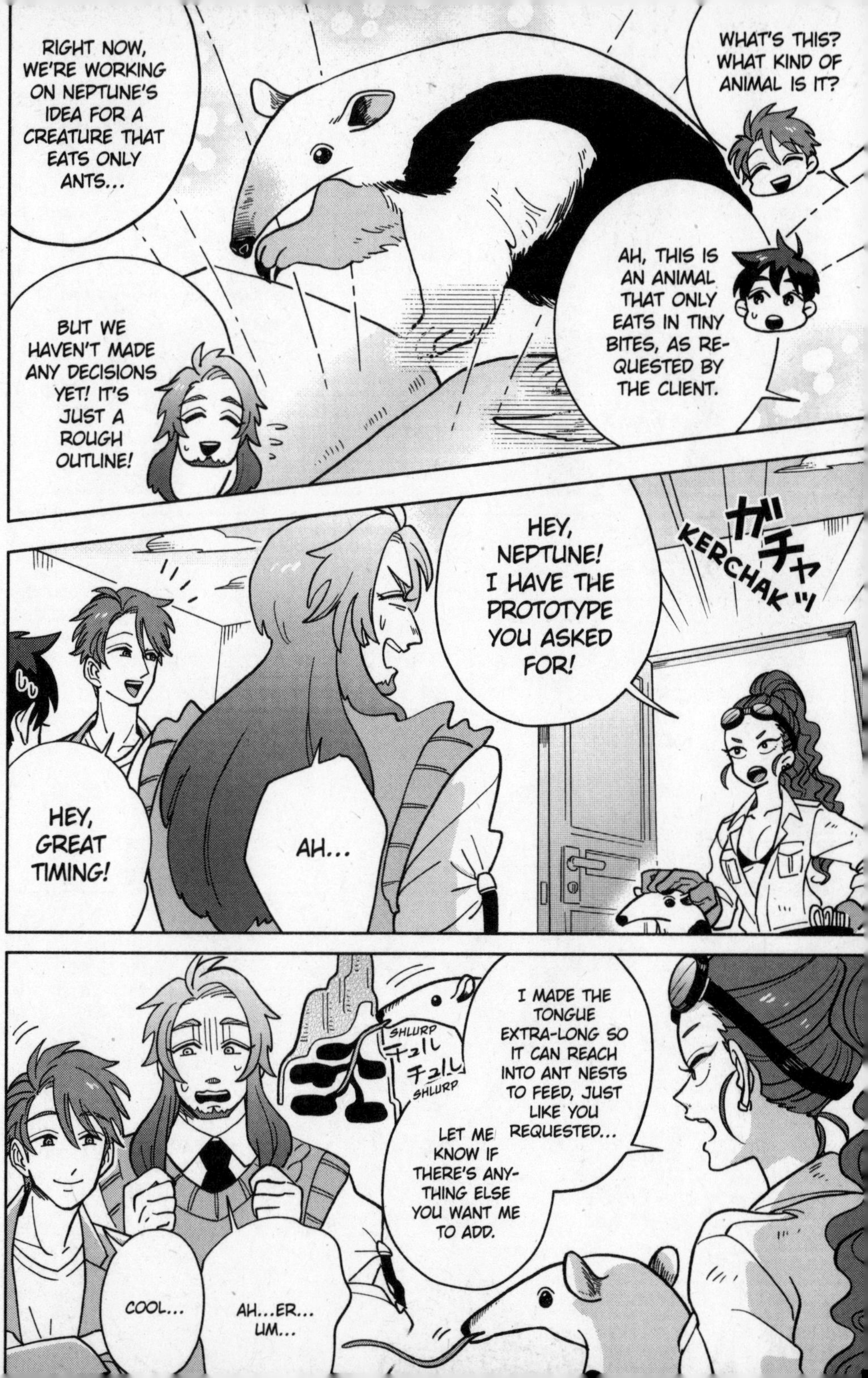
WHAT'S THIS? WHAT KIND OF ANIMAL IS IT?
AH, THIS IS AN ANIMAL THAT ONLY EATS IN TINY BITES, AS RE-QUESTED BY THE CLIENT.
RIGHT NOW, WE'RE WORKING ON NEPTUNE'S IDEA FOR A CREATURE THAT EATS ONLY ANTS...
BUT WE HAVEN'T MADE ANY DECISIONS YET! IT'S JUST A ROUGH OUTLINE!
ガチャッ
KERCHAK
HEY, NEPTUNE! I HAVE THE PROTOTYPE YOU ASKED FOR!
AH...
HEY, GREAT TIMING!
I MADE THE TONGUE EXTRA-LONG SO IT CAN REACH INTO ANT NESTS TO FEED, JUST LIKE YOU REQUESTED...
チュル
SHLURP
チュル
SHLURP
LET ME KNOW IF THERE'S ANY-THING ELSE YOU WANT ME TO ADD.
AH...ER... UM...
COOL...

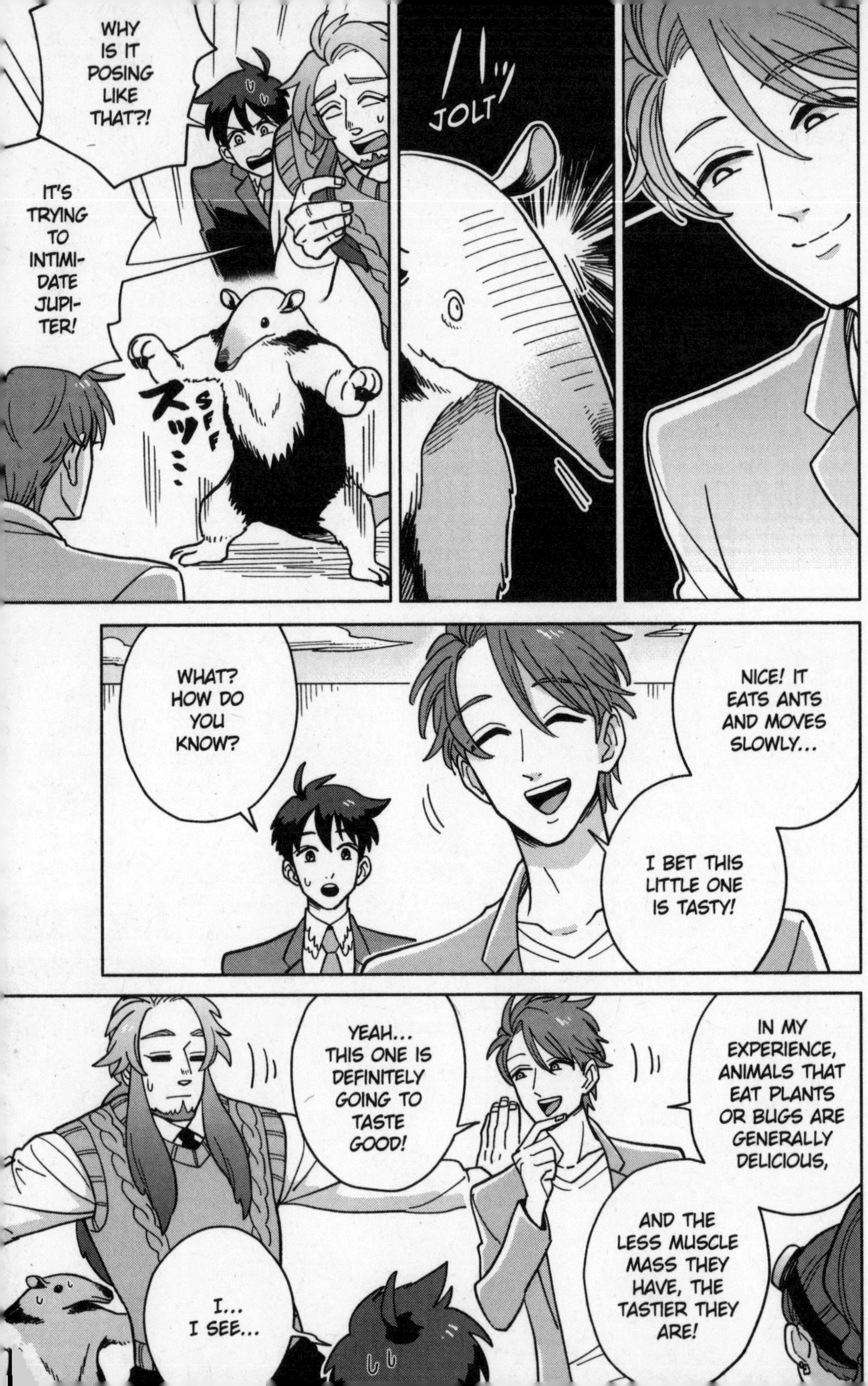
JOLT
WHY IS IT POSING LIKE THAT?!
IT'S TRYING TO INTIMIDATE JUPITER!
スッ… SFF
NICE! IT EATS ANTS AND MOVES SLOWLY...
I BET THIS LITTLE ONE IS TASTY!
WHAT? HOW DO YOU KNOW?
IN MY EXPERIENCE, ANIMALS THAT EAT PLANTS OR BUGS ARE GENERALLY DELICIOUS,
AND THE LESS MUSCLE MASS THEY HAVE, THE TASTIER THEY ARE!
YEAH... THIS ONE IS DEFINITELY GOING TO TASTE GOOD!
I... I SEE...

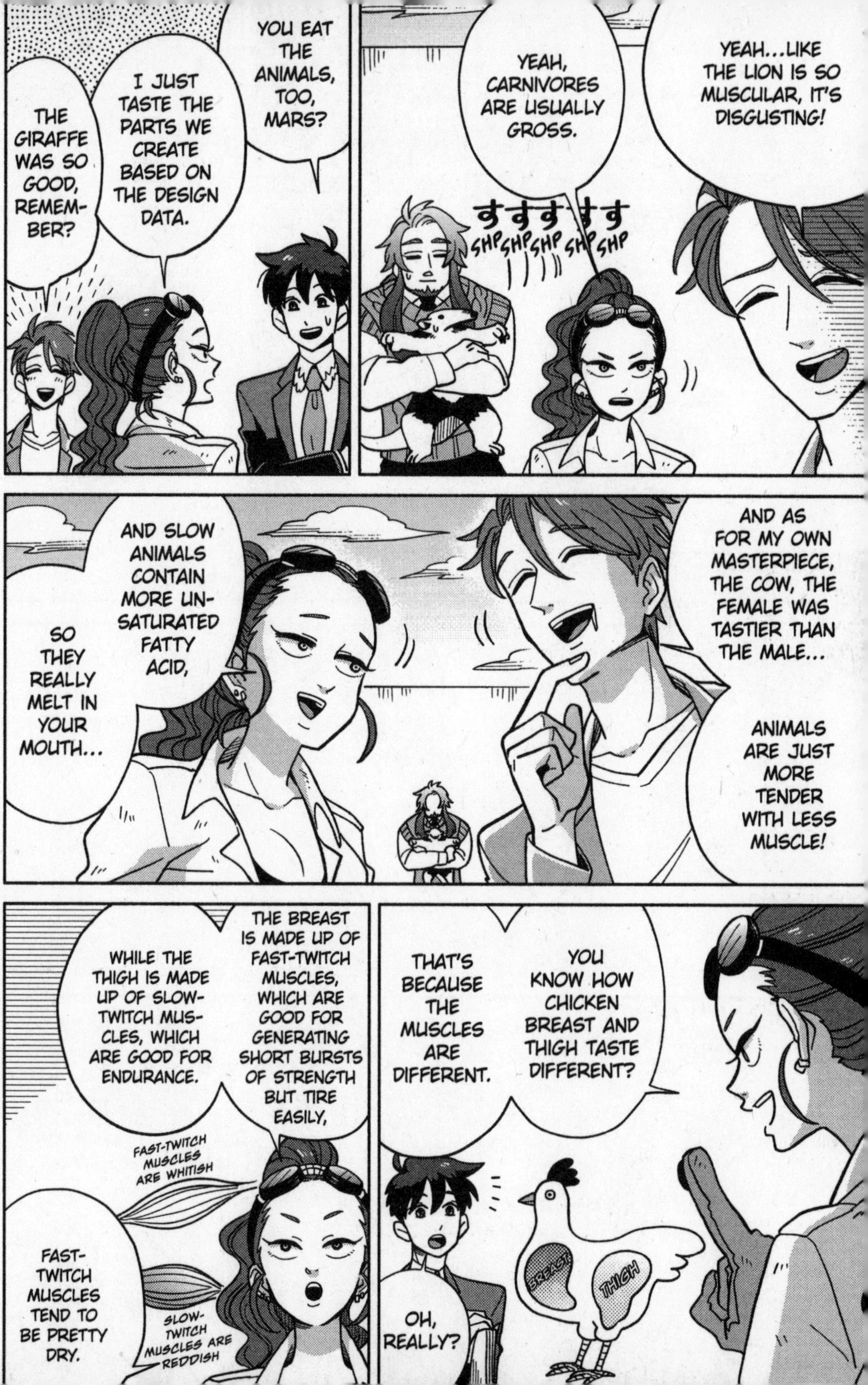
YEAH…LIKE THE LION IS SO MUSCULAR, IT'S DISGUSTING!
YEAH, CARNIVORES ARE USUALLY GROSS.
すすすすす
SHP SHP SHP SHP SHP
YOU EAT THE ANIMALS, TOO, MARS?
I JUST TASTE THE PARTS WE CREATE BASED ON THE DESIGN DATA.
THE GIRAFFE WAS SO GOOD, REMEMBER?
AND AS FOR MY OWN MASTERPIECE, THE COW, THE FEMALE WAS TASTIER THAN THE MALE…
ANIMALS ARE JUST MORE TENDER WITH LESS MUSCLE!
AND SLOW ANIMALS CONTAIN MORE UN-SATURATED FATTY ACID,
SO THEY REALLY MELT IN YOUR MOUTH…
YOU KNOW HOW CHICKEN BREAST AND THIGH TASTE DIFFERENT?
THAT'S BECAUSE THE MUSCLES ARE DIFFERENT.
BREAST
THIGH
OH, REALLY?
THE BREAST IS MADE UP OF FAST-TWITCH MUSCLES, WHICH ARE GOOD FOR GENERATING SHORT BURSTS OF STRENGTH BUT TIRE EASILY,
WHILE THE THIGH IS MADE UP OF SLOW-TWITCH MUS-CLES, WHICH ARE GOOD FOR ENDURANCE.
FAST-TWITCH MUSCLES ARE WHITISH
FAST-TWITCH MUSCLES TEND TO BE PRETTY DRY.
SLOW-TWITCH MUSCLES ARE REDDISH

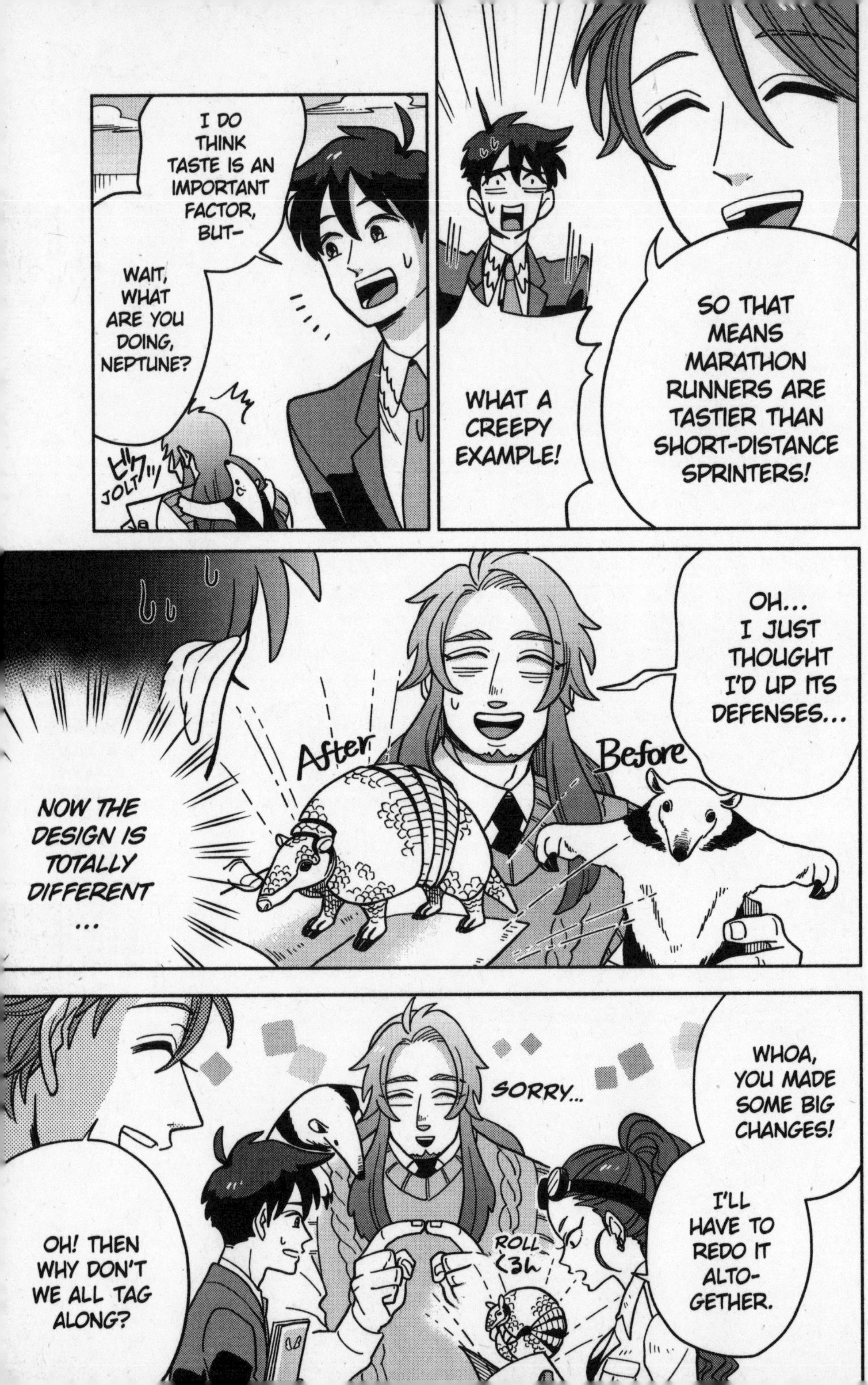
SO THAT MEANS MARATHON RUNNERS ARE TASTIER THAN SHORT-DISTANCE SPRINTERS!
WHAT A CREEPY EXAMPLE!
I DO THINK TASTE IS AN IMPORTANT FACTOR, BUT-
WAIT, WHAT ARE YOU DOING, NEPTUNE?
ビクッ JOLT
OH... I JUST THOUGHT I'D UP ITS DEFENSES...
Before
After
NOW THE DESIGN IS TOTALLY DIFFERENT...
WHOA, YOU MADE SOME BIG CHANGES!
I'LL HAVE TO REDO IT ALTO-GETHER.
SORRY...
ROLL くるん
OH! THEN WHY DON'T WE ALL TAG ALONG?

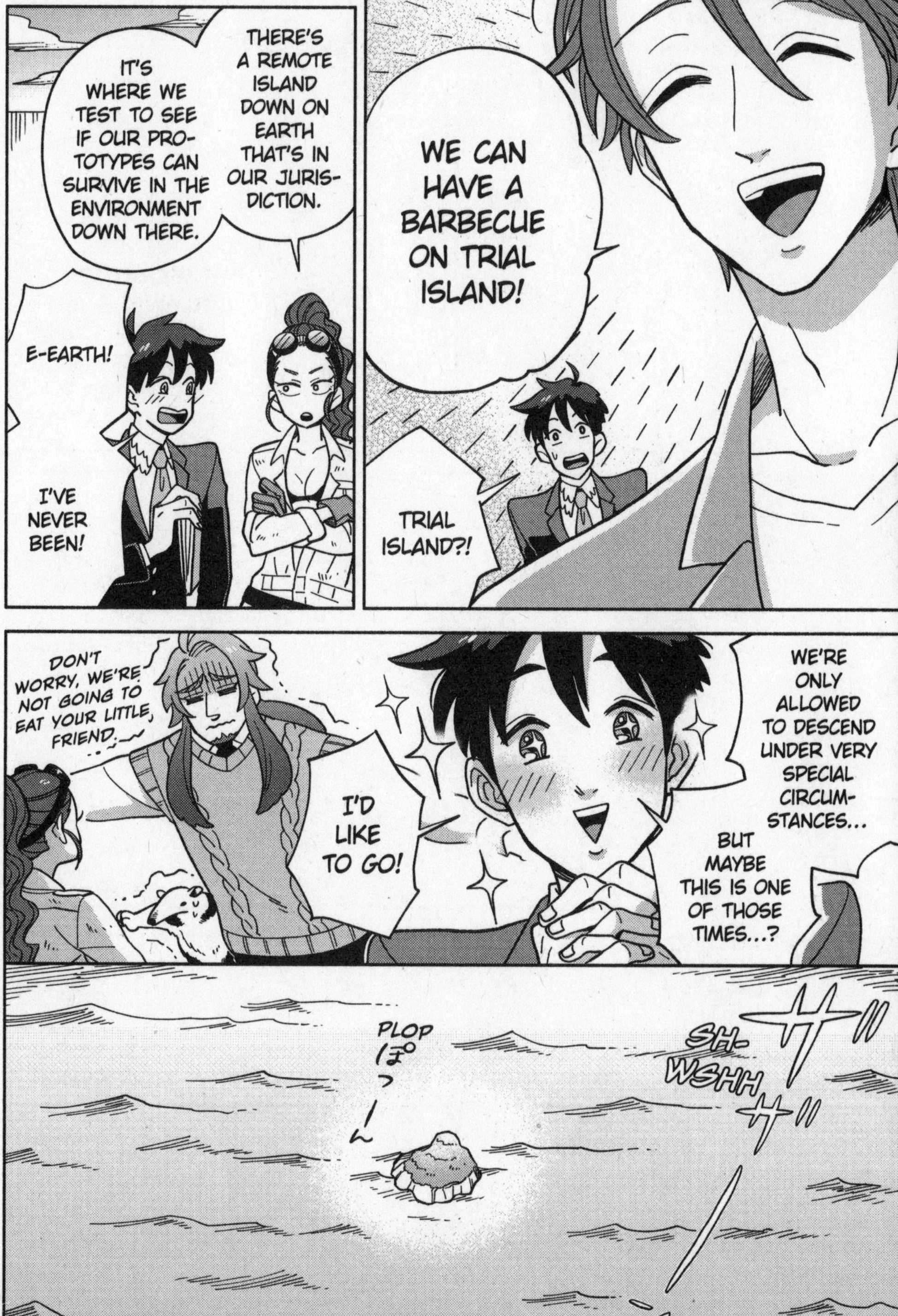
WE CAN HAVE A BARBECUE ON TRIAL ISLAND!
TRIAL ISLAND?!
THERE'S A REMOTE ISLAND DOWN ON EARTH THAT'S IN OUR JURIS-DICTION.
IT'S WHERE WE TEST TO SEE IF OUR PRO-TOTYPES CAN SURVIVE IN THE ENVIRONMENT DOWN THERE.
E-EARTH!
I'VE NEVER BEEN!
WE'RE ONLY ALLOWED TO DESCEND UNDER VERY SPECIAL CIRCUM-STANCES...
BUT MAYBE THIS IS ONE OF THOSE TIMES...?
I'D LIKE TO GO!
DON'T WORRY, WE'RE NOT GOING TO EAT YOUR LITTLE FRIEND.
SH-WSHH
PLOP

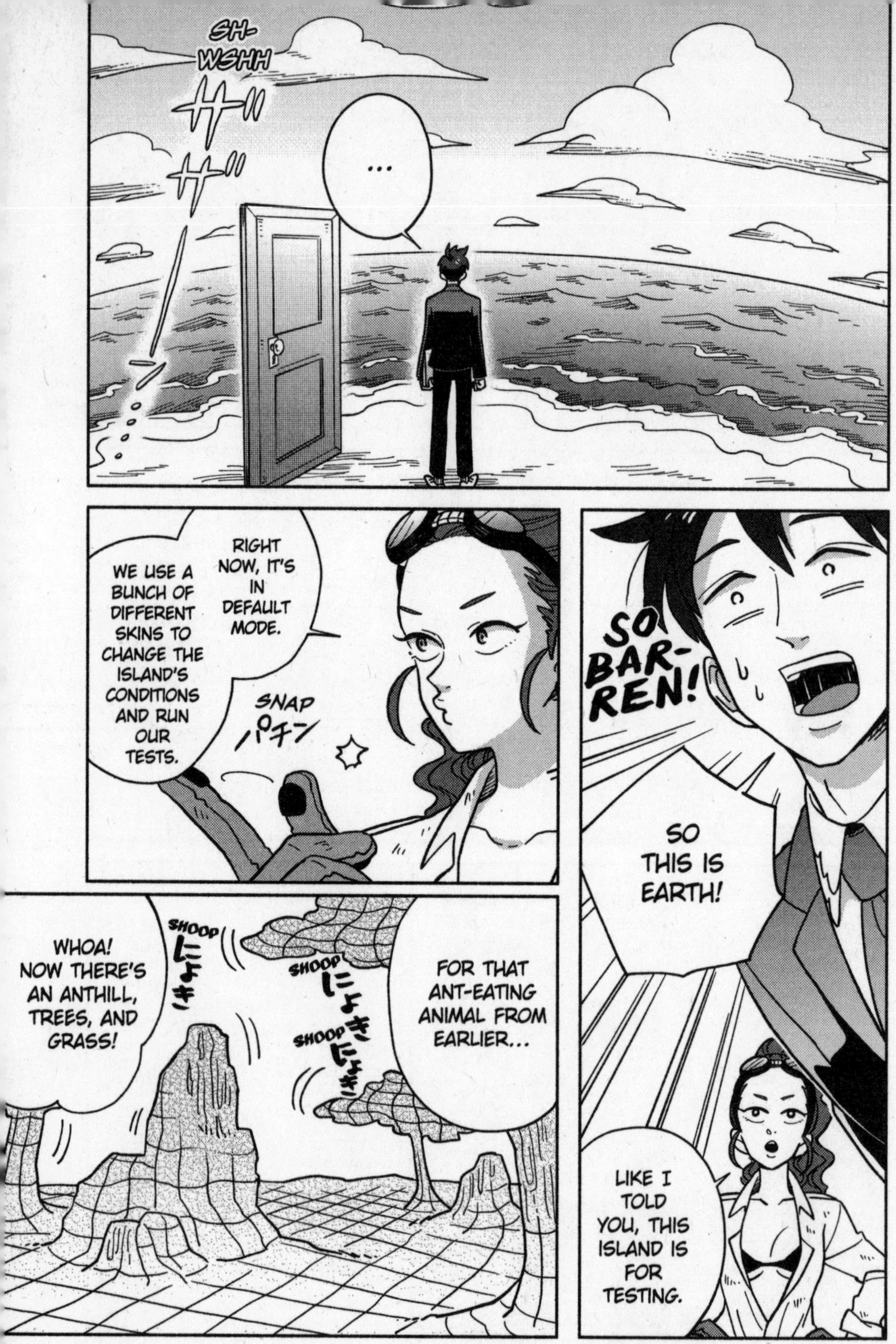
SH-WSHH
ザッ
ザッ
...
SO BAR-REN!
SO THIS IS EARTH!
LIKE I TOLD YOU, THIS ISLAND IS FOR TESTING.
RIGHT NOW, IT'S IN DEFAULT MODE.
WE USE A BUNCH OF DIFFERENT SKINS TO CHANGE THE ISLAND'S CONDITIONS AND RUN OUR TESTS.
SNAP
パチン
FOR THAT ANT-EATING ANIMAL FROM EARLIER...
SHOOP
にょき
SHOOP
にょき
SHOOP
にょき
WHOA! NOW THERE'S AN ANTHILL, TREES, AND GRASS!

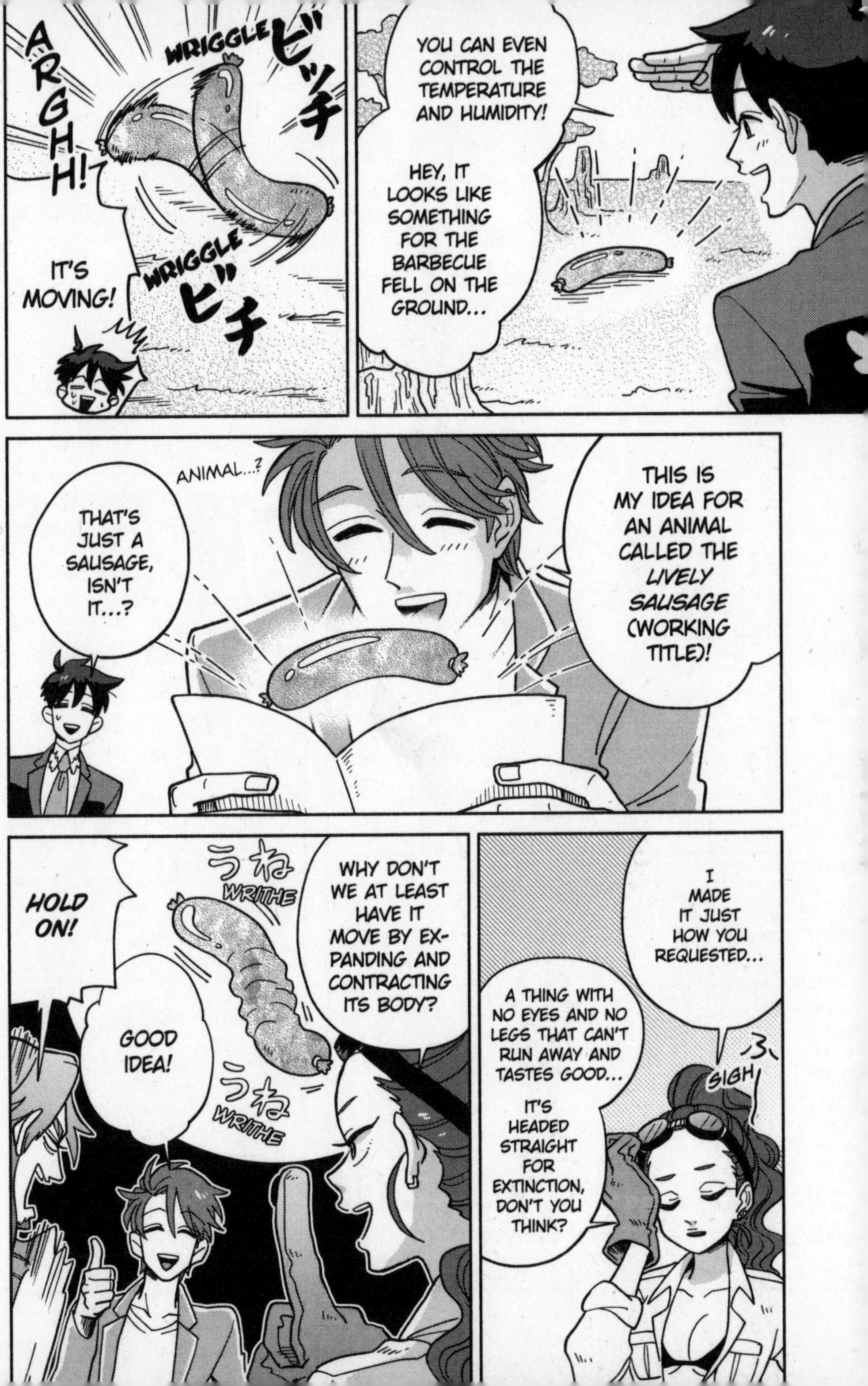
YOU CAN EVEN CONTROL THE TEMPERATURE AND HUMIDITY!
HEY, IT LOOKS LIKE SOMETHING FOR THE BARBECUE FELL ON THE GROUND...
WRIGGLE ビッチ
ARGHH!
WRIGGLE ビチ
IT'S MOVING!
THIS IS MY IDEA FOR AN ANIMAL CALLED THE *LIVELY SAUSAGE* (WORKING TITLE)!
ANIMAL...?
THAT'S JUST A SAUSAGE, ISN'T IT...?
I MADE IT JUST HOW YOU REQUESTED...
A THING WITH NO EYES AND NO LEGS THAT CAN'T RUN AWAY AND TASTES GOOD...
ふ SIGH
IT'S HEADED STRAIGHT FOR EXTINCTION, DON'T YOU THINK?
WHY DON'T WE AT LEAST HAVE IT MOVE BY EXPANDING AND CONTRACTING ITS BODY?
うね WRITHE
HOLD ON!
GOOD IDEA!
うね WRITHE

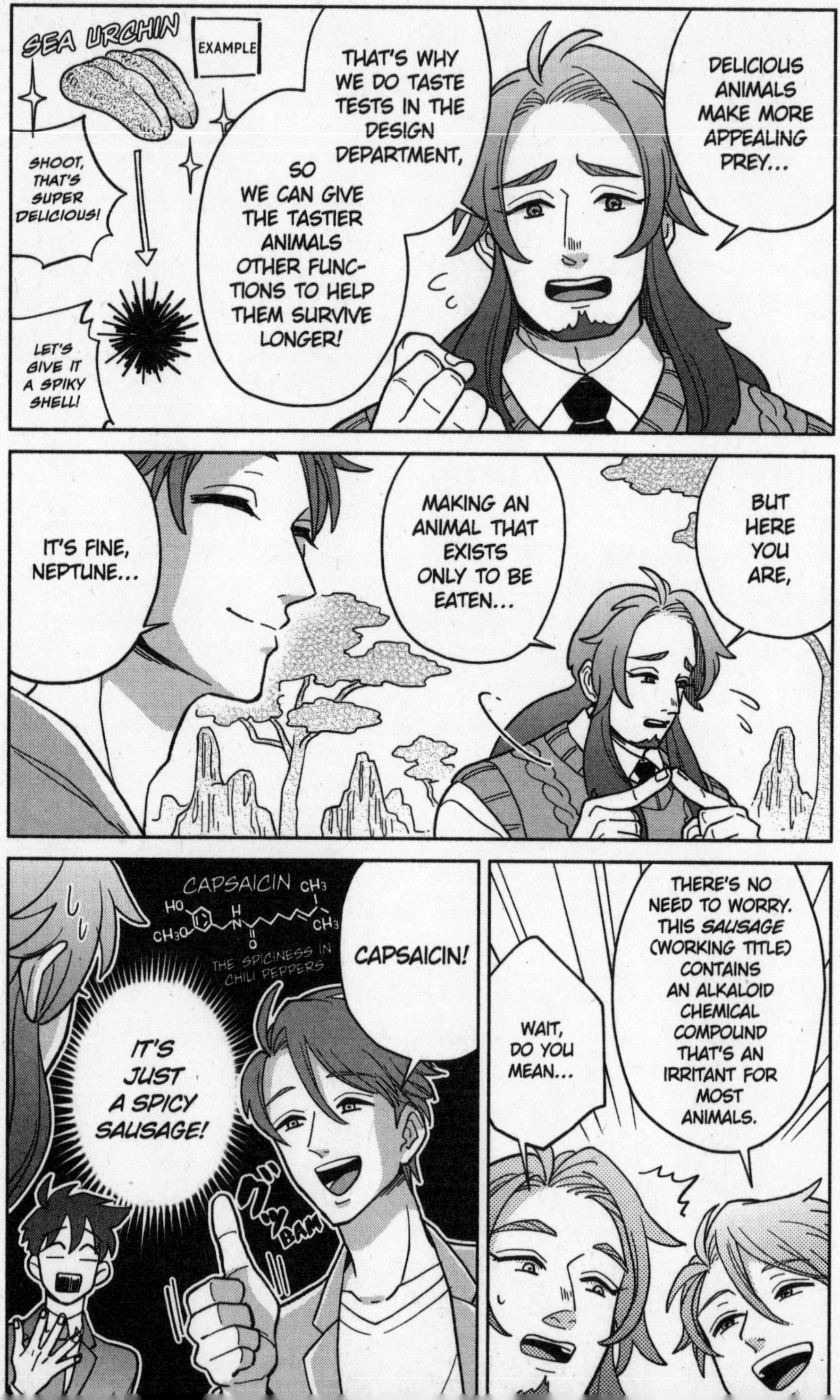
DELICIOUS ANIMALS MAKE MORE APPEALING PREY...
THAT'S WHY WE DO TASTE TESTS IN THE DESIGN DEPARTMENT,
SO WE CAN GIVE THE TASTIER ANIMALS OTHER FUNCTIONS TO HELP THEM SURVIVE LONGER!
EXAMPLE
SEA URCHIN
SHOOT, THAT'S SUPER DELICIOUS!
LET'S GIVE IT A SPIKY SHELL!
BUT HERE YOU ARE,
MAKING AN ANIMAL THAT EXISTS ONLY TO BE EATEN...
IT'S FINE, NEPTUNE...
THERE'S NO NEED TO WORRY. THIS *SAUSAGE* (WORKING TITLE) CONTAINS AN ALKALOID CHEMICAL COMPOUND THAT'S AN IRRITANT FOR MOST ANIMALS.
WAIT, DO YOU MEAN...
CAPSAICIN!
CAPSAICIN
THE SPICINESS IN CHILI PEPPERS
IT'S JUST A SPICY SAUSAGE!
BAM

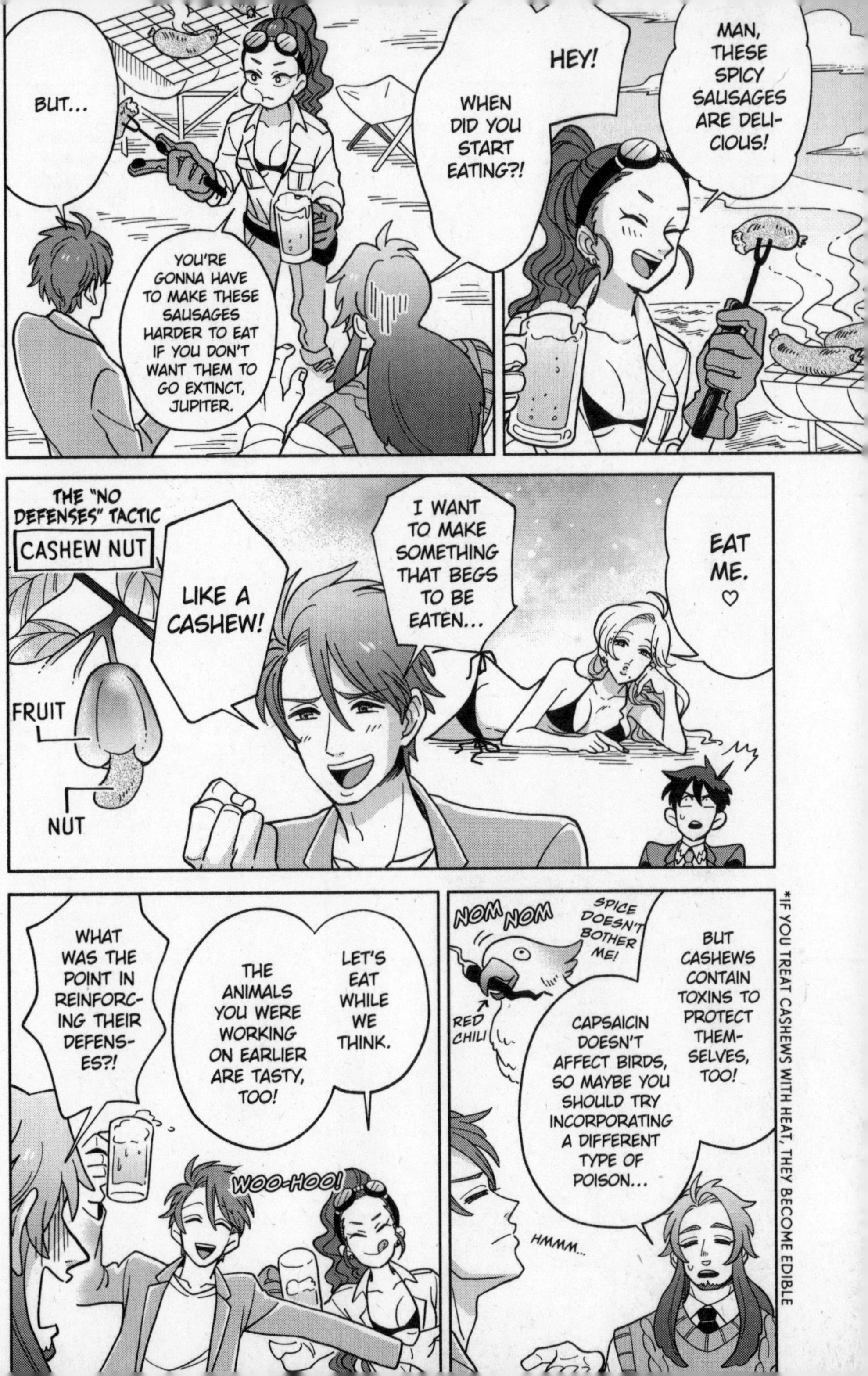
MAN, THESE SPICY SAUSAGES ARE DELI-CIOUS!
HEY!
WHEN DID YOU START EATING?!
BUT...
YOU'RE GONNA HAVE TO MAKE THESE SAUSAGES HARDER TO EAT IF YOU DON'T WANT THEM TO GO EXTINCT, JUPITER.
EAT ME. ♡
I WANT TO MAKE SOMETHING THAT BEGS TO BE EATEN...
LIKE A CASHEW!
THE "NO DEFENSES" TACTIC
CASHEW NUT
FRUIT
NUT
SPICE DOESN'T BOTHER ME!
NOM NOM
RED CHILI
BUT CASHEWS CONTAIN TOXINS TO PROTECT THEM-SELVES, TOO!
CAPSAICIN DOESN'T AFFECT BIRDS, SO MAYBE YOU SHOULD TRY INCORPORATING A DIFFERENT TYPE OF POISON...
HMMM...
LET'S EAT WHILE WE THINK.
THE ANIMALS YOU WERE WORKING ON EARLIER ARE TASTY, TOO!
WOO-HOO!
WHAT WAS THE POINT IN REINFORC-ING THEIR DEFENS-ES?!

*IF YOU TREAT CASHEWS WITH HEAT, THEY BECOME EDIBLE

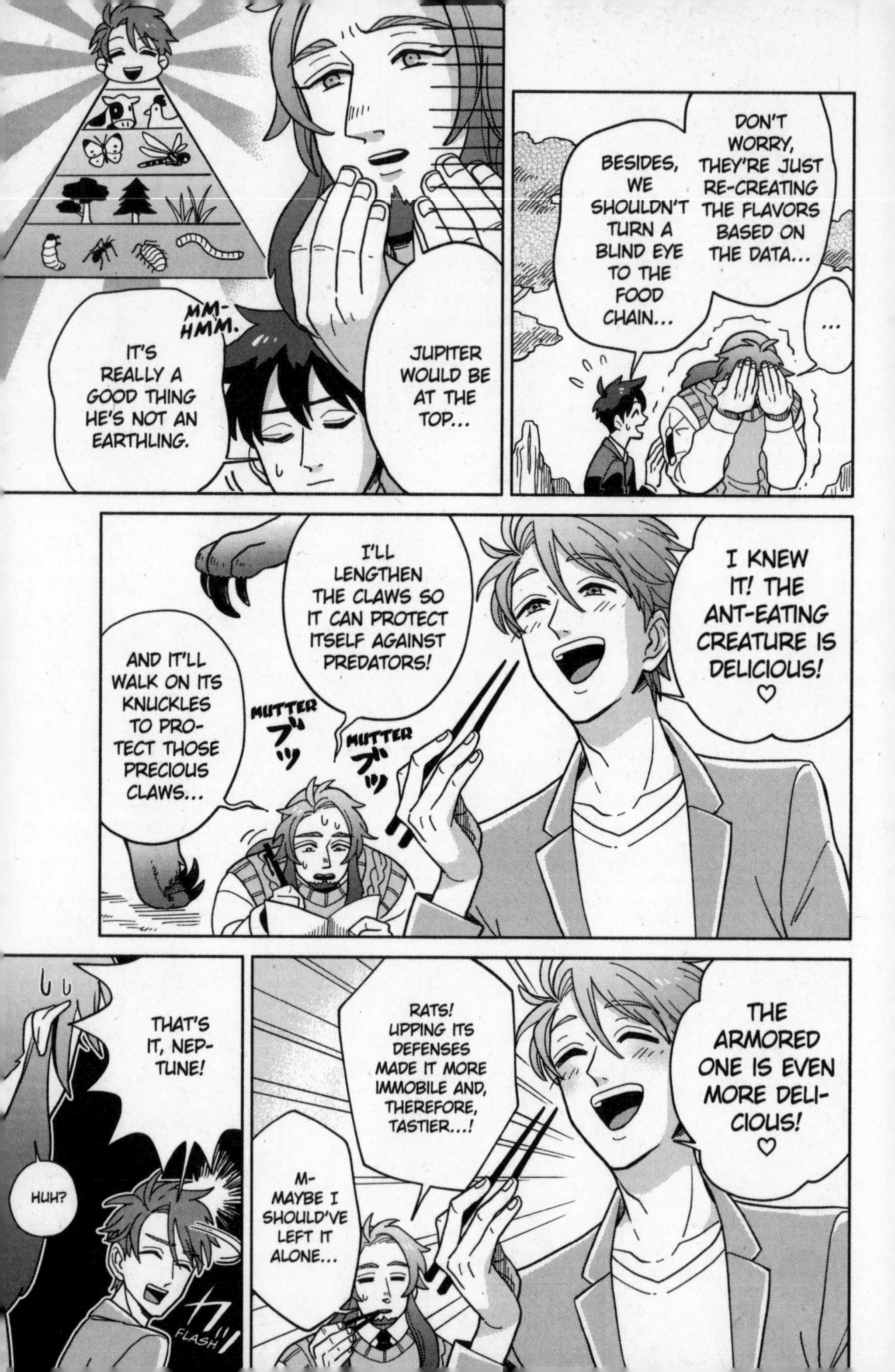

DON'T WORRY, THEY'RE JUST RE-CREATING THE FLAVORS BASED ON THE DATA...
BESIDES, WE SHOULDN'T TURN A BLIND EYE TO THE FOOD CHAIN...
...
JUPITER WOULD BE AT THE TOP...
MM-HMM.
IT'S REALLY A GOOD THING HE'S NOT AN EARTHLING.
I KNEW IT! THE ANT-EATING CREATURE IS DELICIOUS! ♡
I'LL LENGTHEN THE CLAWS SO IT CAN PROTECT ITSELF AGAINST PREDATORS!
MUTTER ブツ
MUTTER ブツ
AND IT'LL WALK ON ITS KNUCKLES TO PROTECT THOSE PRECIOUS CLAWS...
THE ARMORED ONE IS EVEN MORE DELICIOUS! ♡
RATS! UPPING ITS DEFENSES MADE IT MORE IMMOBILE AND, THEREFORE, TASTIER...!
M-MAYBE I SHOULD'VE LEFT IT ALONE...
THAT'S IT, NEPTUNE!
HUH?
FLASH

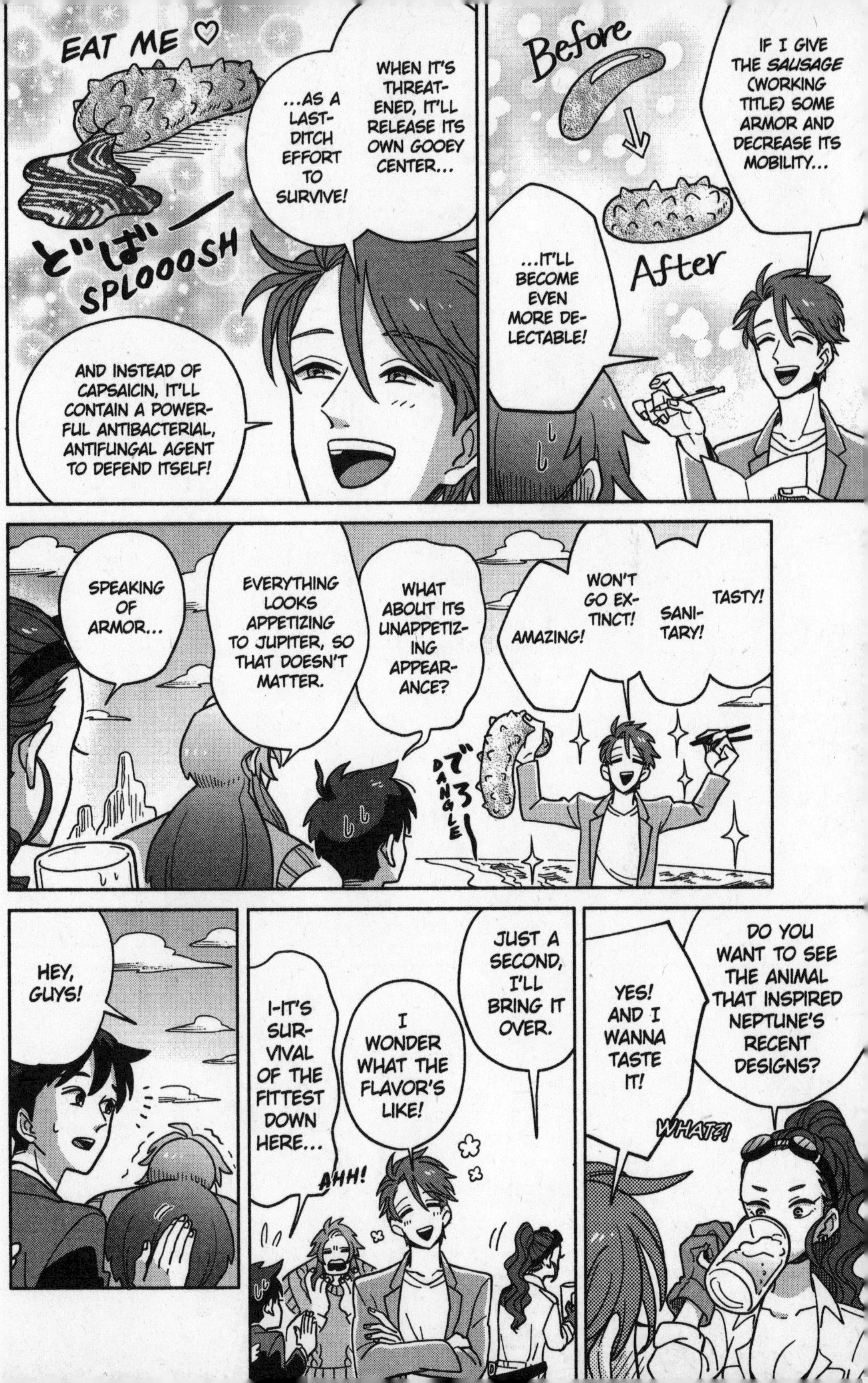
Before
IF I GIVE THE *SAUSAGE* (WORKING TITLE) SOME ARMOR AND DECREASE ITS MOBILITY...
After
...IT'LL BECOME EVEN MORE DE-LECTABLE!
WHEN IT'S THREAT-ENED, IT'LL RELEASE ITS OWN GOOEY CENTER...
...AS A LAST-DITCH EFFORT TO SURVIVE!
EAT ME ♡
どばー
SPLOOOSH
AND INSTEAD OF CAPSAICIN, IT'LL CONTAIN A POWER-FUL ANTIBACTERIAL, ANTIFUNGAL AGENT TO DEFEND ITSELF!
TASTY!
WON'T GO EX-TINCT!
SANI-TARY!
AMAZING!
WHAT ABOUT ITS UNAPPETIZ-ING APPEAR-ANCE?
EVERYTHING LOOKS APPETIZING TO JUPITER, SO THAT DOESN'T MATTER.
SPEAKING OF ARMOR...
でろ
DANGLE
DO YOU WANT TO SEE THE ANIMAL THAT INSPIRED NEPTUNE'S RECENT DESIGNS?
YES! AND I WANNA TASTE IT!
WHAT?!
JUST A SECOND, I'LL BRING IT OVER.
I WONDER WHAT THE FLAVOR'S LIKE!
I-IT'S SUR-VIVAL OF THE FITTEST DOWN HERE...
AHH!
HEY, GUYS!

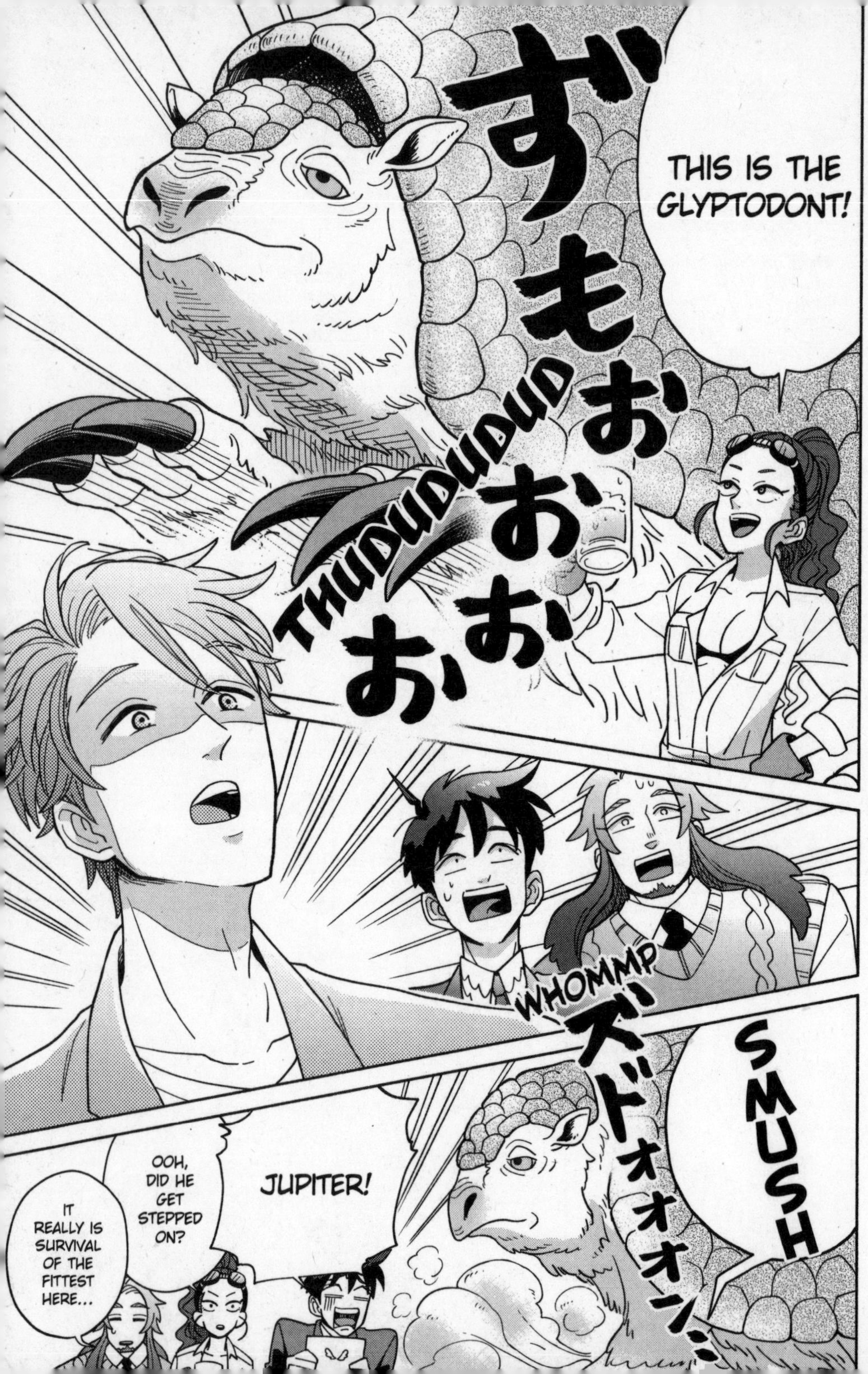
THIS IS THE GLYPTODONT!
ずもおおおお
THUDUDUDUD
SMUSH
ズドォオオン
WHOMMP
JUPITER!
OOH, DID HE GET STEPPED ON?
IT REALLY IS SURVIVAL OF THE FITTEST HERE...

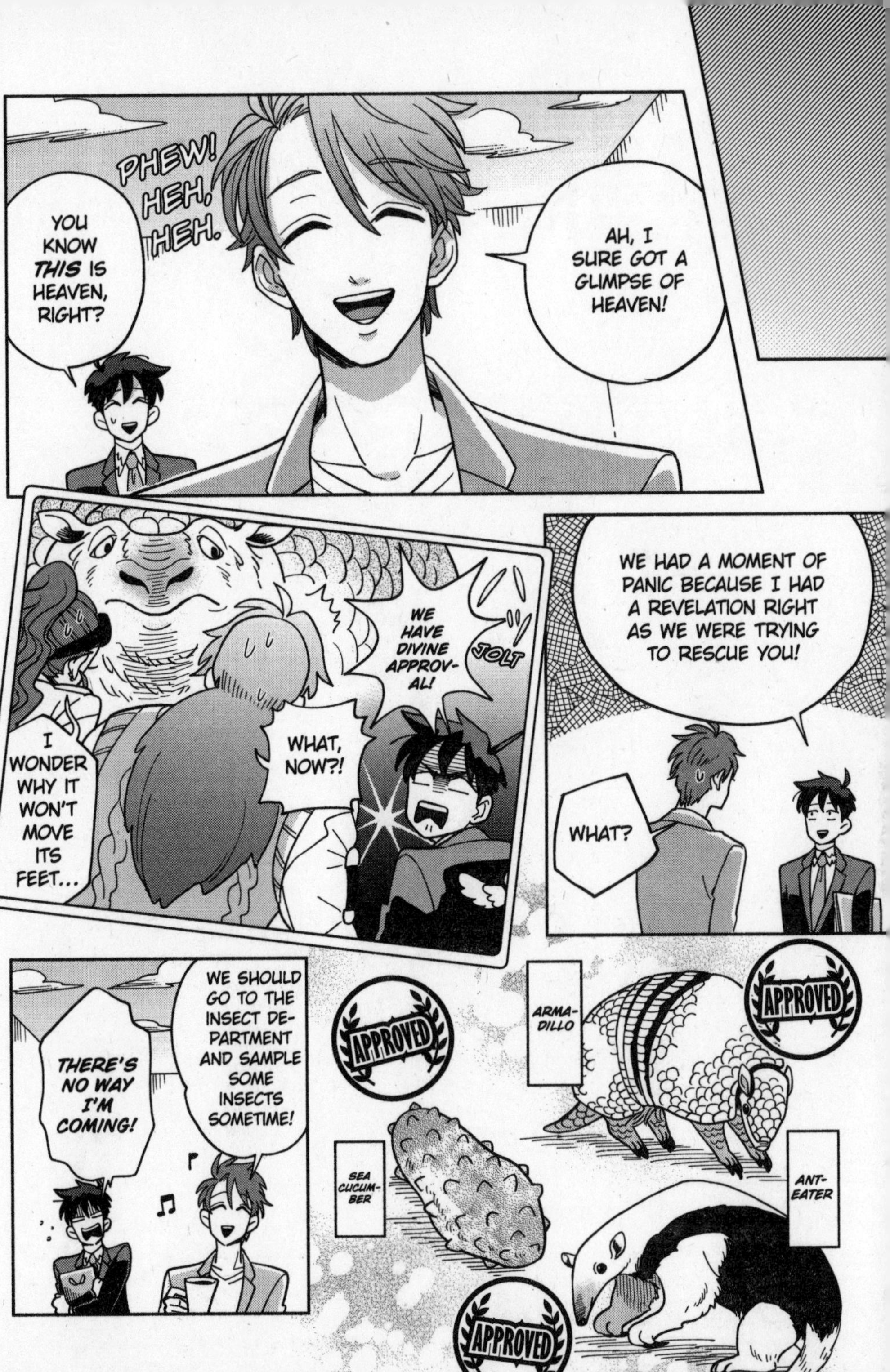
AH, I SURE GOT A GLIMPSE OF HEAVEN!
PHEW! HEH, HEH.
YOU KNOW THIS IS HEAVEN, RIGHT?
WE HAD A MOMENT OF PANIC BECAUSE I HAD A REVELATION RIGHT AS WE WERE TRYING TO RESCUE YOU!
WHAT?
WE HAVE DIVINE APPROV-AL!
JOLT
WHAT, NOW?!
I WONDER WHY IT WON'T MOVE ITS FEET...
APPROVED
ARMA-DILLO
APPROVED
ANT-EATER
SEA CUCUM-BER
APPROVED
WE SHOULD GO TO THE INSECT DE-PARTMENT AND SAMPLE SOME INSECTS SOMETIME!
THERE'S NO WAY I'M COMING!

THE ENCYCLOPEDIA OF REAL ANIMALS 04

ANIMAL ENCYCLOPEDIA

ANIMAL 10 ARMADILLO

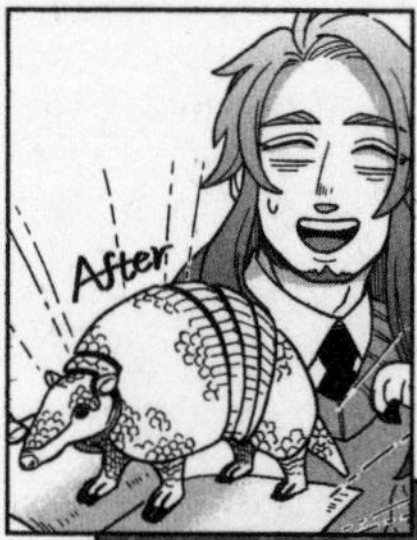
After

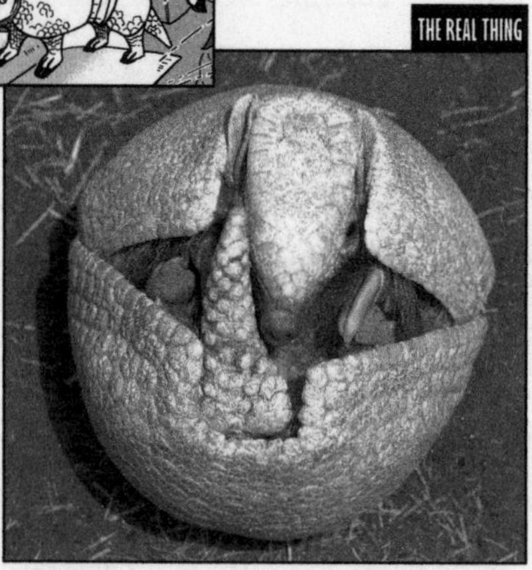
THE REAL THING

Only certain species in the armadillo family can curl into a ball.

Photo: Ardea/Aflo

[Name] Armadillo
[Classification] Class: Mammalia
Superorder: Xenarthra
Order: Cingulata
Family: Dasypodidae
[Range] Southern North America, Central and South America
[Length] 10-100cm (4 in-3 ft)

The armadillo's skin is covered in hard scales, but it is an animal commonly eaten in South America. It's thought that the anteater and armadillo evolved over time to represent an armored and unarmored version of the same creature. It is even more closely related to the glyptodont, a giant animal that measured over three meters (nine-and-a-half-feet) long and lived in South America until 10,000 years ago. Research suggests that glyptodonts may have gone extinct due to overhunting by early humans, who hunted them for their meat and used their hard shells to make tools.

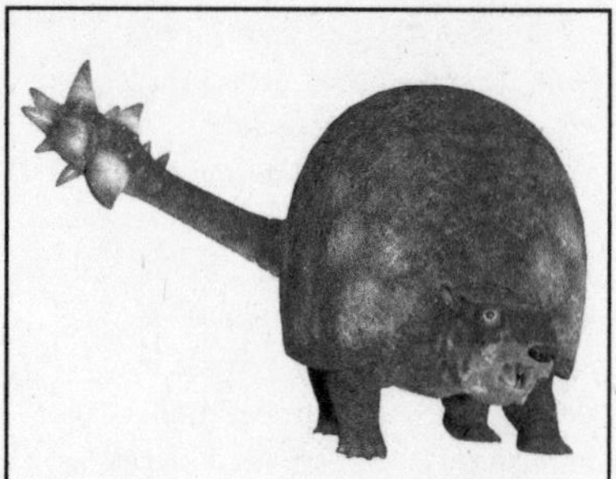

An imagined reproduction of the extinct glyptodont.

ANIMAL 11 | ANTEATER

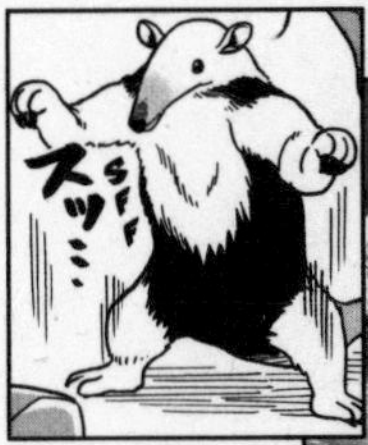
スッ…
SFF

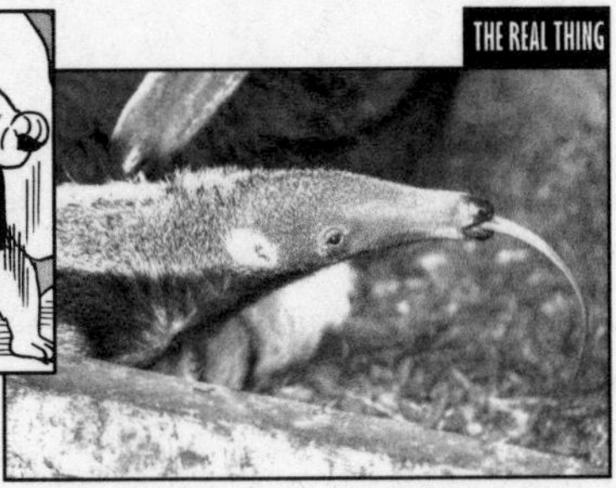
THE REAL THING

The largest of the anteater family, the giant anteater also eats insects and fruit.
Photo: Alamy/Aflo

[Name] Anteater
[Classification] Class: Mammalia
Superorder: Xenarthra
Order: Pilosa
Family: Vermilingua
[Range] Central and South America
[Length] 15-130 cm (6 in-4 ft)

The anteater eats its prey using its long, thin tongue, which is covered in sticky saliva. Its toothless mouth opens only by approximately two centimeters (one inch). The anteater's tongue is exceptionally long, and in the case of the giant anteater, can measure up to 60 centimeters (2 feet). The southern tamandua, introduced in this chapter, stands on its hind legs when threatened by predators. It is not very aggressive but defends itself with its sharp claws when attacked.

ANIMAL 12 | SEA CUCUMBER

Currently, there are over 1,400 species of sea cucumber. The holotoxins they contain have antifungal properties and have been used in medications for infections such as athlete's foot. Some species expel their intestines when attacked. *Konowata* is a rare Japanese delicacy made from salted and fermented sea cucumber intestines, while *kuchiko* is another unusual dish made by drying or salting and fermenting the ovaries. Sea cucumbers are highly regenerative, and can regrow lost organs.

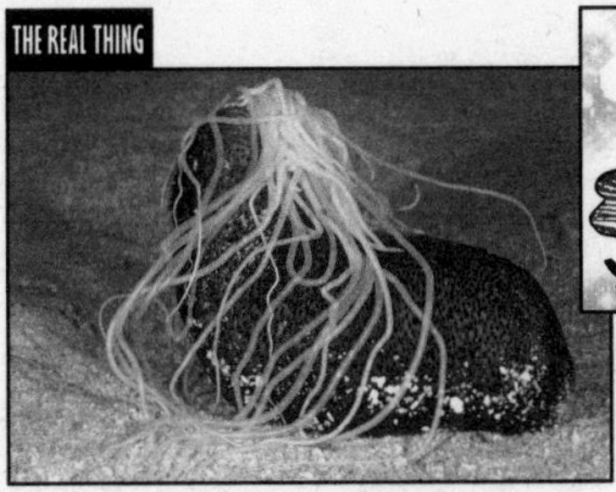
THE REAL THING

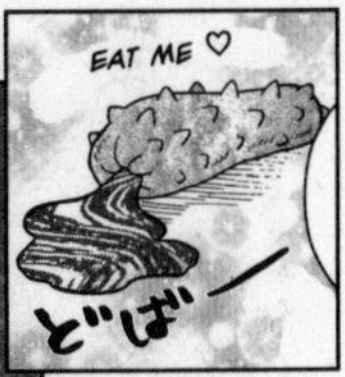
EAT ME ♡
どばー

Certain sea cucumber species protect themselves by expelling sticky cuvierian tubules to immobilize predators.
Photo: Alamy/Aflo

Name] Sea cucumber
[Classification] Phylum: Echinodermata
Class: Holothuroidea
[Habitat] Oceans around the world (They are exclusively marine.)
[Length] 10 cm-4.5 m (4 in-15 ft)

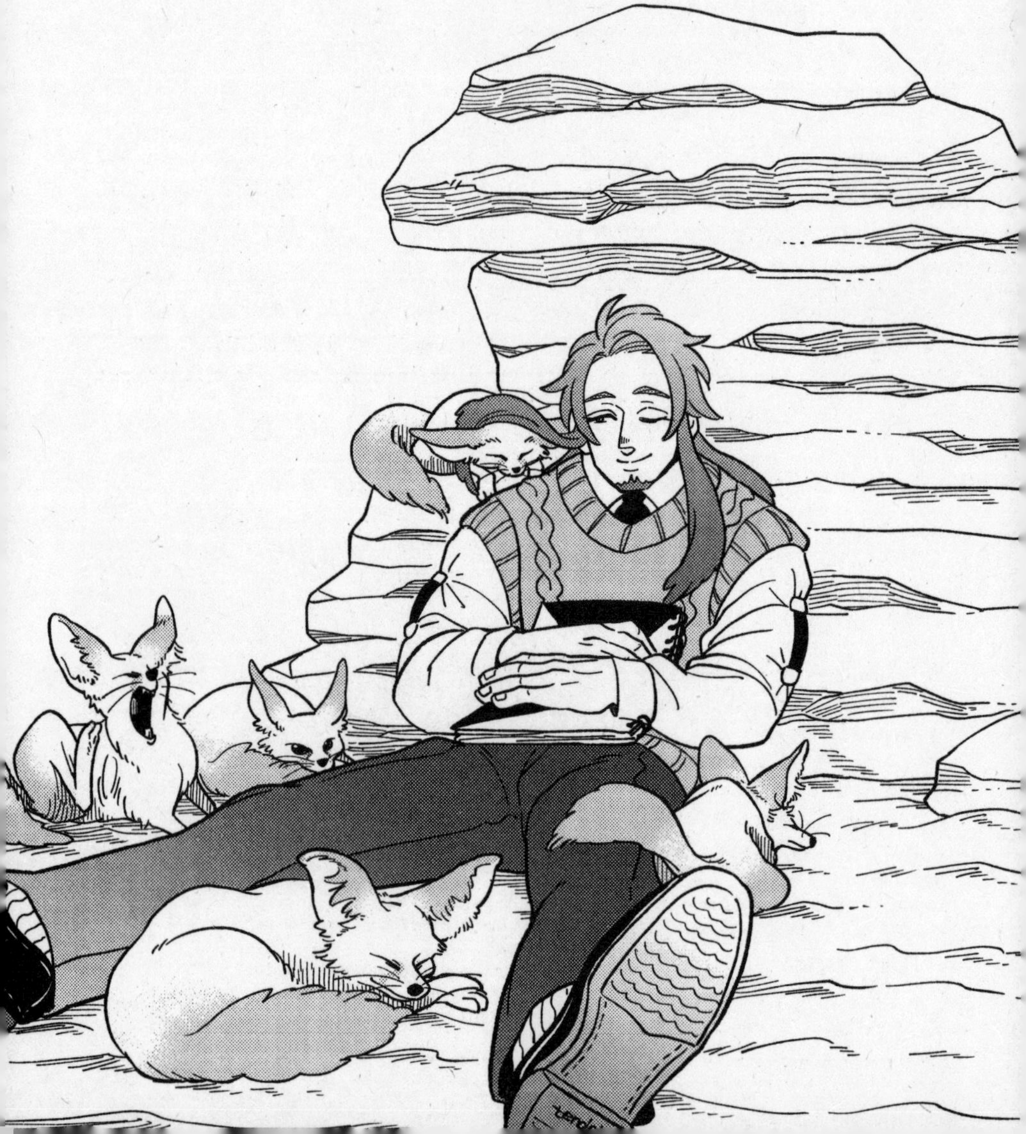

HEAVEN'S DESIGN TEAM

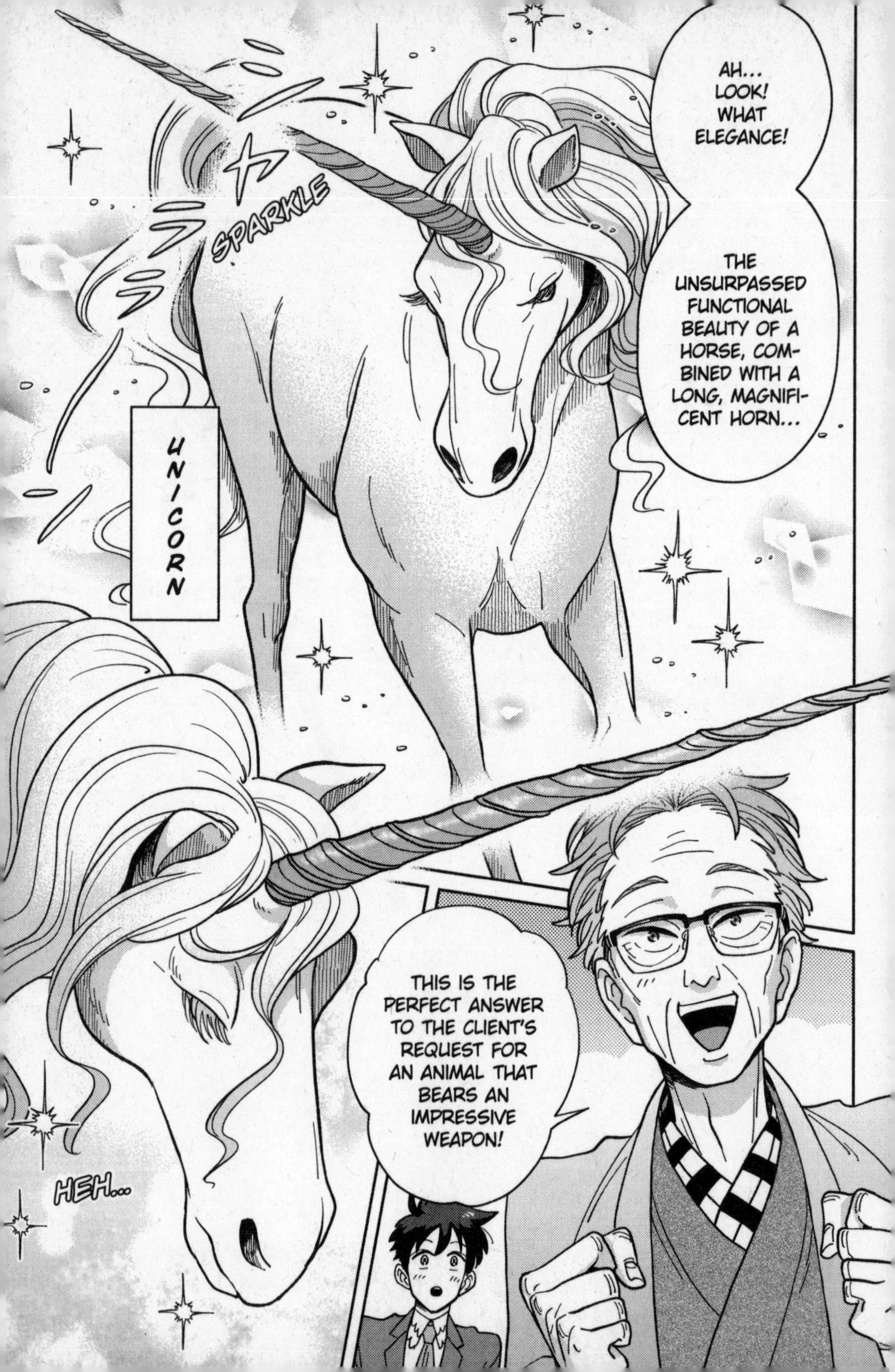
AH... LOOK! WHAT ELEGANCE!
THE UNSURPASSED FUNCTIONAL BEAUTY OF A HORSE, COMBINED WITH A LONG, MAGNIFICENT HORN...
SPARKLE
UNICORN
THIS IS THE PERFECT ANSWER TO THE CLIENT'S REQUEST FOR AN ANIMAL THAT BEARS AN IMPRESSIVE WEAPON!
HEH...

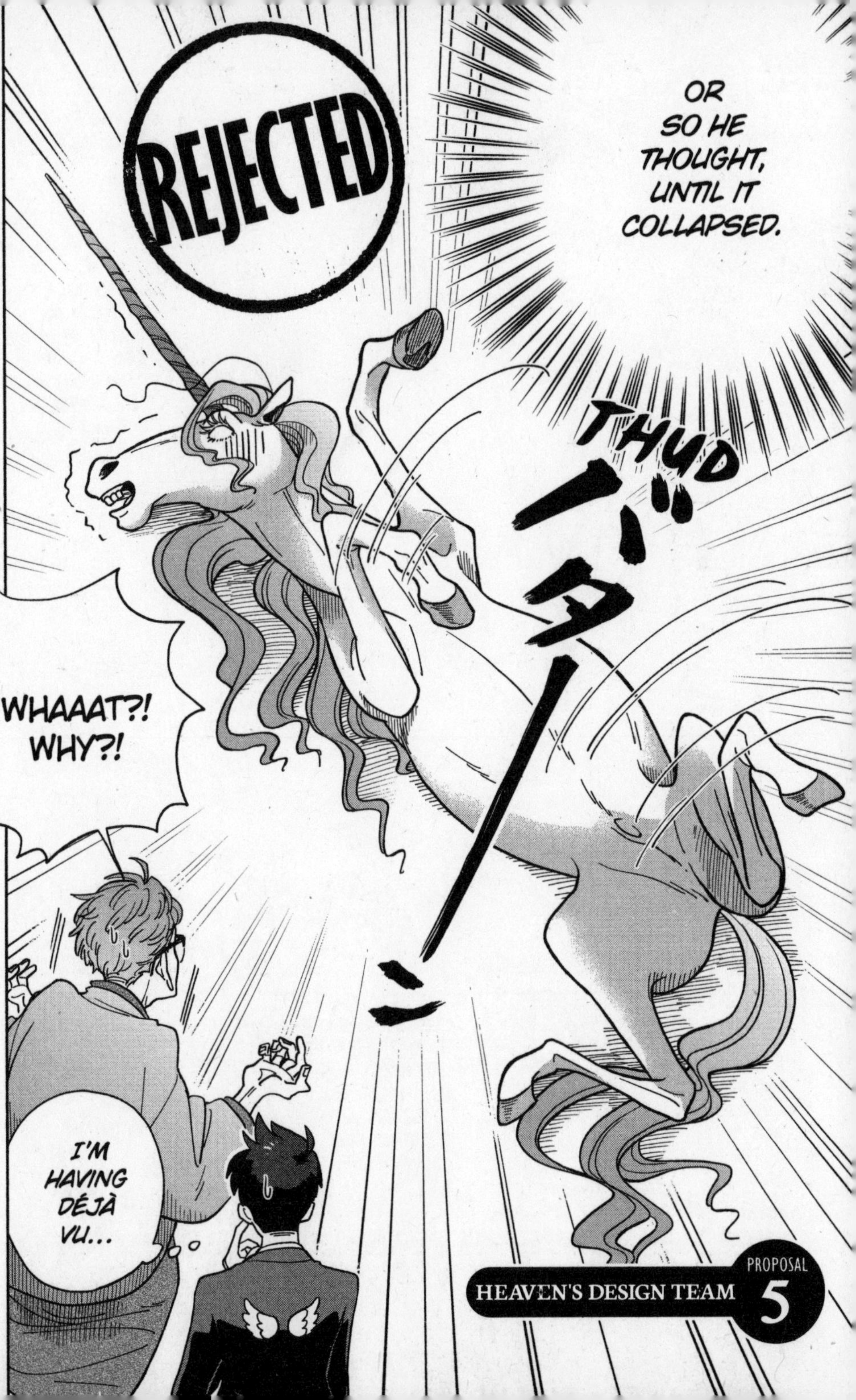
OR SO HE THOUGHT, UNTIL IT COLLAPSED.
REJECTED
THUD
WHAAAT?! WHY?!
I'M HAVING DÉJÀ VU...
HEAVEN'S DESIGN TEAM
PROPOSAL 5

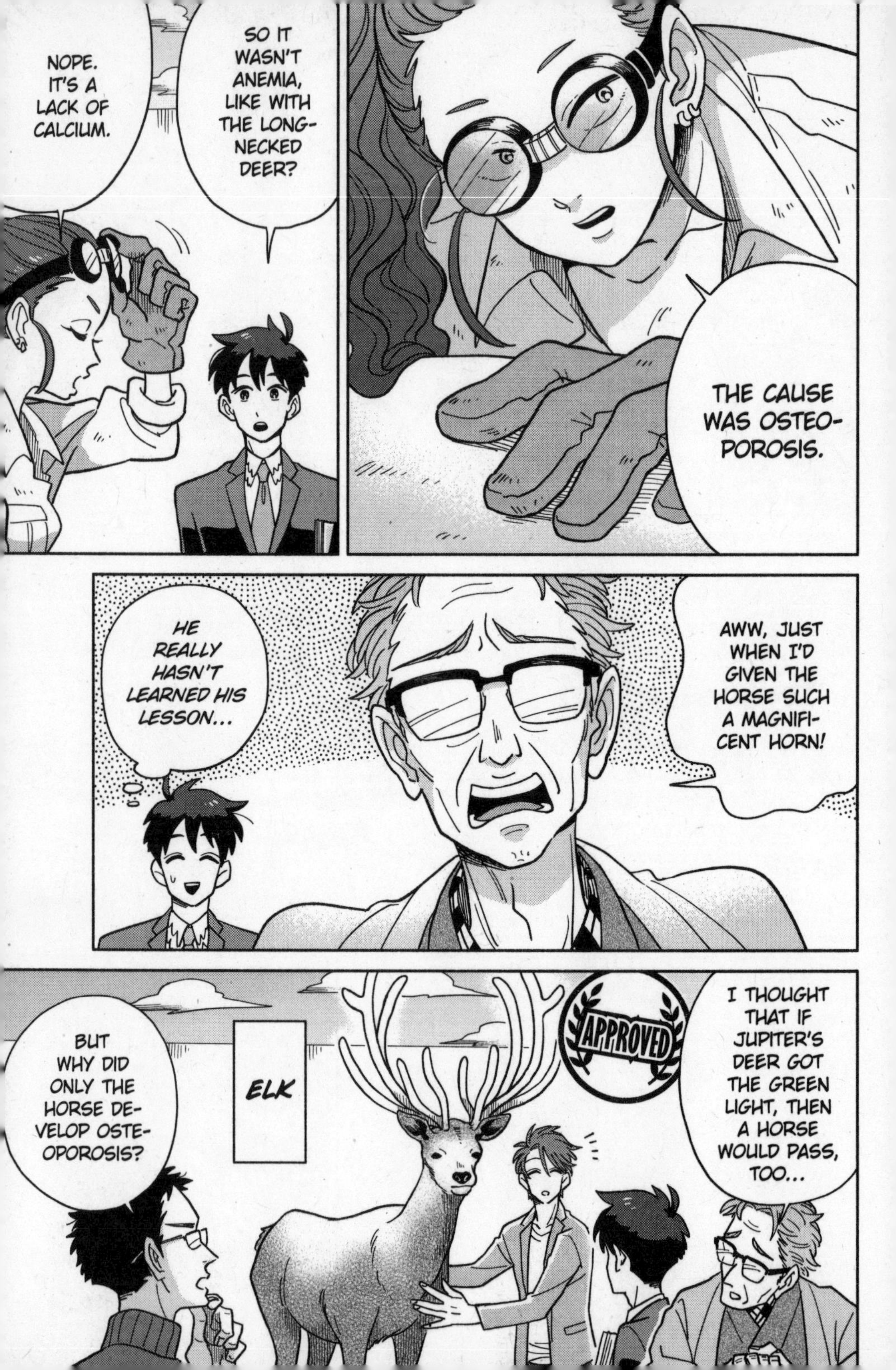
THE CAUSE WAS OSTEO-POROSIS.
SO IT WASN'T ANEMIA, LIKE WITH THE LONG-NECKED DEER?
NOPE. IT'S A LACK OF CALCIUM.
AWW, JUST WHEN I'D GIVEN THE HORSE SUCH A MAGNIFI-CENT HORN!
HE REALLY HASN'T LEARNED HIS LESSON...
I THOUGHT THAT IF JUPITER'S DEER GOT THE GREEN LIGHT, THEN A HORSE WOULD PASS, TOO...
APPROVED
ELK
BUT WHY DID ONLY THE HORSE DE-VELOP OSTE-OPOROSIS?

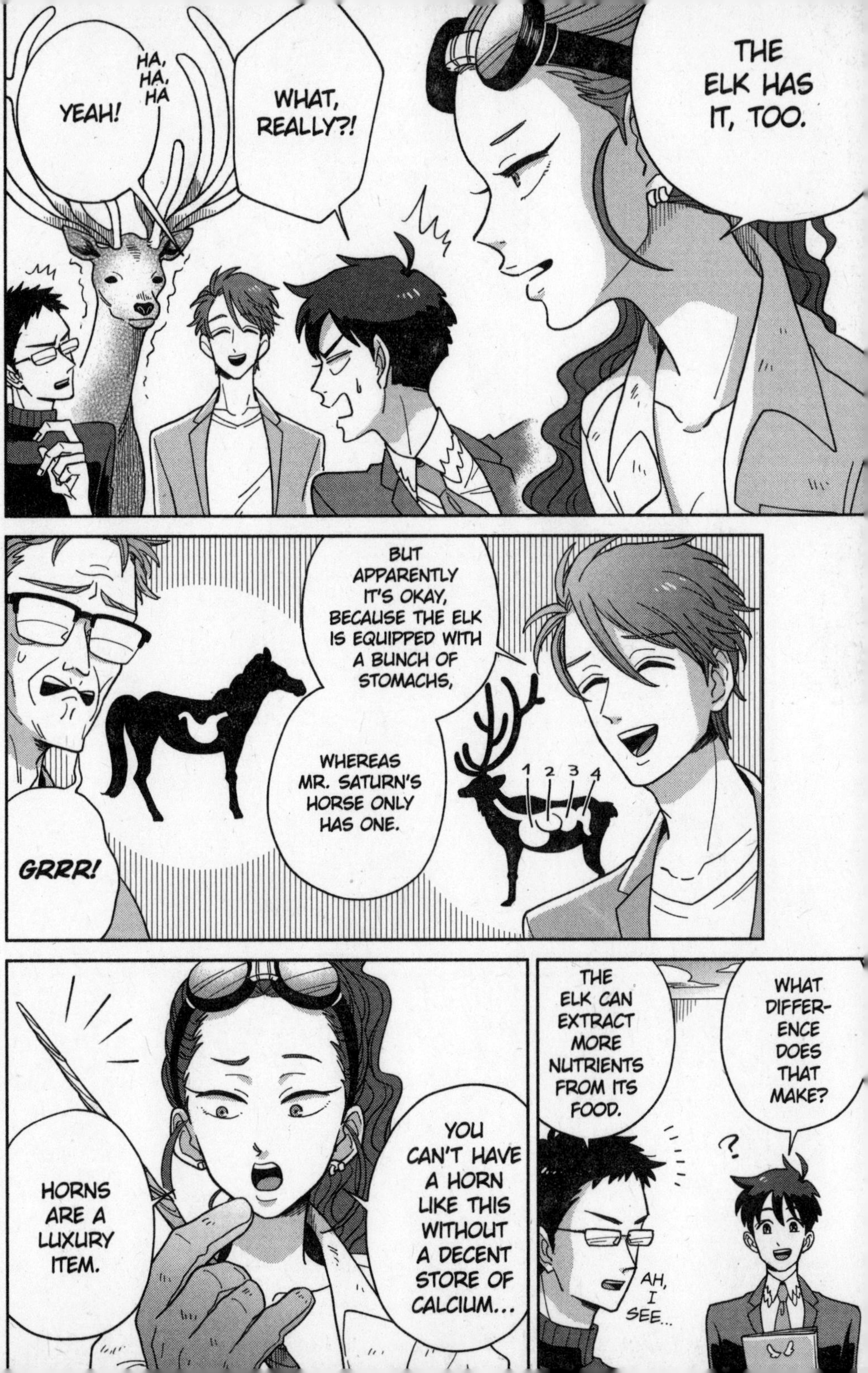

THE ELK HAS IT, TOO.
WHAT, REALLY?!
HA, HA, HA
YEAH!
BUT APPARENTLY IT'S OKAY, BECAUSE THE ELK IS EQUIPPED WITH A BUNCH OF STOMACHS,
WHEREAS MR. SATURN'S HORSE ONLY HAS ONE.
1 2 3 4
GRRR!
WHAT DIFFER-ENCE DOES THAT MAKE?
THE ELK CAN EXTRACT MORE NUTRIENTS FROM ITS FOOD.
AH, I SEE...
YOU CAN'T HAVE A HORN LIKE THIS WITHOUT A DECENT STORE OF CALCIUM...
HORNS ARE A LUXURY ITEM.

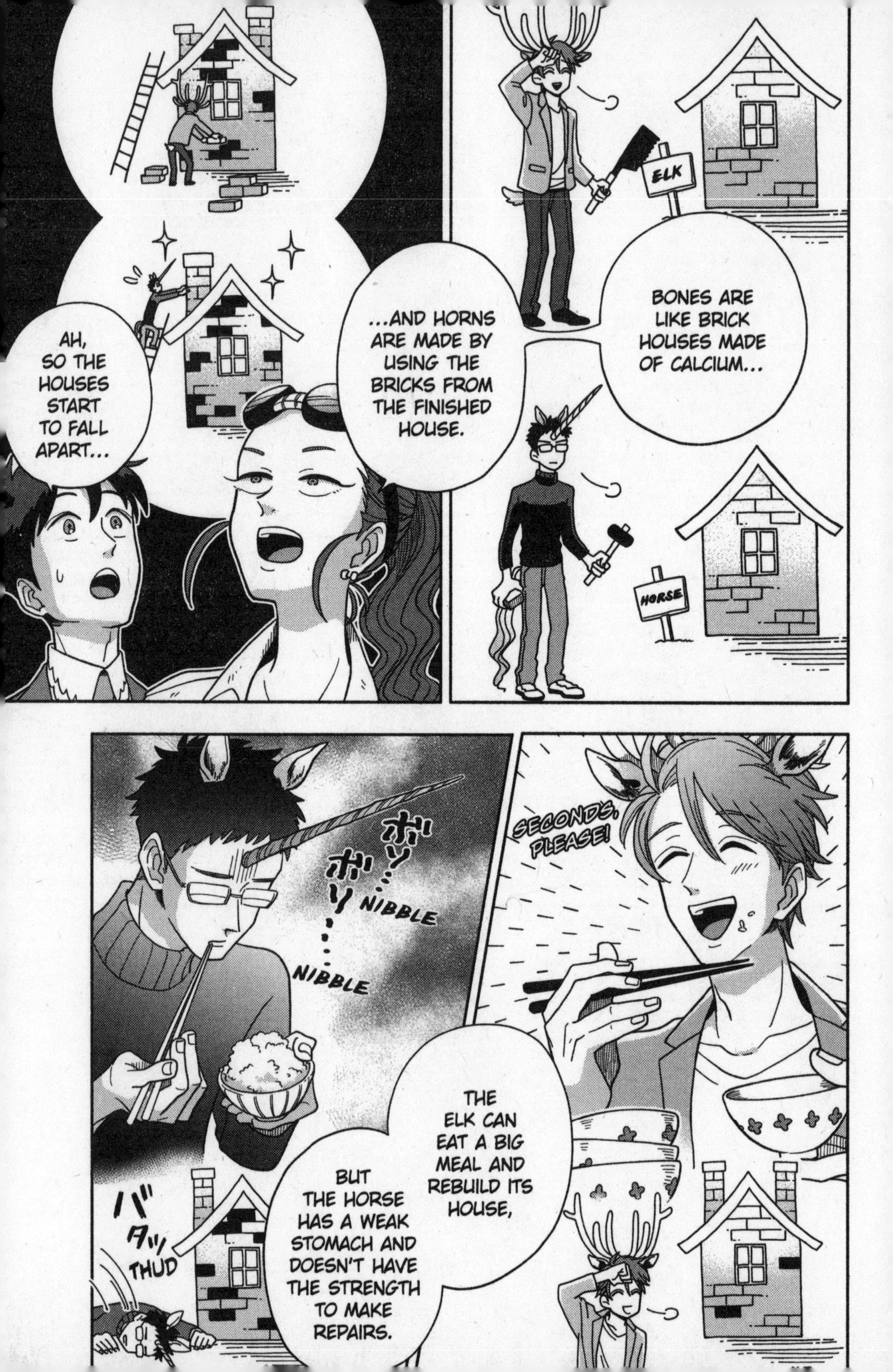
ELK
BONES ARE LIKE BRICK HOUSES MADE OF CALCIUM...
HORSE
...AND HORNS ARE MADE BY USING THE BRICKS FROM THE FINISHED HOUSE.
AH, SO THE HOUSES START TO FALL APART...
SECONDS, PLEASE!
THE ELK CAN EAT A BIG MEAL AND REBUILD ITS HOUSE,
BUT THE HORSE HAS A WEAK STOMACH AND DOESN'T HAVE THE STRENGTH TO MAKE REPAIRS.
ボリ… NIBBLE
ボリ… NIBBLE
バタッ THUD

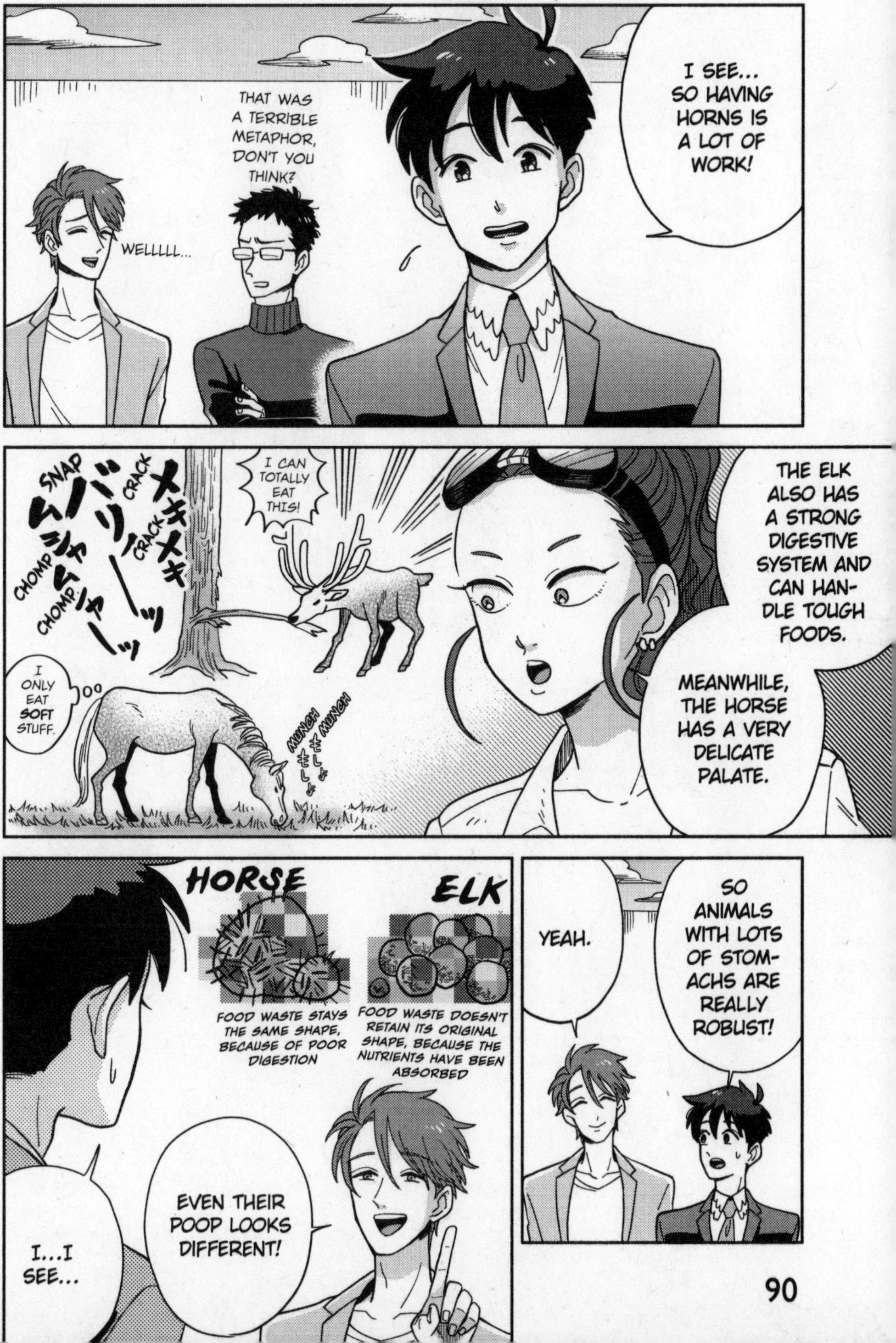
I SEE... SO HAVING HORNS IS A LOT OF WORK!
THAT WAS A TERRIBLE METAPHOR, DON'T YOU THINK?
WELLLLL...
THE ELK ALSO HAS A STRONG DIGESTIVE SYSTEM AND CAN HANDLE TOUGH FOODS.
MEANWHILE, THE HORSE HAS A VERY DELICATE PALATE.
I CAN TOTALLY EAT THIS!
メキメキ CRACK CRACK
バリーッ SNAP
ムシャムシャーッ CHOMP CHOMP
I ONLY EAT **SOFT** STUFF.
もしょもしょ MUNCH MUNCH
SO ANIMALS WITH LOTS OF STOMACHS ARE REALLY ROBUST!
YEAH.
ELK
FOOD WASTE DOESN'T RETAIN ITS ORIGINAL SHAPE, BECAUSE THE NUTRIENTS HAVE BEEN ABSORBED
HORSE
FOOD WASTE STAYS THE SAME SHAPE, BECAUSE OF POOR DIGESTION
EVEN THEIR POOP LOOKS DIFFERENT!
I...I SEE...

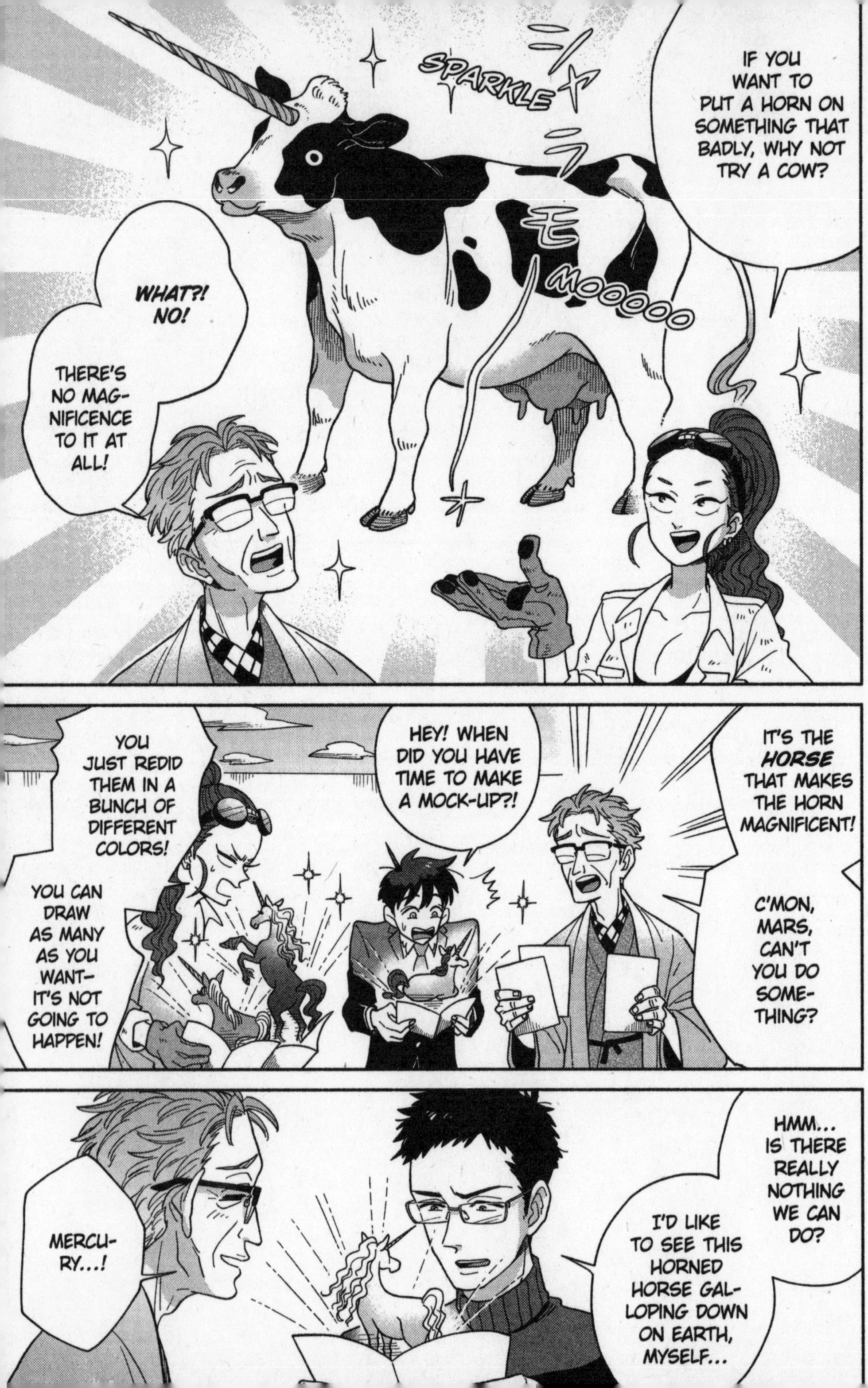
IF YOU WANT TO PUT A HORN ON SOMETHING THAT BADLY, WHY NOT TRY A COW?
SPARKLE
MOOOOOO
WHAT?! NO!
THERE'S NO MAGNIFICENCE TO IT AT ALL!
IT'S THE HORSE THAT MAKES THE HORN MAGNIFICENT!
C'MON, MARS, CAN'T YOU DO SOMETHING?
HEY! WHEN DID YOU HAVE TIME TO MAKE A MOCK-UP?!
YOU JUST REDID THEM IN A BUNCH OF DIFFERENT COLORS!
YOU CAN DRAW AS MANY AS YOU WANT-IT'S NOT GOING TO HAPPEN!
HMM... IS THERE REALLY NOTHING WE CAN DO?
I'D LIKE TO SEE THIS HORNED HORSE GALLOPING DOWN ON EARTH, MYSELF...
MERCURY...!

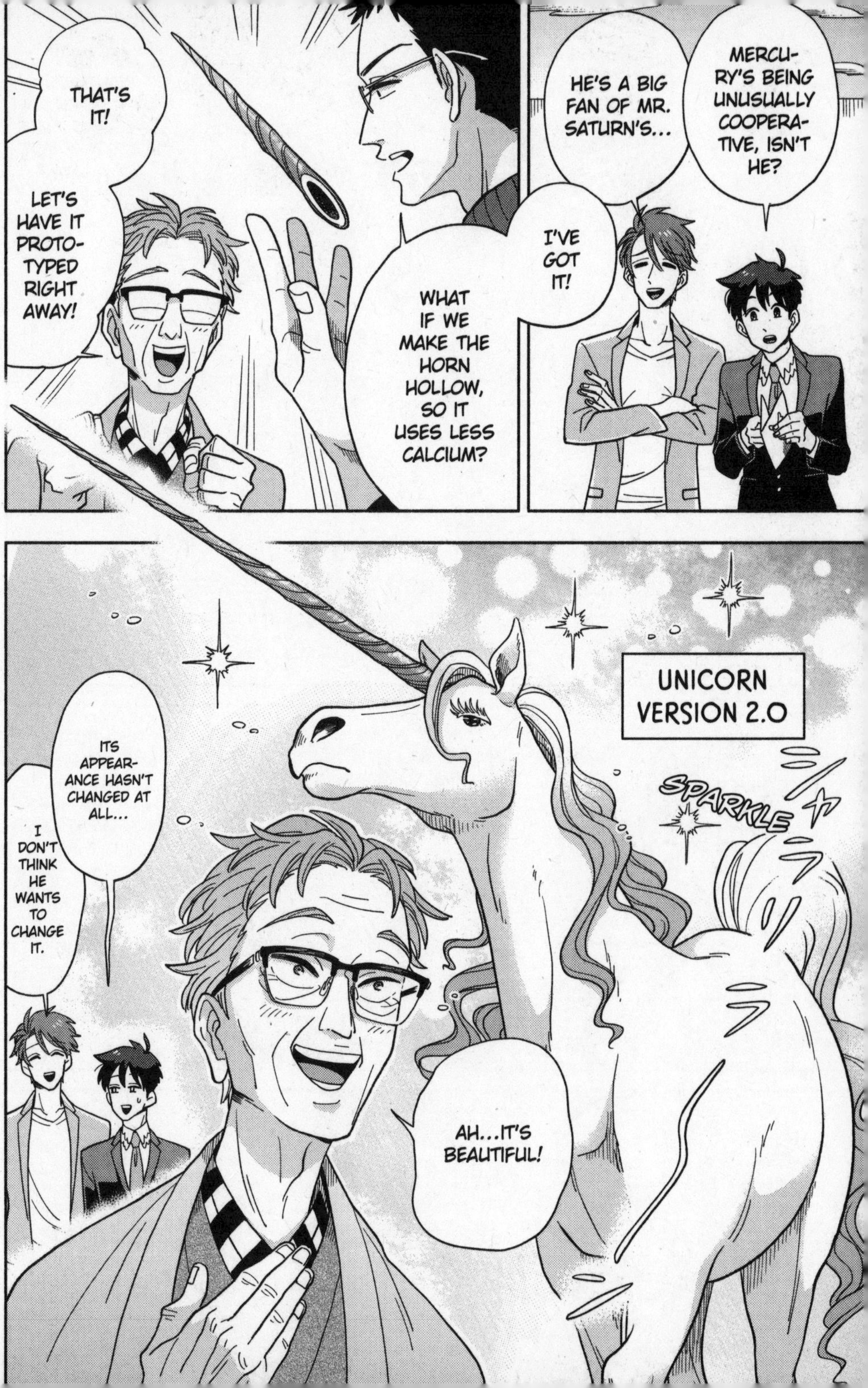
MERCURY'S BEING UNUSUALLY COOPERATIVE, ISN'T HE?
HE'S A BIG FAN OF MR. SATURN'S...
I'VE GOT IT!
WHAT IF WE MAKE THE HORN HOLLOW, SO IT USES LESS CALCIUM?
THAT'S IT!
LET'S HAVE IT PROTOTYPED RIGHT AWAY!
UNICORN VERSION 2.0
SPARKLE
AH...IT'S BEAUTIFUL!
ITS APPEARANCE HASN'T CHANGED AT ALL...
I DON'T THINK HE WANTS TO CHANGE IT.

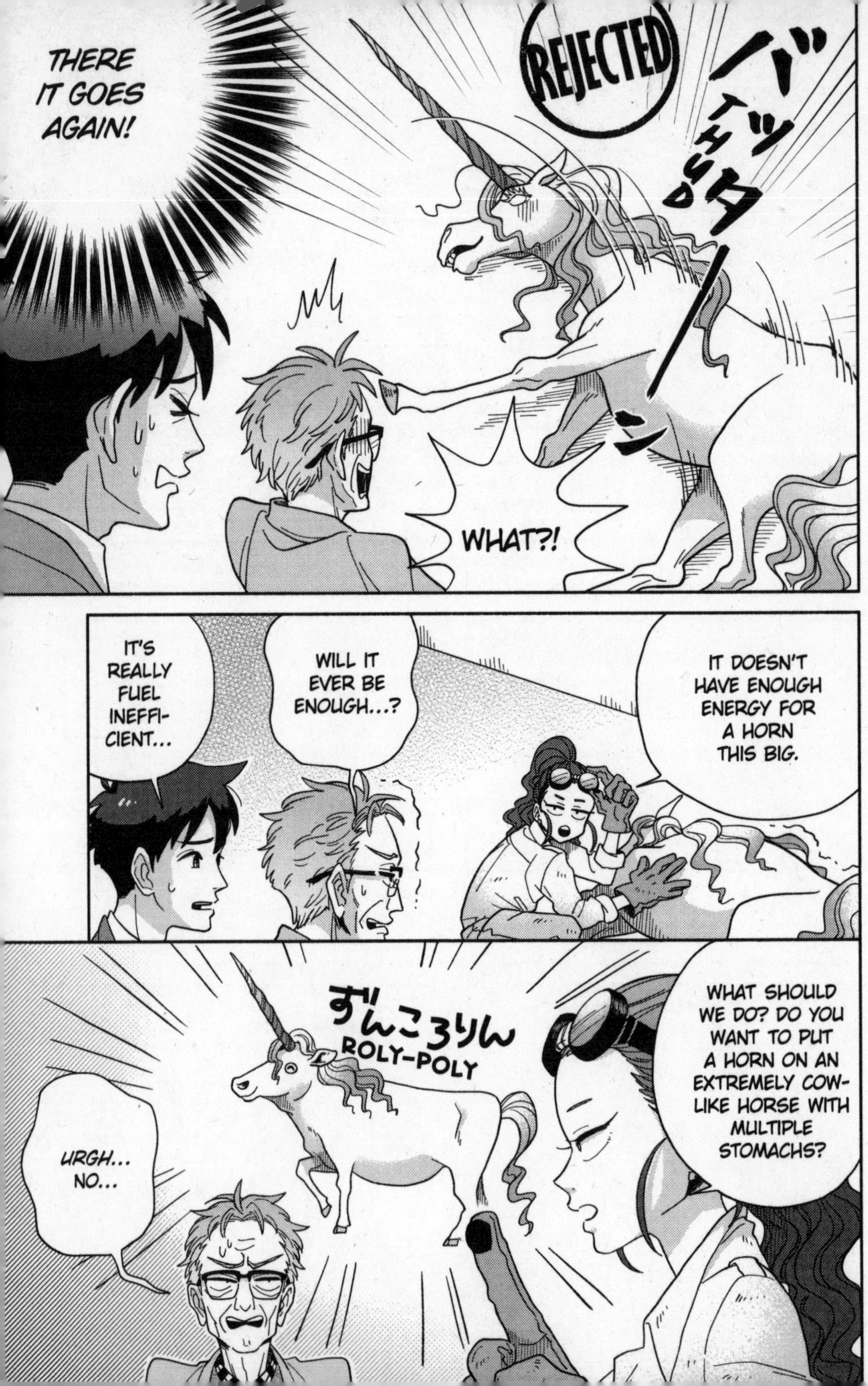
REJECTED
バッターン
THUD
THERE IT GOES AGAIN!
WHAT?!
IT DOESN'T HAVE ENOUGH ENERGY FOR A HORN THIS BIG.
WILL IT EVER BE ENOUGH...?
IT'S REALLY FUEL INEFFI-CIENT...
WHAT SHOULD WE DO? DO YOU WANT TO PUT A HORN ON AN EXTREMELY COW-LIKE HORSE WITH MULTIPLE STOMACHS?
ずんころりん
ROLY-POLY
URGH... NO...

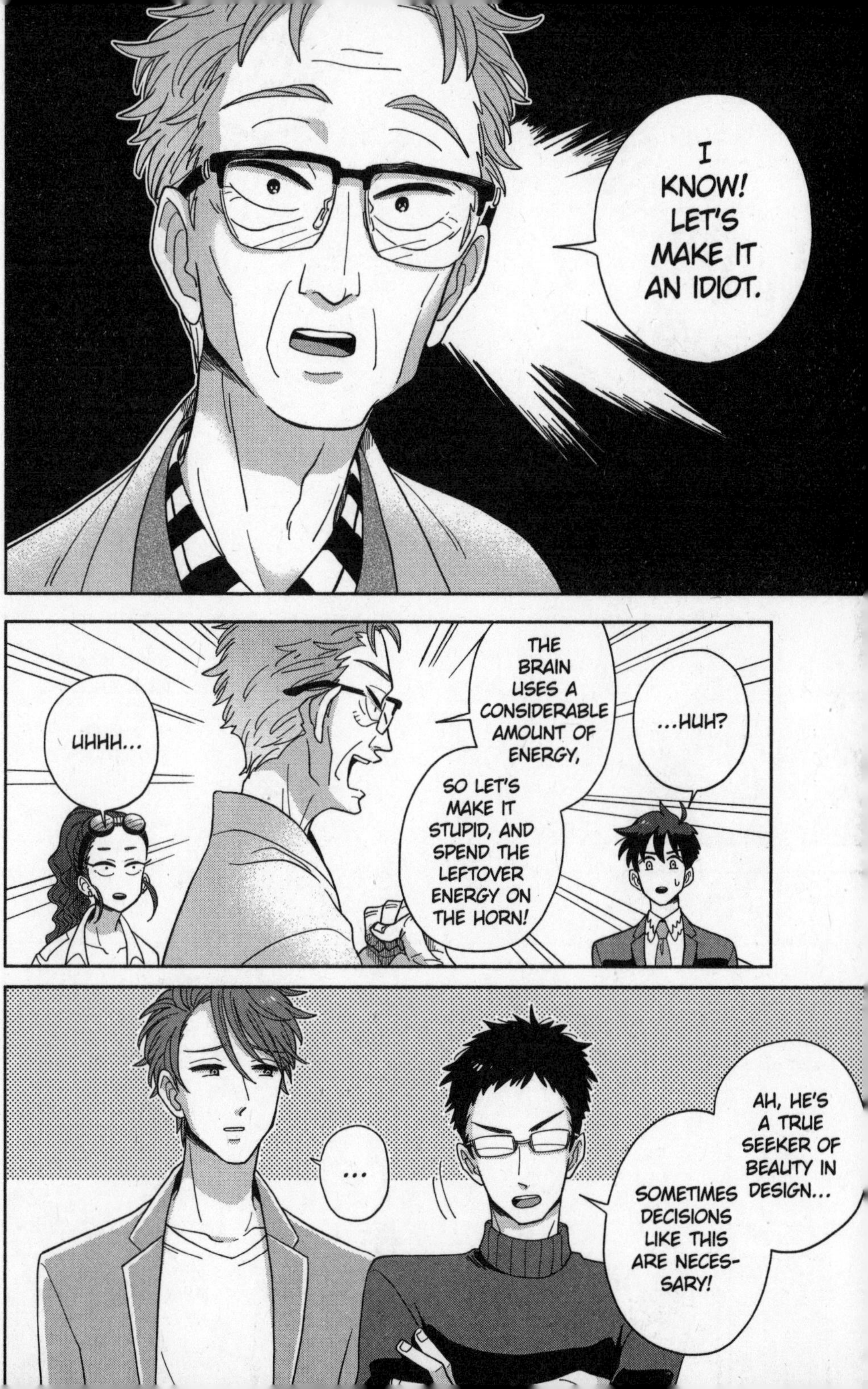
I KNOW! LET'S MAKE IT AN IDIOT.
...HUH?
THE BRAIN USES A CONSIDERABLE AMOUNT OF ENERGY,
SO LET'S MAKE IT STUPID, AND SPEND THE LEFTOVER ENERGY ON THE HORN!
UHHH...
AH, HE'S A TRUE SEEKER OF BEAUTY IN DESIGN...
SOMETIMES DECISIONS LIKE THIS ARE NECES-SARY!
...

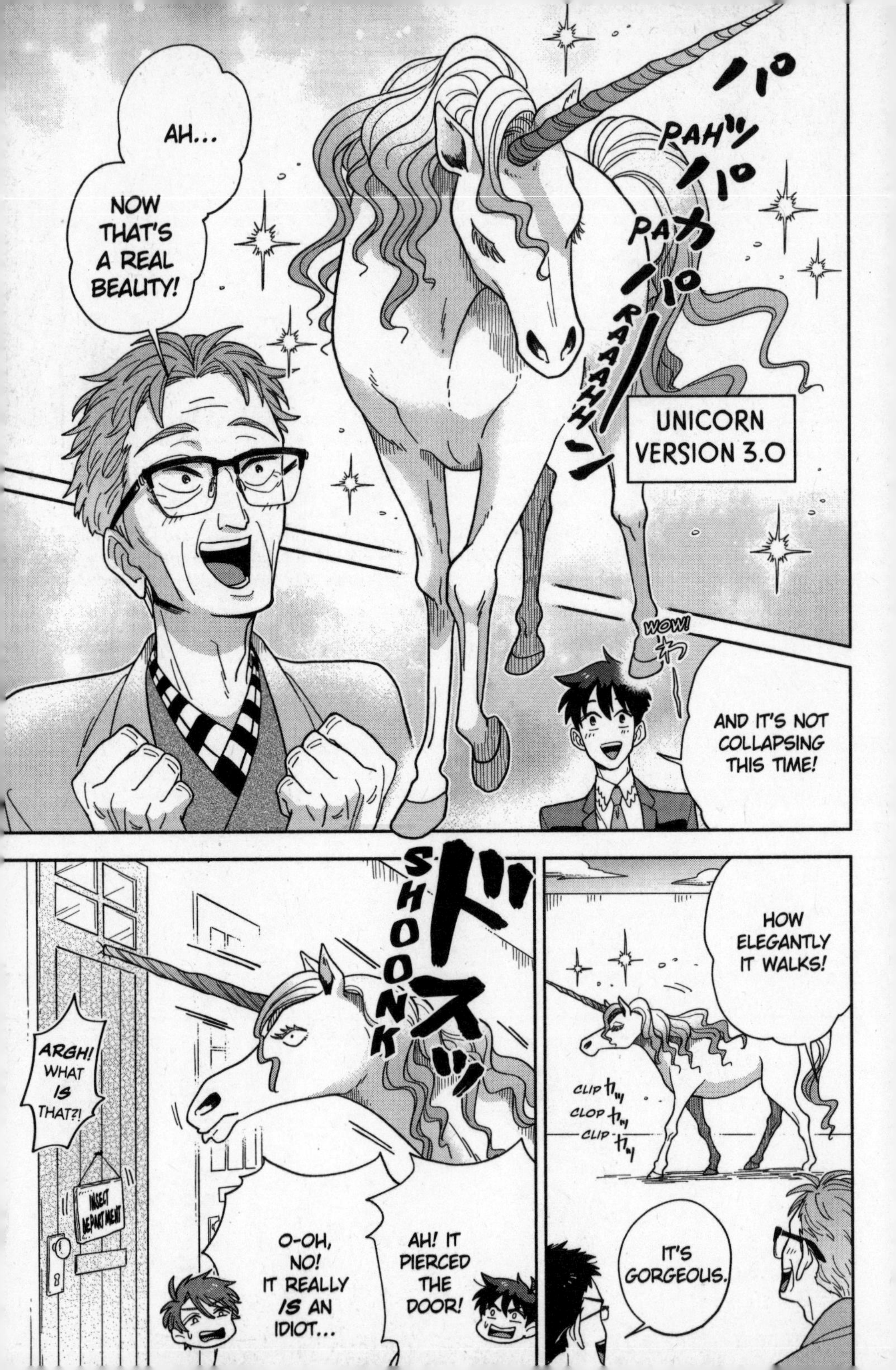
PAH
PA
RAAAAHHN
UNICORN VERSION 3.0
AH...
NOW THAT'S A REAL BEAUTY!
WOW!
AND IT'S NOT COLLAPSING THIS TIME!
HOW ELEGANTLY IT WALKS!
CLIP
CLOP
CLIP
IT'S GORGEOUS.
SHOONK
ARGH! WHAT IS THAT?!
INSECT DEPARTMENT
AH! IT PIERCED THE DOOR!
O-OH, NO! IT REALLY IS AN IDIOT...

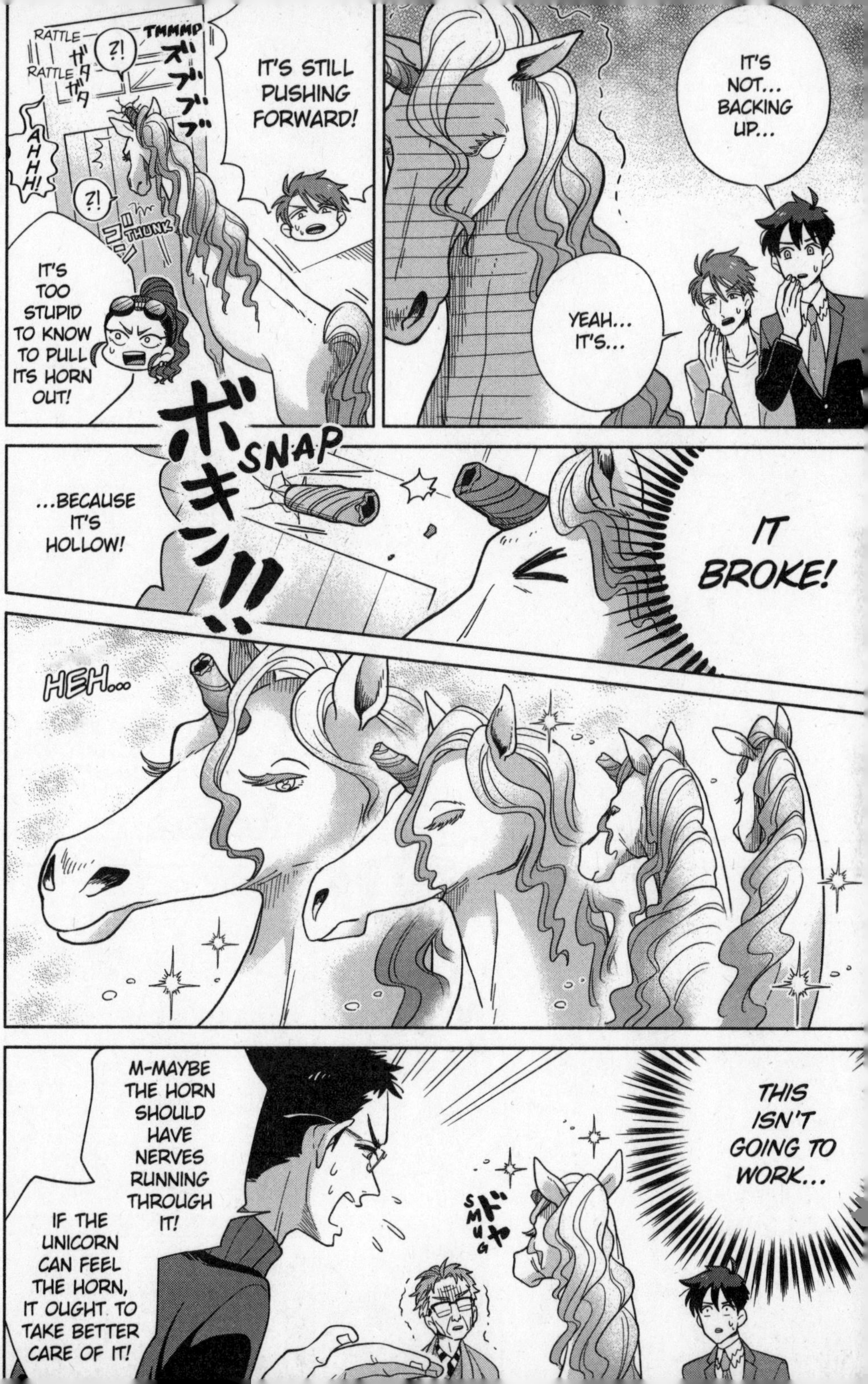

IT'S NOT... BACKING UP...
YEAH... IT'S...
RATTLE ガタ RATTLE ガタ
TMMMP ズブブブ
?!
AHHHH!
?!
THUNK
IT'S STILL PUSHING FORWARD!
IT'S TOO STUPID TO KNOW TO PULL ITS HORN OUT!
IT BROKE!
ボキン!! SNAP
...BECAUSE IT'S HOLLOW!
HEH...
THIS ISN'T GOING TO WORK...
ドヤ SMUG
M-MAYBE THE HORN SHOULD HAVE NERVES RUNNING THROUGH IT!
IF THE UNICORN CAN FEEL THE HORN, IT OUGHT TO TAKE BETTER CARE OF IT!

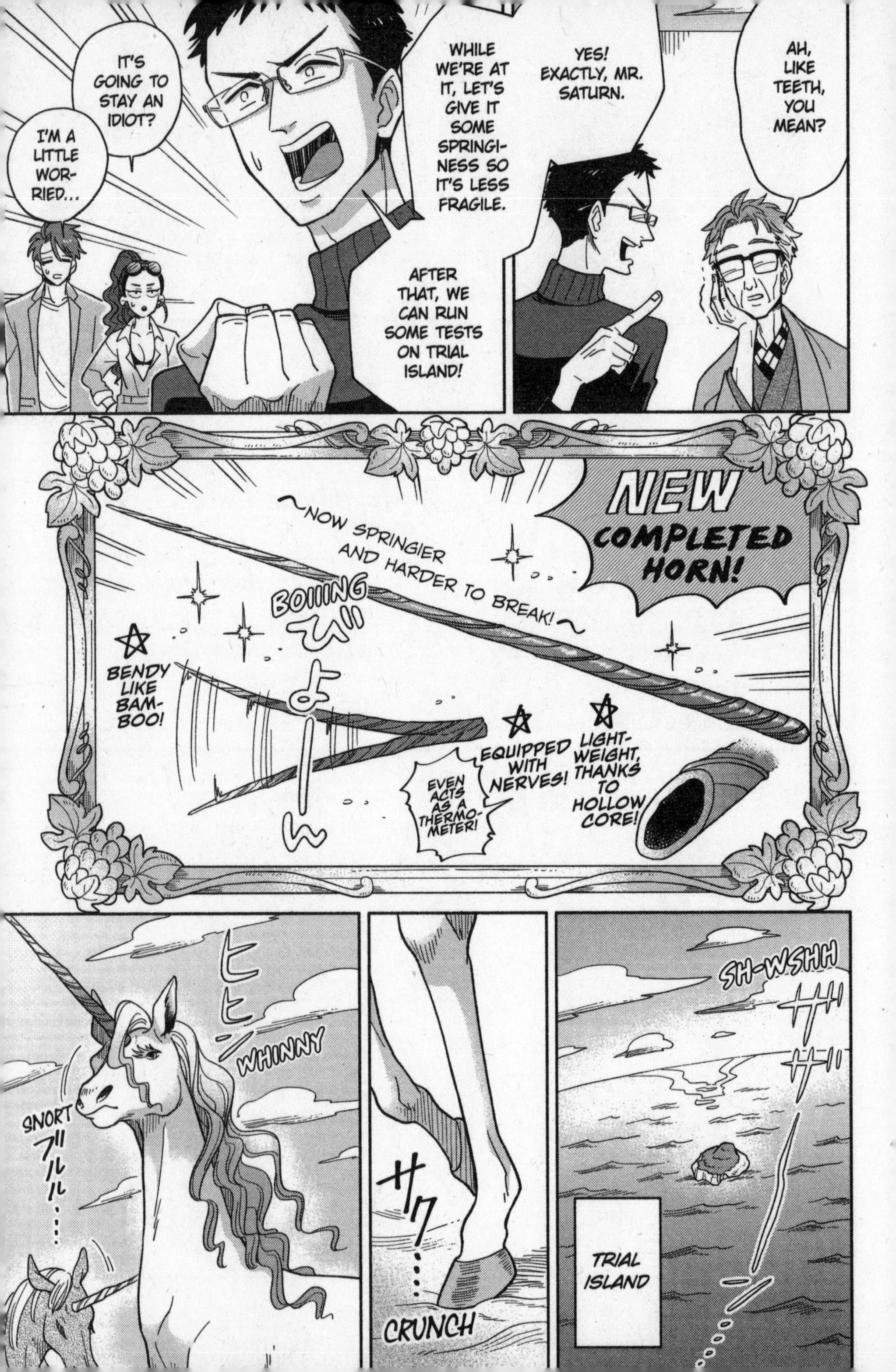

AH, LIKE TEETH, YOU MEAN?
YES! EXACTLY, MR. SATURN.
WHILE WE'RE AT IT, LET'S GIVE IT SOME SPRINGI-NESS SO IT'S LESS FRAGILE.
AFTER THAT, WE CAN RUN SOME TESTS ON TRIAL ISLAND!
IT'S GOING TO STAY AN IDIOT?
I'M A LITTLE WOR-RIED...
NEW COMPLETED HORN!
~NOW SPRINGIER AND HARDER TO BREAK!~
BOIIING
LIGHT-WEIGHT, THANKS TO HOLLOW CORE!
EQUIPPED WITH NERVES!
EVEN ACTS AS A THERMO-METER!
BENDY LIKE BAM-BOO!
SH-WSHH
TRIAL ISLAND
CRUNCH
WHINNY
SNORT

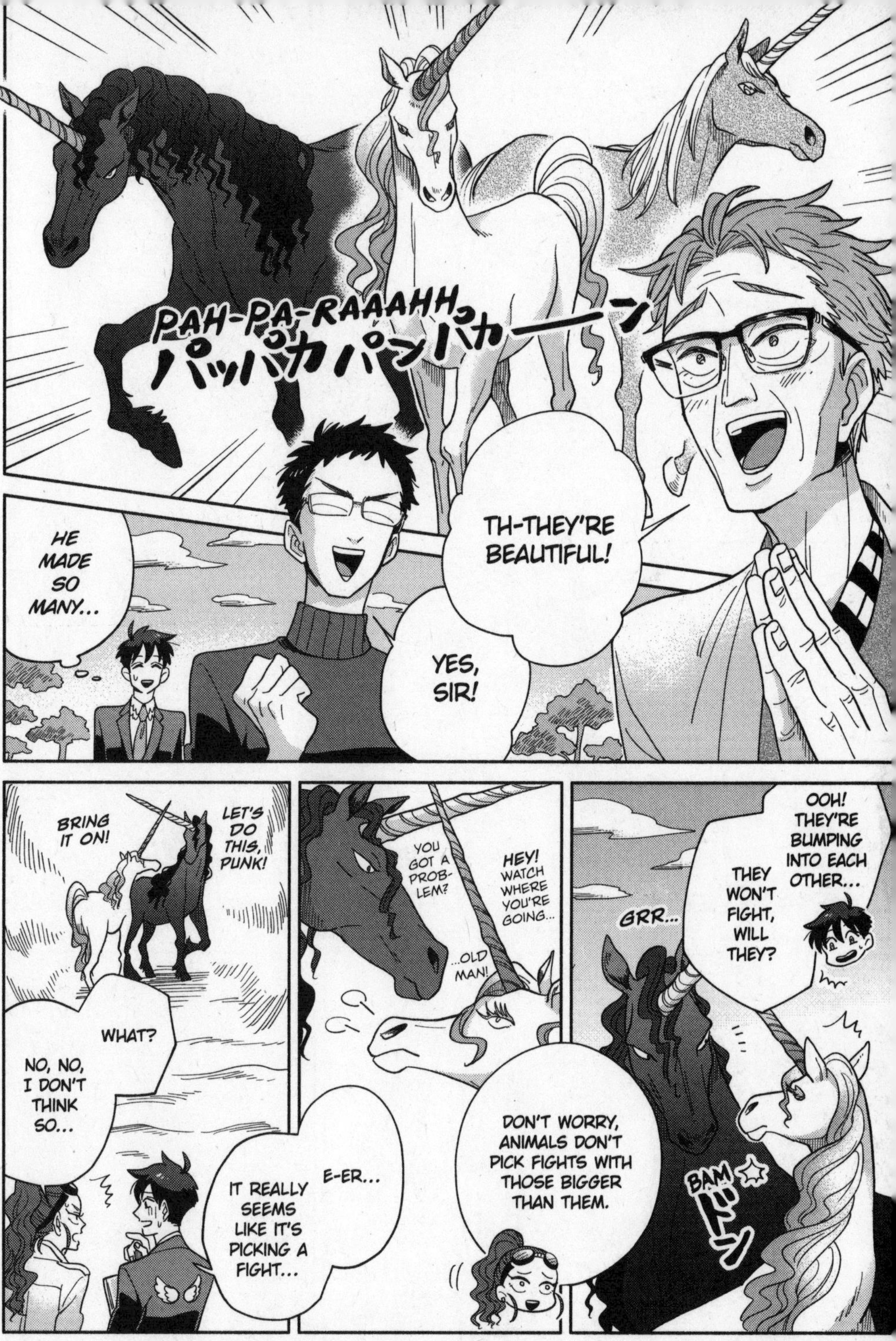
PAH-PA-RAAAHH
パッパカパーン
TH-THEY'RE BEAUTIFUL!
YES, SIR!
HE MADE SO MANY...
OOH! THEY'RE BUMPING INTO EACH OTHER...
THEY WON'T FIGHT, WILL THEY?
GRR...
DON'T WORRY, ANIMALS DON'T PICK FIGHTS WITH THOSE BIGGER THAN THEM.
BAM
ドン
HEY! WATCH WHERE YOU'RE GOING...
YOU GOT A PROB-LEM?
...OLD MAN!
E-ER...
IT REALLY SEEMS LIKE IT'S PICKING A FIGHT...
LET'S DO THIS, PUNK!
BRING IT ON!
WHAT?
NO, NO, I DON'T THINK SO...

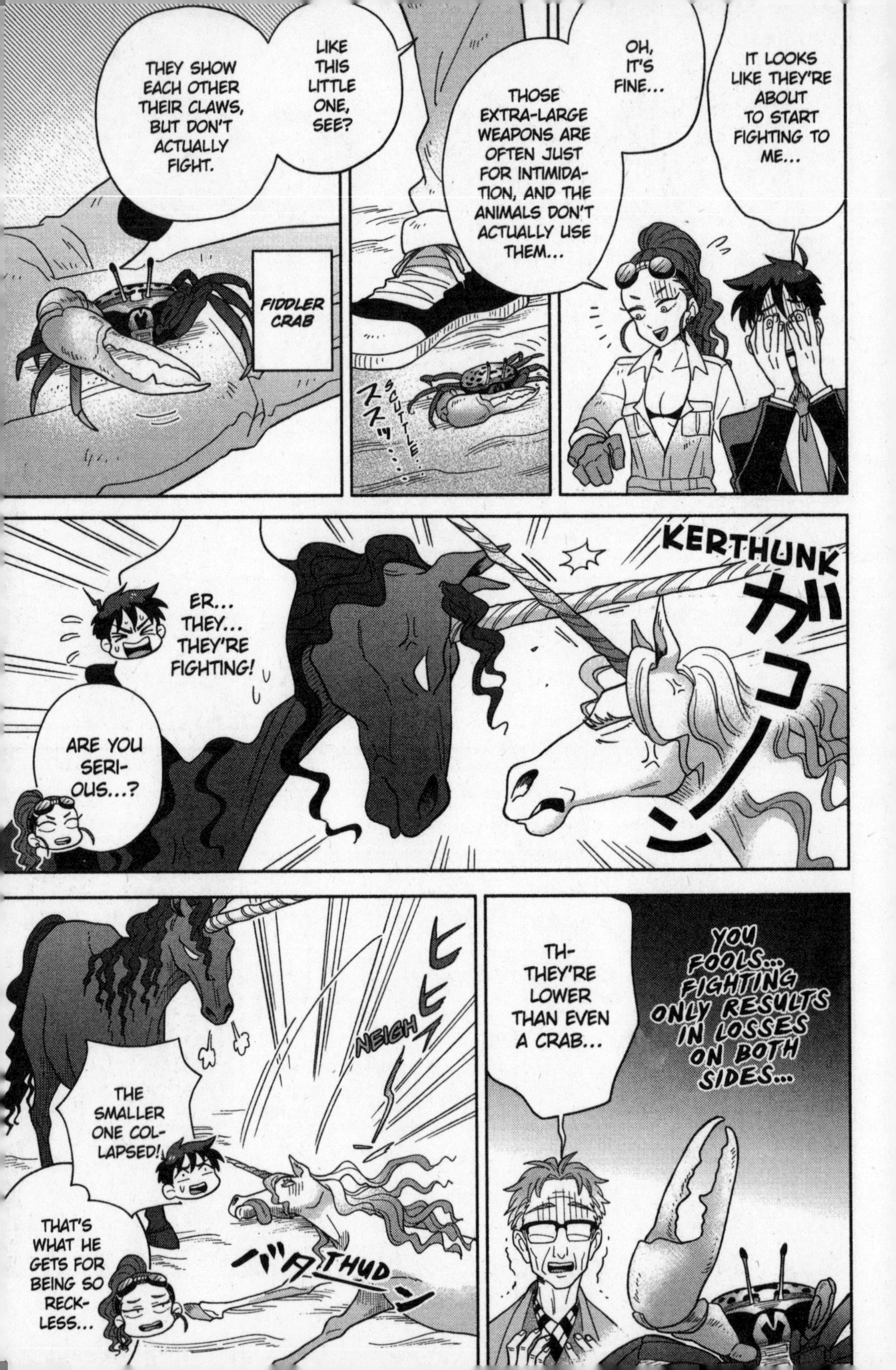

IT LOOKS LIKE THEY'RE ABOUT TO START FIGHTING TO ME...
OH, IT'S FINE...
THOSE EXTRA-LARGE WEAPONS ARE OFTEN JUST FOR INTIMIDATION, AND THE ANIMALS DON'T ACTUALLY USE THEM...
ススッ SCUTTLE...
LIKE THIS LITTLE ONE, SEE?
THEY SHOW EACH OTHER THEIR CLAWS, BUT DON'T ACTUALLY FIGHT.
FIDDLER CRAB
KERTHUNK
ガコーン
ER... THEY... THEY'RE FIGHTING!
ARE YOU SERIOUS...?
YOU FOOLS... FIGHTING ONLY RESULTS IN LOSSES ON BOTH SIDES...
TH-THEY'RE LOWER THAN EVEN A CRAB...
ヒヒン
NEIGH
THE SMALLER ONE COLLAPSED!
THAT'S WHAT HE GETS FOR BEING SO RECKLESS...
バタン THUD

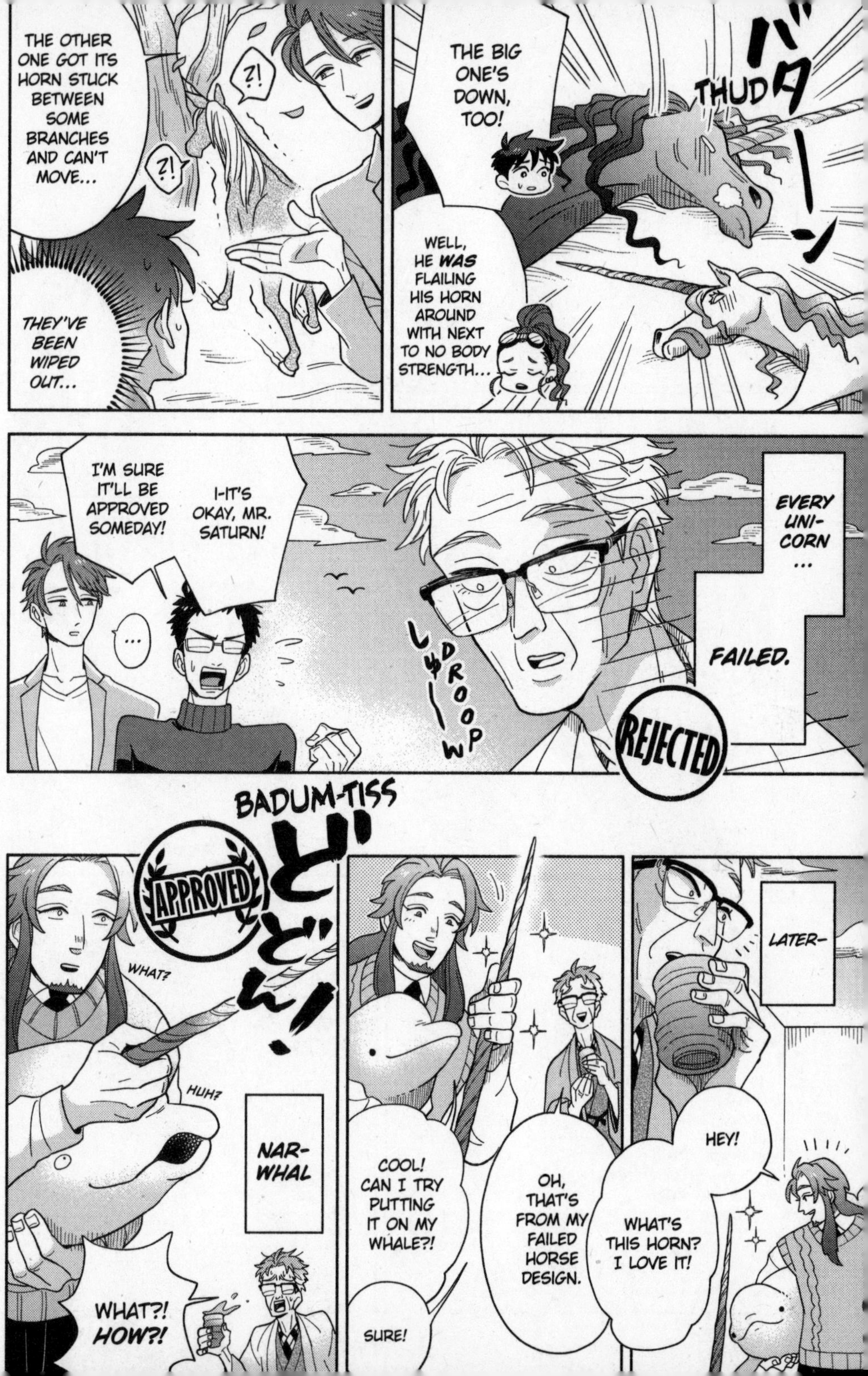
THE BIG ONE'S DOWN, TOO!
THUD
WELL, HE *WAS* FLAILING HIS HORN AROUND WITH NEXT TO NO BODY STRENGTH...
THE OTHER ONE GOT ITS HORN STUCK BETWEEN SOME BRANCHES AND CAN'T MOVE...
?!
?!
THEY'VE BEEN WIPED OUT...
EVERY UNI-CORN...
FAILED.
REJECTED
DROOP
I-IT'S OKAY, MR. SATURN!
I'M SURE IT'LL BE APPROVED SOMEDAY!
...
LATER-
HEY!
WHAT'S THIS HORN? I LOVE IT!
OH, THAT'S FROM MY FAILED HORSE DESIGN.
COOL! CAN I TRY PUTTING IT ON MY WHALE?!
SURE!
BADUM-TISS
APPROVED
WHAT?
HUH?
NAR-WHAL
WHAT?! HOW?!

THE ENCYCLOPEDIA OF
REAL ANIMALS 05

ANIMAL ENCYCLOPEDIA

ANIMAL 13	ELK

THE REAL THING

Even big antlers like these fall off during winter.
Photo: WESTEND61/Aflo

Male elk have enormous antlers, the largest of which can weigh up to 18 kilograms (40 pounds). These shed and regrow each year and develop very quickly, in just a few months. To sustain its antlers' growth, the elk requires huge amounts of energy and calcium in a short period. Because its nutritional intake is insufficient, the elk borrows calcium from its bones and uses it as material to build up its antlers instead, resulting in osteoporosis. The elk then grazes constantly to bring its health back to normal. Because growing antlers requires so much effort, they stay small if the elk is in poor health. Therefore, antlers serve as an indicator of the male's health for the female. Males also use antlers to assess one another's strength before conflict to avoid unnecessary fighting.

[Type species] *Cervus canadensis*
[Classification] Class: Mammalia
Order: Artiodactyla
Family: Cervidae
Genus: *Cervinae*
[Range] North America, Central and Eastern Asia
[Height] Approximately 2 m (6 ft)

ANIMAL 14 | FIDDLER CRAB

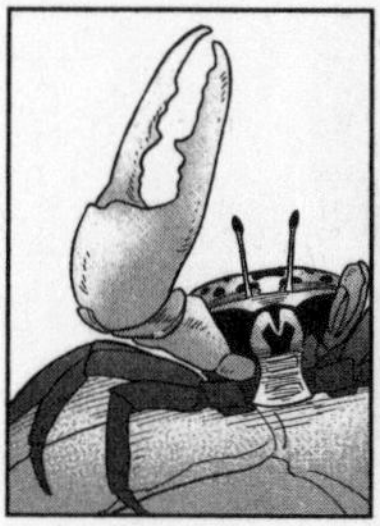

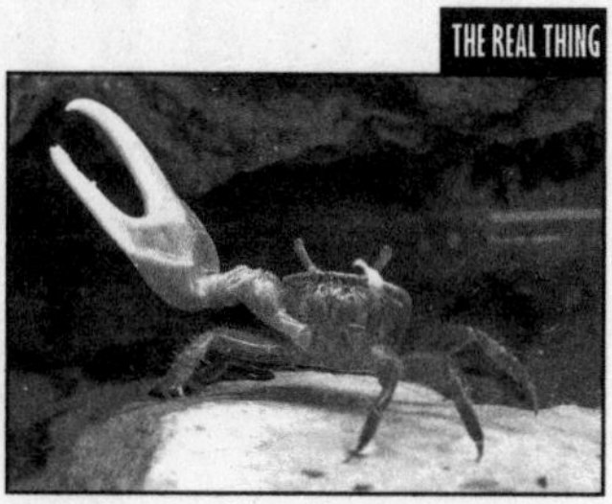
THE REAL THING
Only the male crab has an extra-large claw.

Photo: Mark Newman/Aflo

The fiddler crab has a giant claw only on one leg. When two males are competing, they wave their claws but don't often use them to attack. Instead, they are apparently able to size one another up, and the crab with the bigger claw wins. In the animal world, using oversized weapons often destroys the bearer, so they are more often used to intimidate (almost in the same way we humans wield our own weapons).

[Name] Fiddler crab
[Classification] Class: Malacostraca
Order: Decapoda
Family: Ocypodidae
Genus: *Uca*
[Range] Japan (Parts of Honshu, Shikoku, Kyushu), Korean Peninsula, China, Taiwan
[Width] 1.5-3.5cm (0.5-1.5 in) (shell only)

ANIMAL 15 | NARWHAL

As introduced in this chapter, the narwhal's light and hollow tusk is a sensory organ that can measure temperature and flex like bamboo. When the tusks made their way to Europe, some believed they were the horns of the legendary unicorn. The narwhal's tusk is in fact an extremely oversized front tooth. Its exact use and the reason it forms a helix spiral are unknown. The narwhal is one of only two members of the monodontidae family, along with the beluga whale (also seen in this chapter).

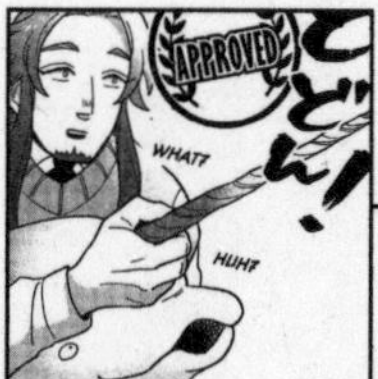
APPROVED
WHAT?
HUH?

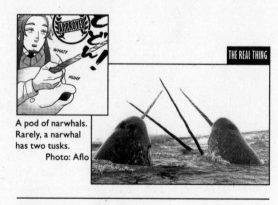

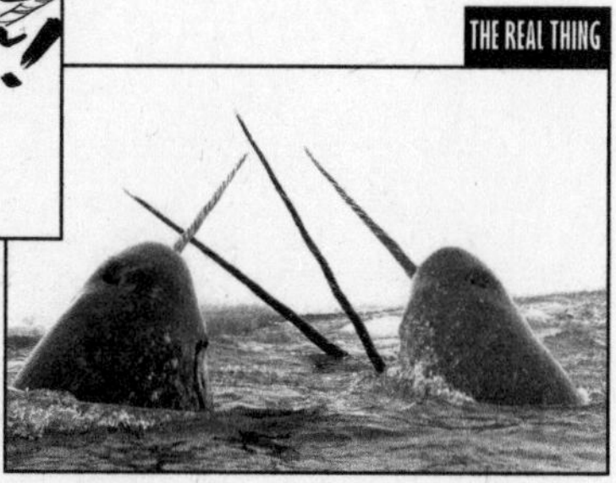
THE REAL THING
A pod of narwhals. Rarely, a narwhal has two tusks.

Photo: Aflo

[Type species] *Monodon monoceros*
[Classification] Class: Mammalia
Order: Artiodactyla
Family: Monodontidae
Genus: *Monodon*
[Habitat] Arctic waters
[Length] Approximately 5 m (16 ft); 8 m (26 ft) including the tusk

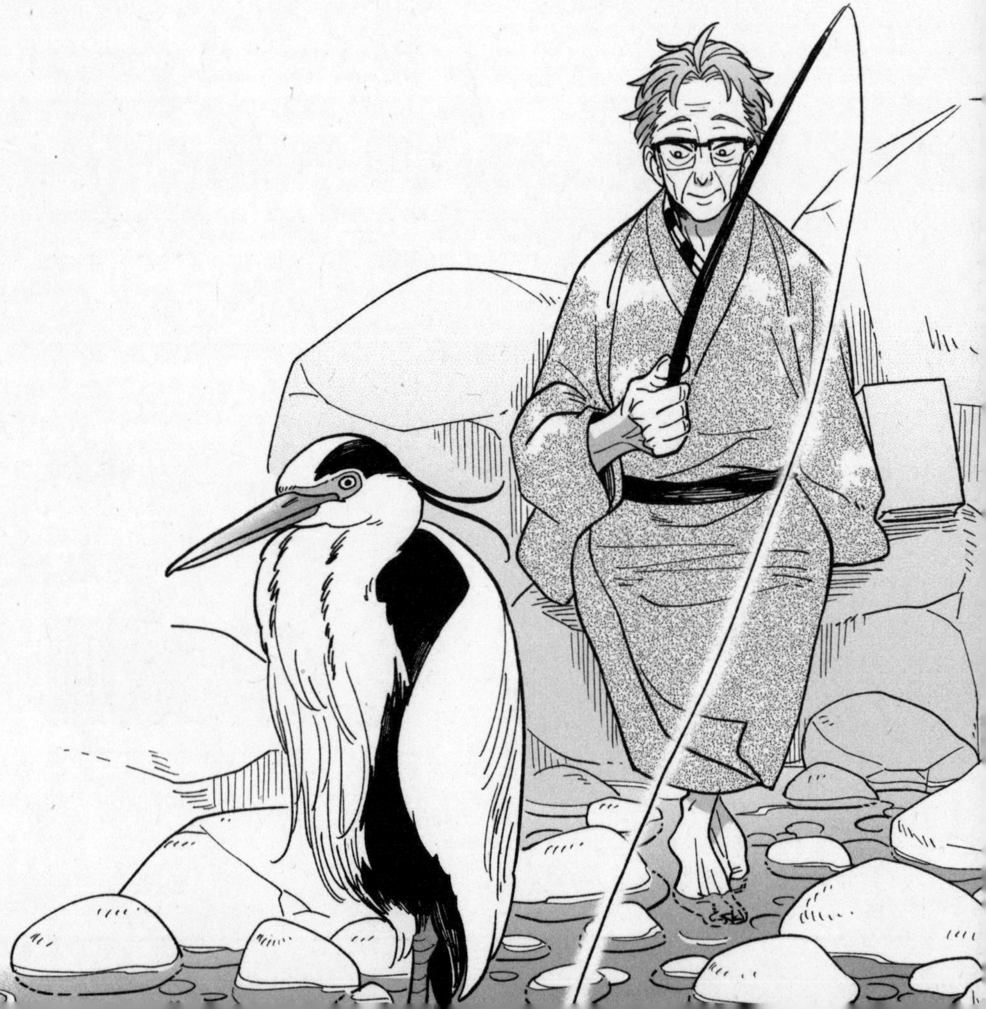

HEAVEN'S
DESIGN TEAM

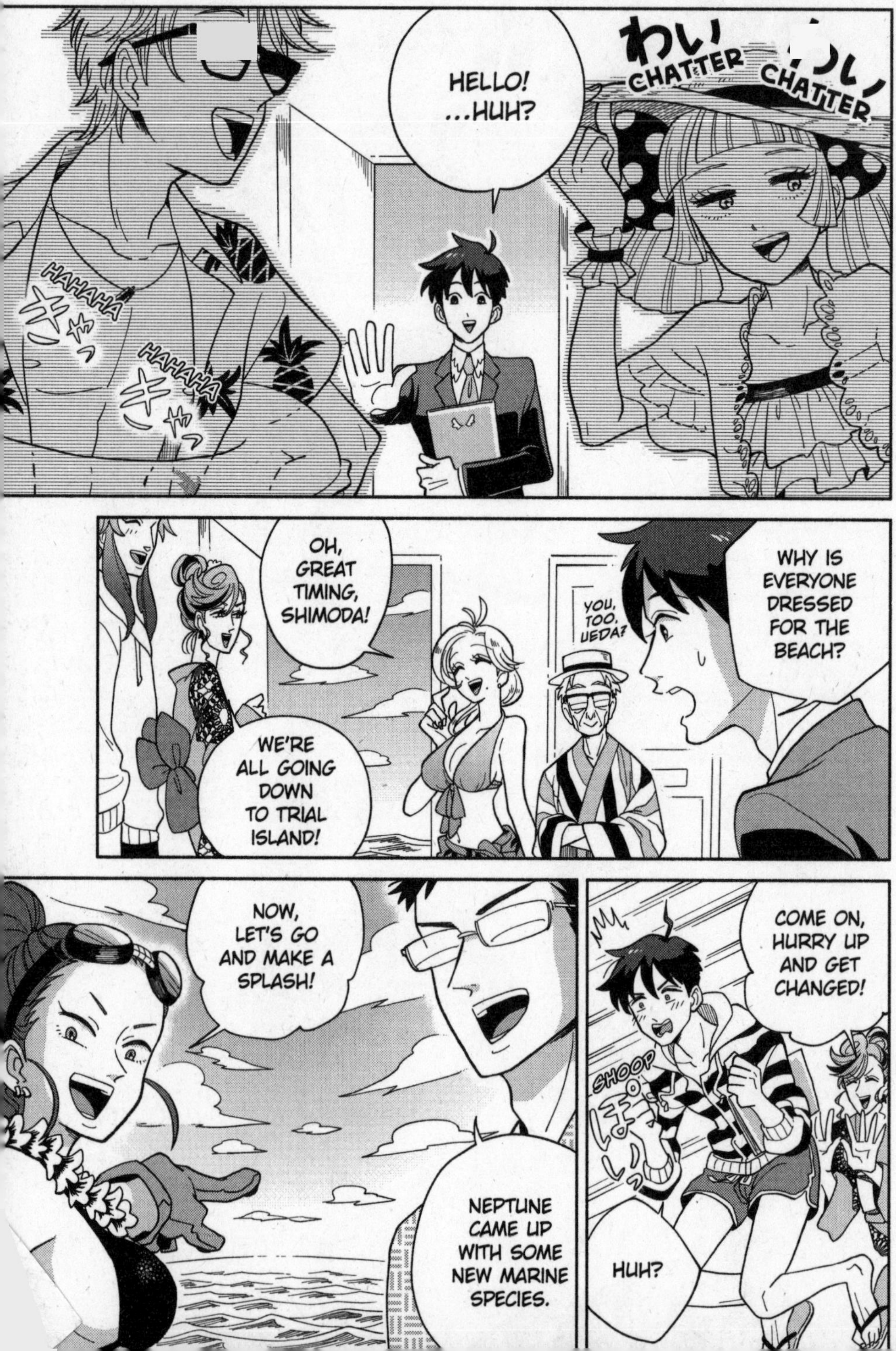
わい CHATTER
CHATTER
HELLO! ...HUH?
HAHAHA きゃっ
HAHAHA きゃっ
WHY IS EVERYONE DRESSED FOR THE BEACH?
YOU, TOO, UEDA?
OH, GREAT TIMING, SHIMODA!
WE'RE ALL GOING DOWN TO TRIAL ISLAND!
COME ON, HURRY UP AND GET CHANGED!
SHOOP ぽいっ
HUH?
NOW, LET'S GO AND MAKE A SPLASH!
NEPTUNE CAME UP WITH SOME NEW MARINE SPECIES.

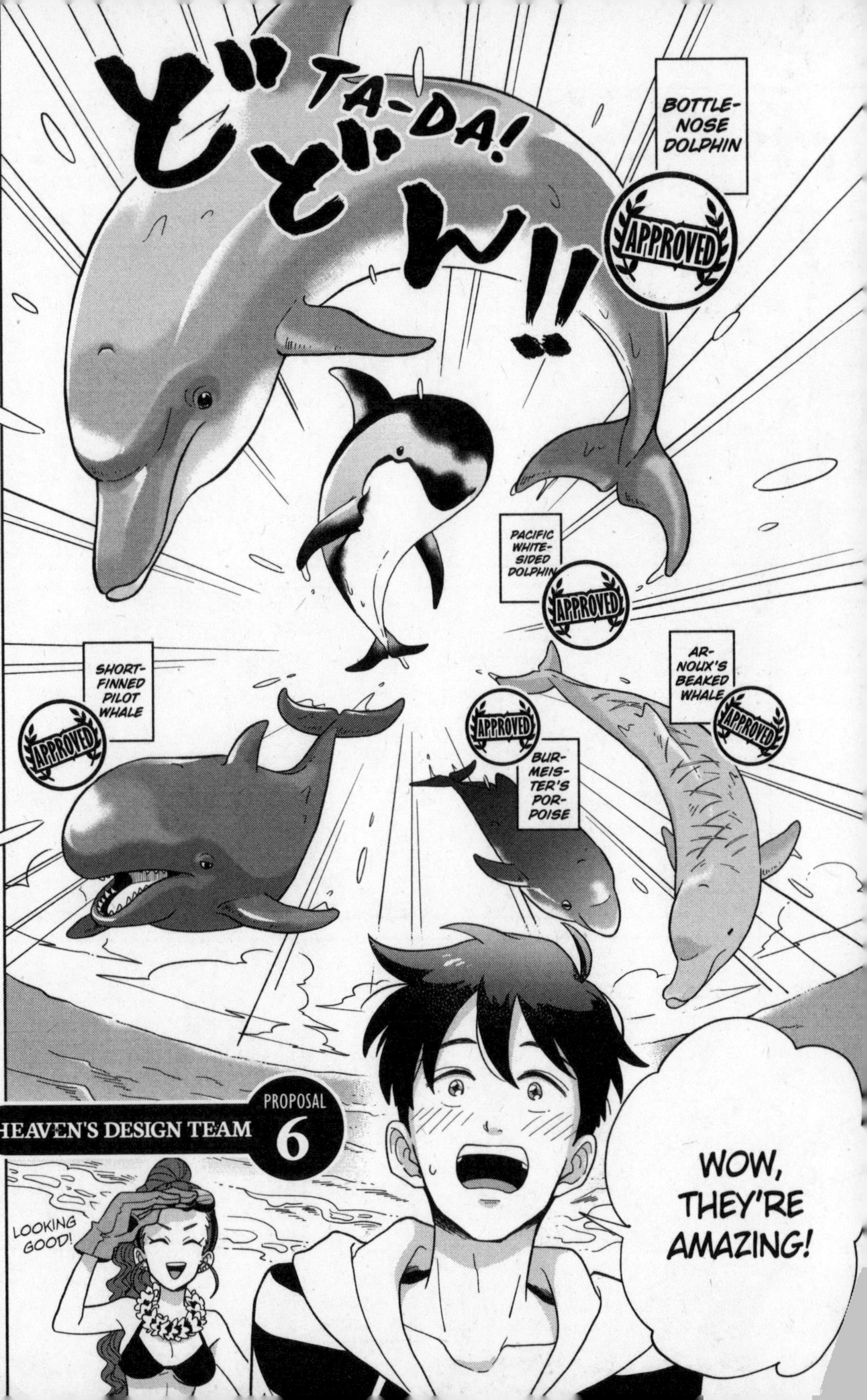
どどん!!
TA-DA!
BOTTLE-NOSE DOLPHIN
APPROVED
PACIFIC WHITE-SIDED DOLPHIN
APPROVED
ARNOUX'S BEAKED WHALE
APPROVED
BURMEISTER'S PORPOISE
APPROVED
SHORT-FINNED PILOT WHALE
APPROVED
HEAVEN'S DESIGN TEAM
PROPOSAL 6
WOW, THEY'RE AMAZING!
LOOKING GOOD!

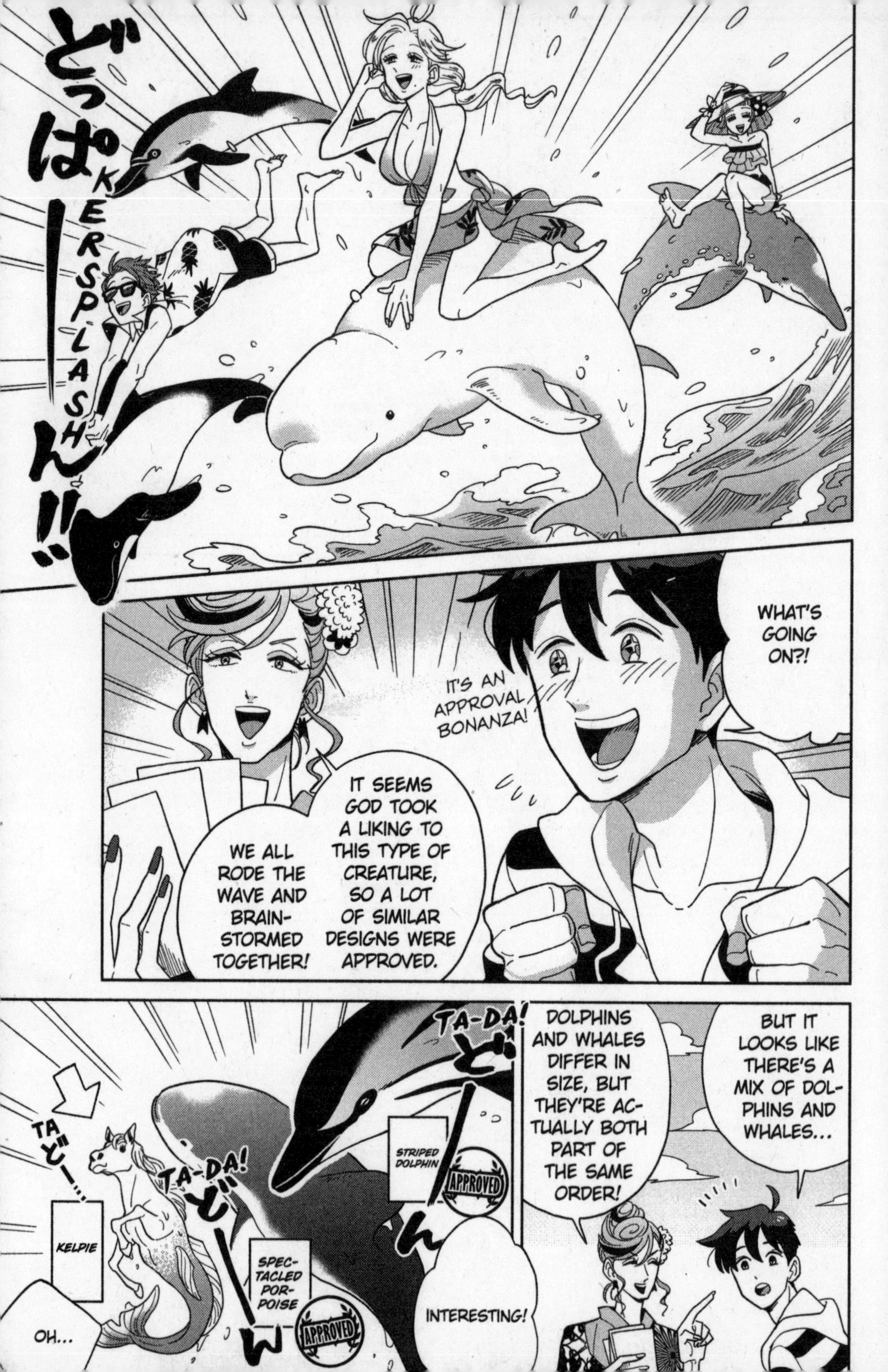
どっぱーん!!
KERSPLASH
WHAT'S GOING ON?!
IT'S AN APPROVAL BONANZA!
IT SEEMS GOD TOOK A LIKING TO THIS TYPE OF CREATURE, SO A LOT OF SIMILAR DESIGNS WERE APPROVED.
WE ALL RODE THE WAVE AND BRAIN-STORMED TOGETHER!
BUT IT LOOKS LIKE THERE'S A MIX OF DOL-PHINS AND WHALES...
DOLPHINS AND WHALES DIFFER IN SIZE, BUT THEY'RE AC-TUALLY BOTH PART OF THE SAME ORDER!
INTERESTING!
TA-DA!
ど
STRIPED DOLPHIN
APPROVED
TA-DA!
どーん
SPEC-TACLED POR-POISE
APPROVED
TA
どー…
KELPIE
OH...

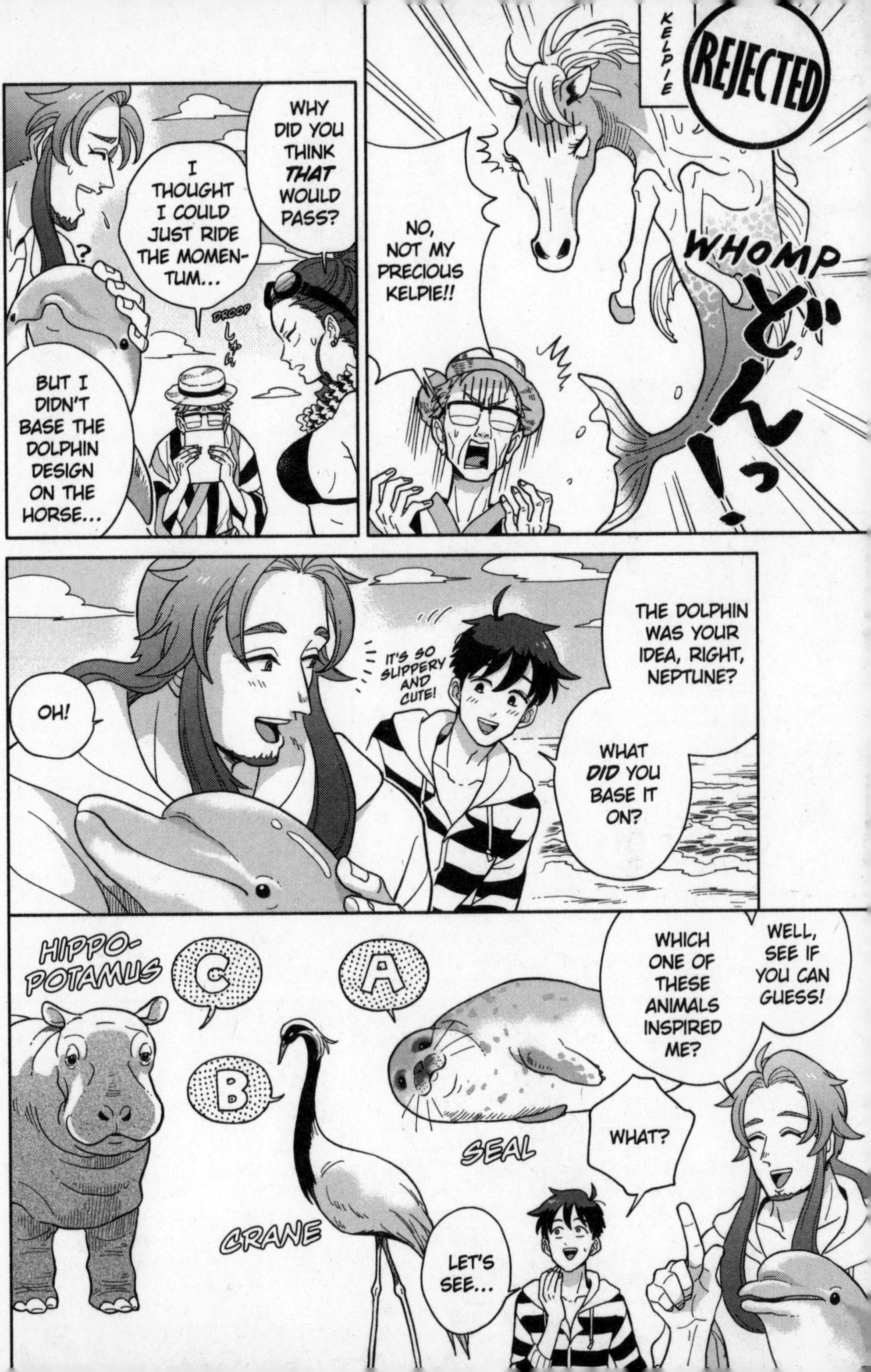

KELPIE
REJECTED
WHOMP
どんっ!
NO, NOT MY PRECIOUS KELPIE!!
WHY DID YOU THINK THAT WOULD PASS?
I THOUGHT I COULD JUST RIDE THE MOMEN-TUM…
?
DROOP
BUT I DIDN'T BASE THE DOLPHIN DESIGN ON THE HORSE…
THE DOLPHIN WAS YOUR IDEA, RIGHT, NEPTUNE?
WHAT DID YOU BASE IT ON?
IT'S SO SLIPPERY AND CUTE!
OH!
WELL, SEE IF YOU CAN GUESS!
WHICH ONE OF THESE ANIMALS INSPIRED ME?
WHAT?
A
SEAL
LET'S SEE…
B
CRANE
C
HIPPO-POTAMUS

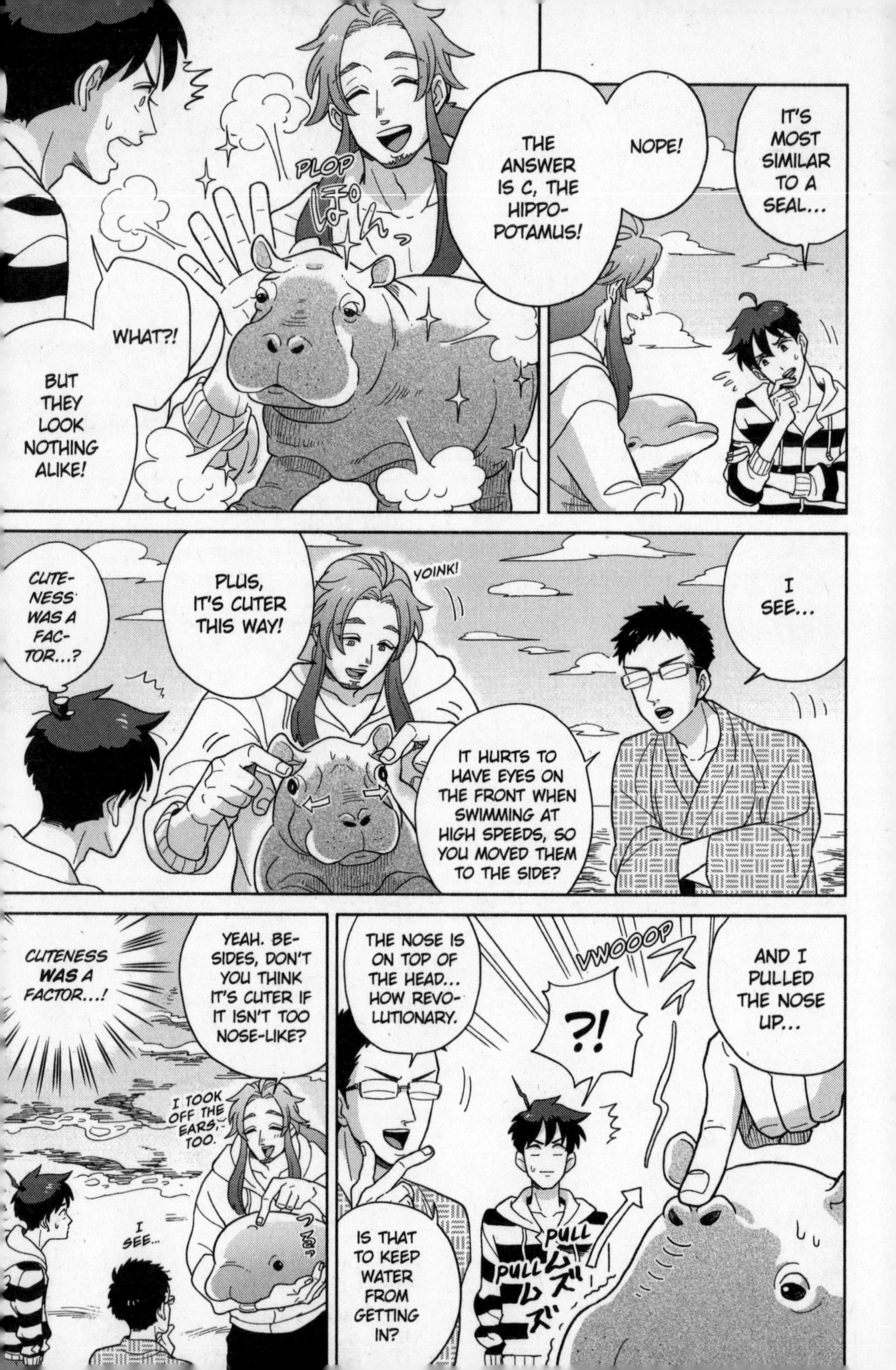
IT'S MOST SIMILAR TO A SEAL...
NOPE!
THE ANSWER IS C, THE HIPPO-POTAMUS!
PLOP
WHAT?!
BUT THEY LOOK NOTHING ALIKE!
I SEE...
YOINK!
PLUS, IT'S CUTER THIS WAY!
CUTE-NESS WAS A FAC-TOR...?
IT HURTS TO HAVE EYES ON THE FRONT WHEN SWIMMING AT HIGH SPEEDS, SO YOU MOVED THEM TO THE SIDE?
AND I PULLED THE NOSE UP...
VWOOOP
?!
THE NOSE IS ON TOP OF THE HEAD... HOW REVO-LUTIONARY.
PULL
PULL
IS THAT TO KEEP WATER FROM GETTING IN?
YEAH. BE-SIDES, DON'T YOU THINK IT'S CUTER IF IT ISN'T TOO NOSE-LIKE?
CUTENESS WAS A FACTOR...!
I TOOK OFF THE EARS, TOO.
I SEE...

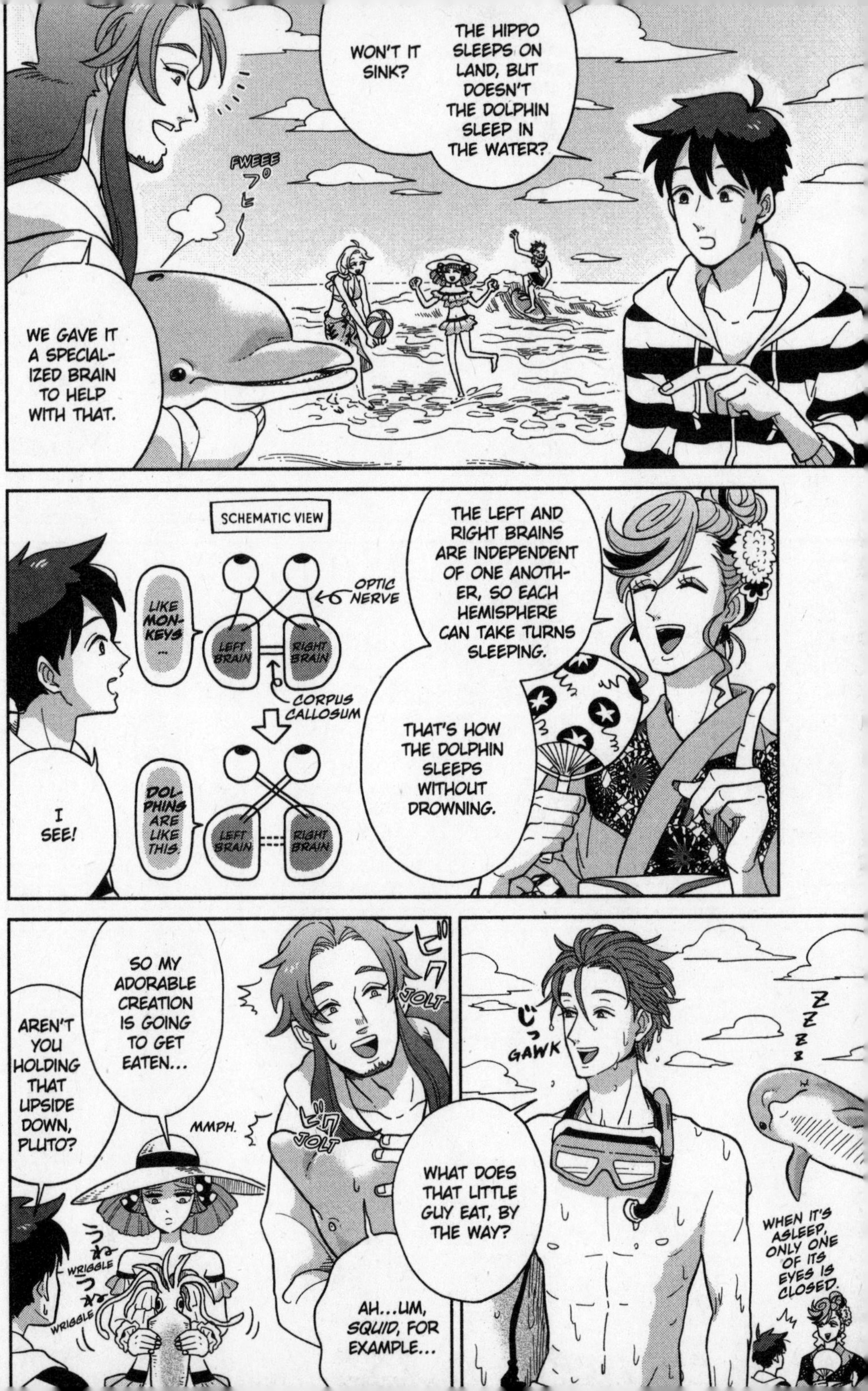
THE HIPPO SLEEPS ON LAND, BUT DOESN'T THE DOLPHIN SLEEP IN THE WATER?
WON'T IT SINK?
FWEEE
WE GAVE IT A SPECIAL-IZED BRAIN TO HELP WITH THAT.
THE LEFT AND RIGHT BRAINS ARE INDEPENDENT OF ONE ANOTH-ER, SO EACH HEMISPHERE CAN TAKE TURNS SLEEPING.
SCHEMATIC VIEW
LIKE MON-KEYS...
LEFT BRAIN
RIGHT BRAIN
OPTIC NERVE
CORPUS CALLOSUM
DOL-PHINS ARE LIKE THIS.
LEFT BRAIN
RIGHT BRAIN
THAT'S HOW THE DOLPHIN SLEEPS WITHOUT DROWNING.
I SEE!
GAWK
WHAT DOES THAT LITTLE GUY EAT, BY THE WAY?
Z Z Z z
WHEN IT'S ASLEEP, ONLY ONE OF ITS EYES IS CLOSED.
AH...UM, SQUID, FOR EXAMPLE...
JOLT
JOLT
SO MY ADORABLE CREATION IS GOING TO GET EATEN...
MMPH.
AREN'T YOU HOLDING THAT UPSIDE DOWN, PLUTO?
WRIGGLE
WRIGGLE

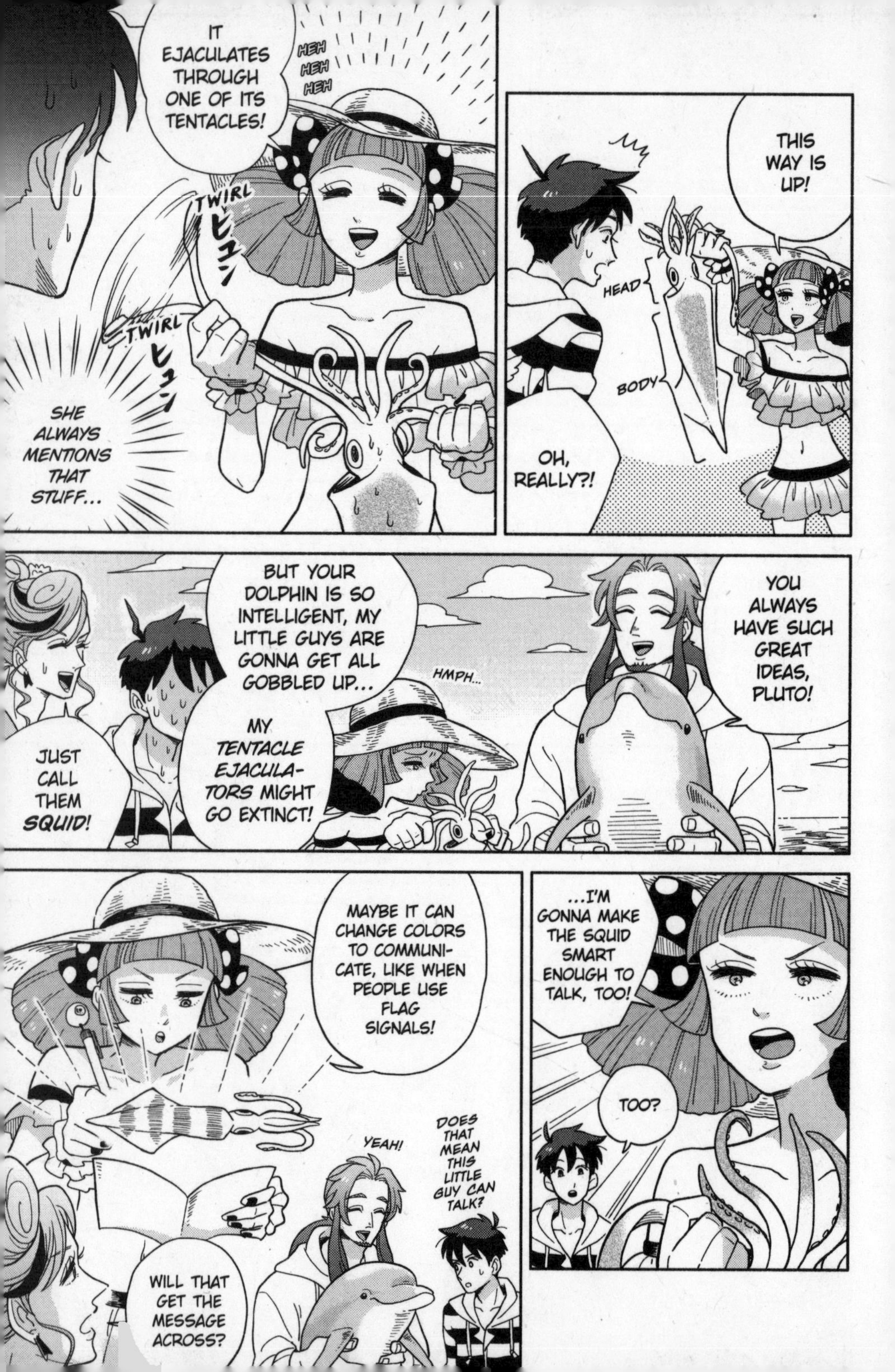

THIS WAY IS UP!
HEAD
BODY
OH, REALLY?!
IT EJACULATES THROUGH ONE OF ITS TENTACLES!
HEH HEH HEH
TWIRL ビュン
TWIRL ヒュン
SHE ALWAYS MENTIONS THAT STUFF...
YOU ALWAYS HAVE SUCH GREAT IDEAS, PLUTO!
HMPH...
BUT YOUR DOLPHIN IS SO INTELLIGENT, MY LITTLE GUYS ARE GONNA GET ALL GOBBLED UP...
MY *TENTACLE EJACULATORS* MIGHT GO EXTINCT!
JUST CALL THEM *SQUID!*
...I'M GONNA MAKE THE SQUID SMART ENOUGH TO TALK, TOO!
TOO?
MAYBE IT CAN CHANGE COLORS TO COMMUNICATE, LIKE WHEN PEOPLE USE FLAG SIGNALS!
DOES THAT MEAN THIS LITTLE GUY CAN TALK?
YEAH!
WILL THAT GET THE MESSAGE ACROSS?

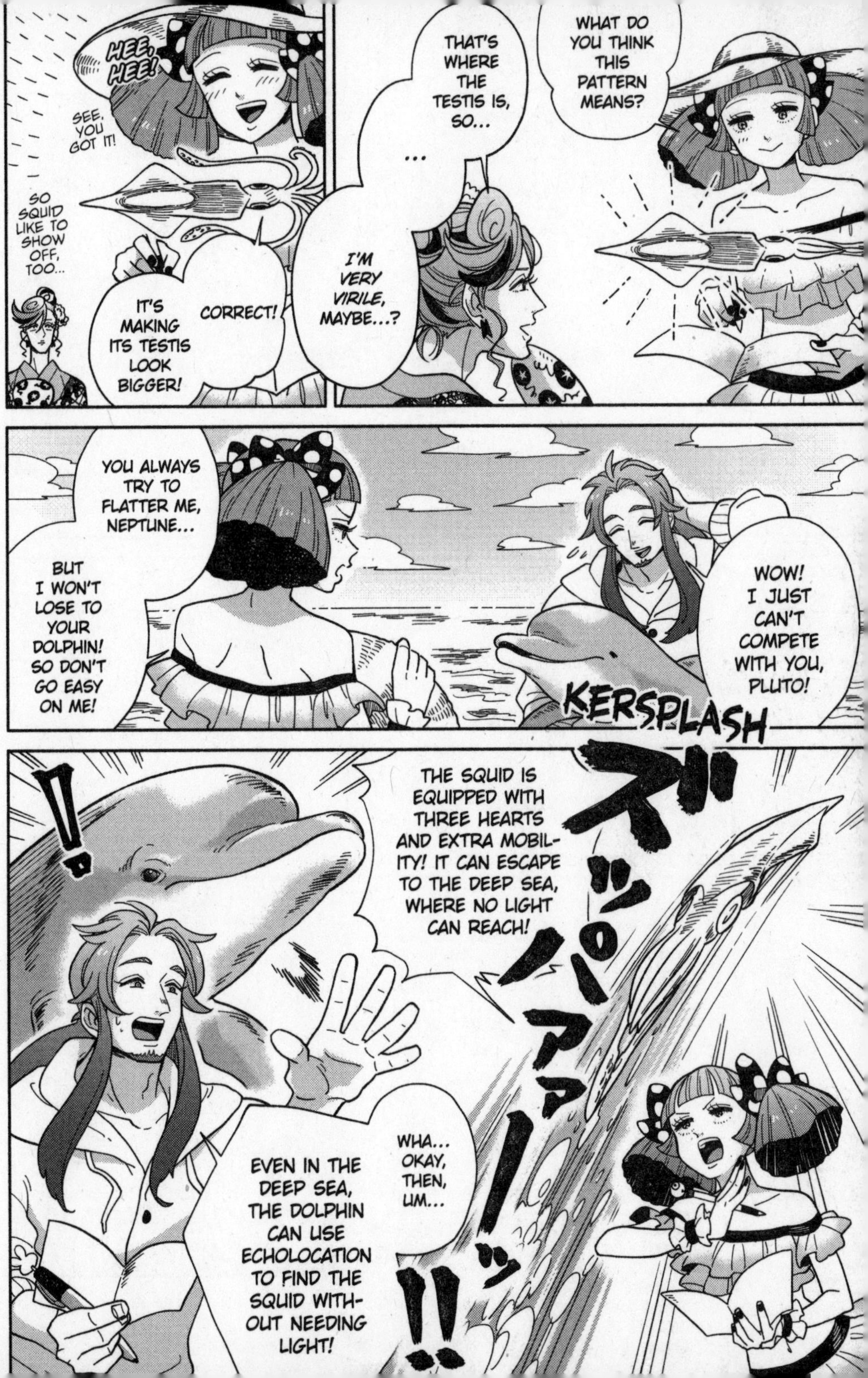
WHAT DO YOU THINK THIS PATTERN MEANS?
THAT'S WHERE THE TESTIS IS, SO...
...
I'M VERY VIRILE, MAYBE...?
HEE, HEE!
CORRECT!
IT'S MAKING ITS TESTIS LOOK BIGGER!
SEE, YOU GOT IT!
SO SQUID LIKE TO SHOW OFF, TOO...
WOW! I JUST CAN'T COMPETE WITH YOU, PLUTO!
KERSPLASH
YOU ALWAYS TRY TO FLATTER ME, NEPTUNE...
BUT I WON'T LOSE TO YOUR DOLPHIN! SO DON'T GO EASY ON ME!
THE SQUID IS EQUIPPED WITH THREE HEARTS AND EXTRA MOBILITY! IT CAN ESCAPE TO THE DEEP SEA, WHERE NO LIGHT CAN REACH!
WHA... OKAY, THEN, UM...
!
EVEN IN THE DEEP SEA, THE DOLPHIN CAN USE ECHOLOCATION TO FIND THE SQUID WITHOUT NEEDING LIGHT!

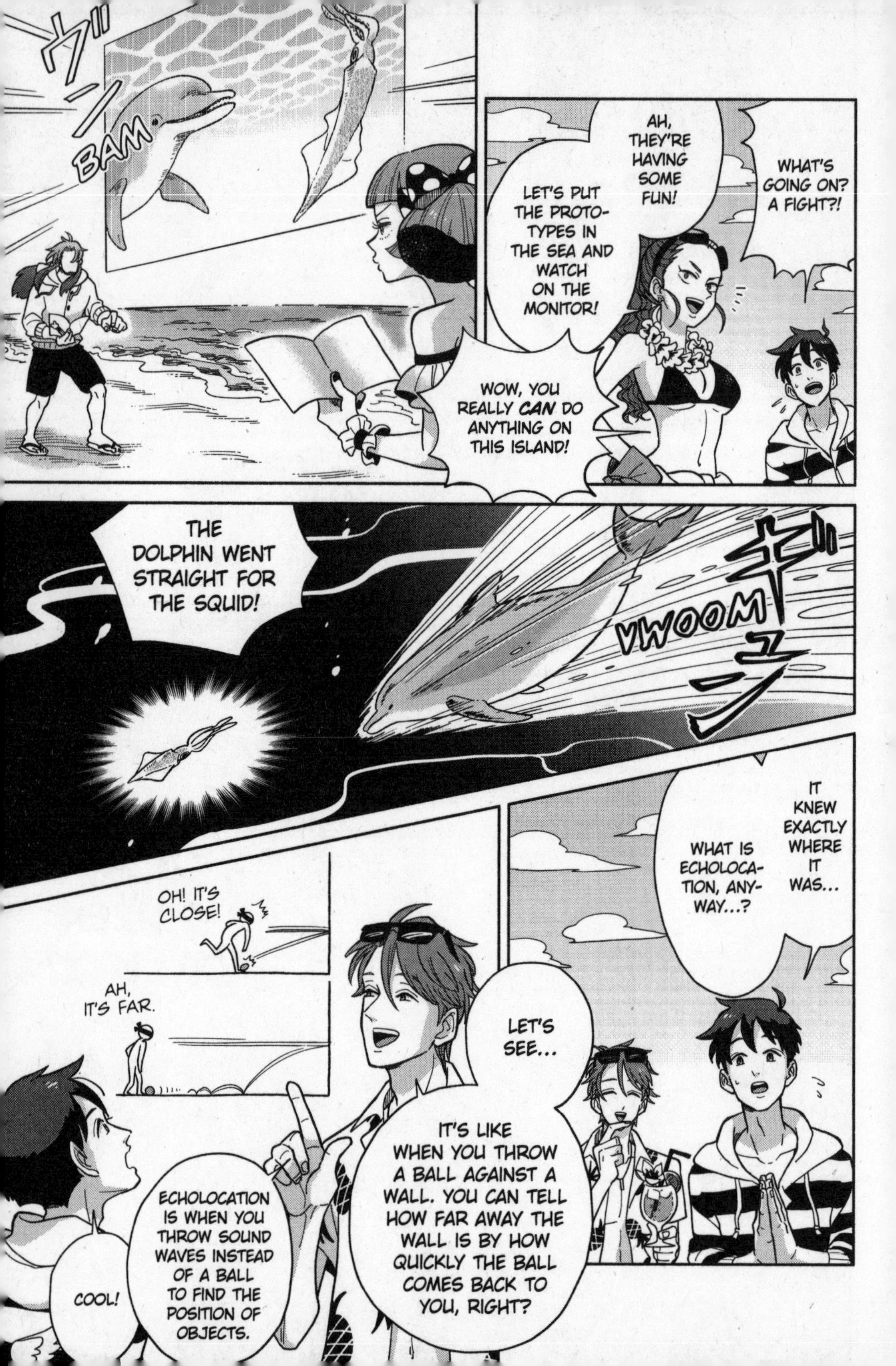
WHAT'S GOING ON? A FIGHT?!
AH, THEY'RE HAVING SOME FUN!
LET'S PUT THE PROTO-TYPES IN THE SEA AND WATCH ON THE MONITOR!
WOW, YOU REALLY *CAN* DO ANYTHING ON THIS ISLAND!
BAM
THE DOLPHIN WENT STRAIGHT FOR THE SQUID!
VWOOM
IT KNEW EXACTLY WHERE IT WAS...
WHAT IS ECHOLOCA-TION, ANY-WAY...?
LET'S SEE...
IT'S LIKE WHEN YOU THROW A BALL AGAINST A WALL. YOU CAN TELL HOW FAR AWAY THE WALL IS BY HOW QUICKLY THE BALL COMES BACK TO YOU, RIGHT?
OH! IT'S CLOSE!
AH, IT'S FAR.
ECHOLOCATION IS WHEN YOU THROW SOUND WAVES INSTEAD OF A BALL TO FIND THE POSITION OF OBJECTS.
COOL!

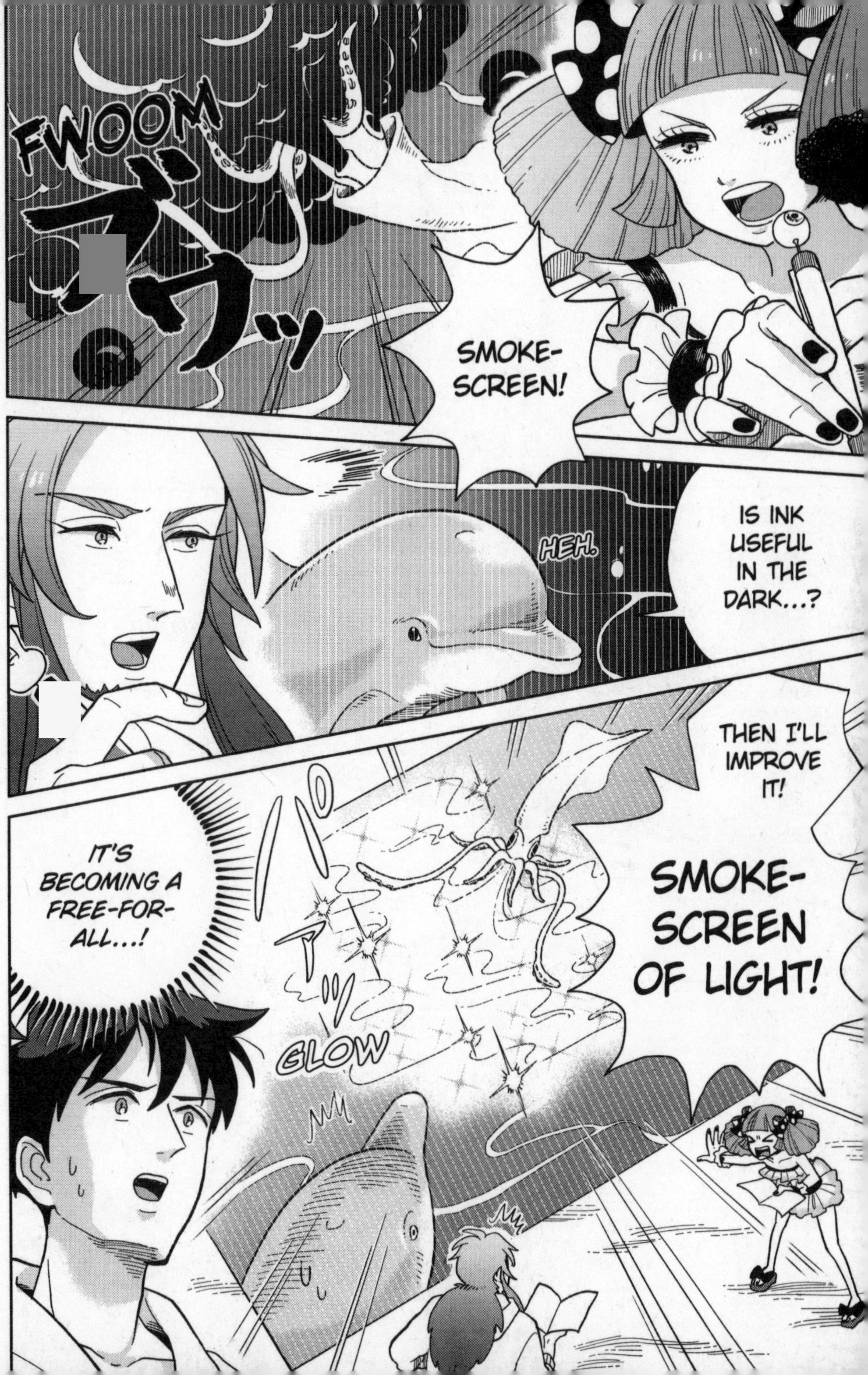
FWOOM
SMOKE-SCREEN!
IS INK USEFUL IN THE DARK...?
HEH.
THEN I'LL IMPROVE IT!
SMOKE-SCREEN OF LIGHT!
IT'S BECOMING A FREE-FOR-ALL...!
GLOW

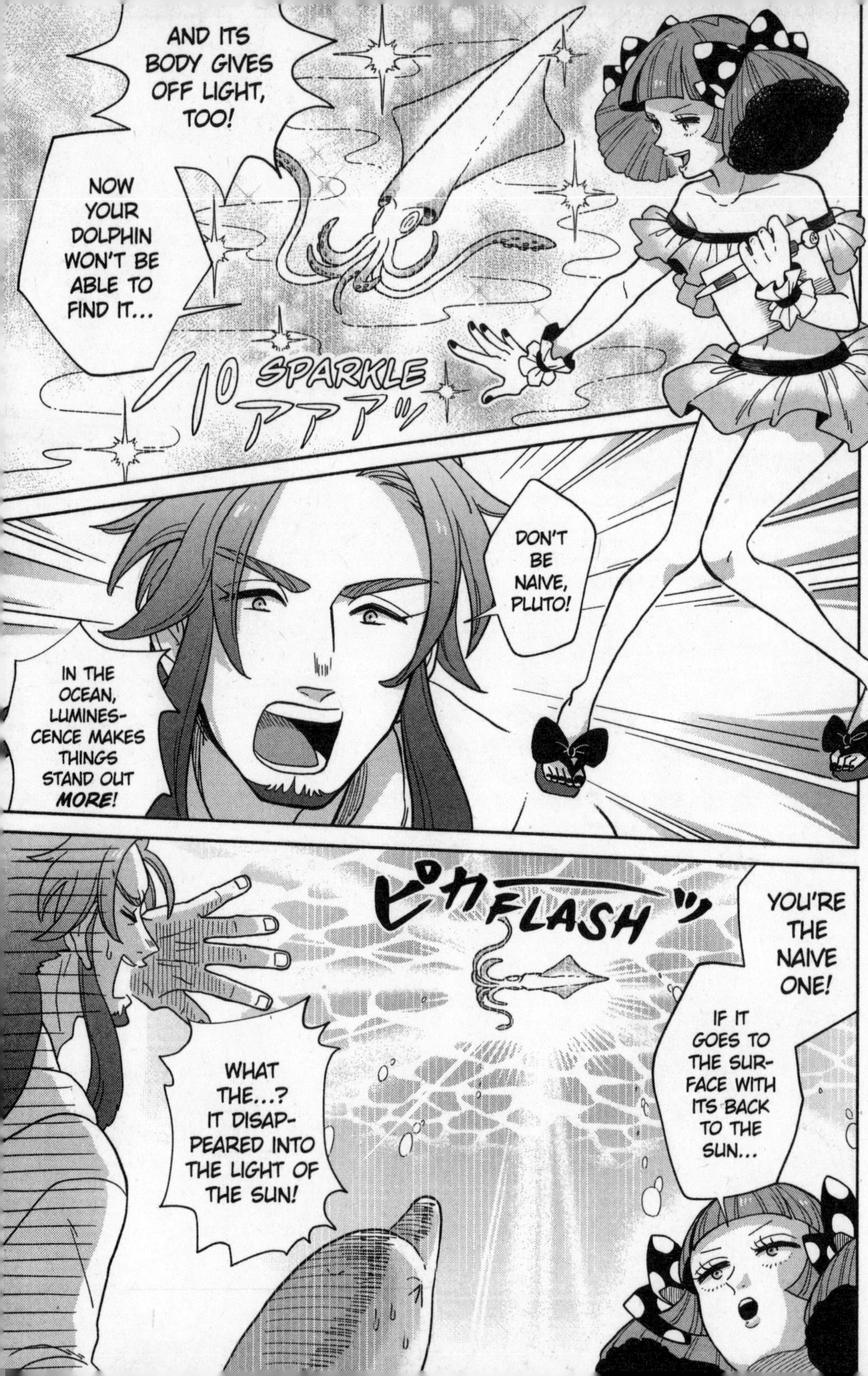
AND ITS BODY GIVES OFF LIGHT, TOO!
NOW YOUR DOLPHIN WON'T BE ABLE TO FIND IT...
パアアアッ SPARKLE
DON'T BE NAIVE, PLUTO!
IN THE OCEAN, LUMINES-CENCE MAKES THINGS STAND OUT *MORE*!
ピカッ FLASH
WHAT THE...? IT DISAP-PEARED INTO THE LIGHT OF THE SUN!
YOU'RE THE NAIVE ONE!
IF IT GOES TO THE SUR-FACE WITH ITS BACK TO THE SUN...

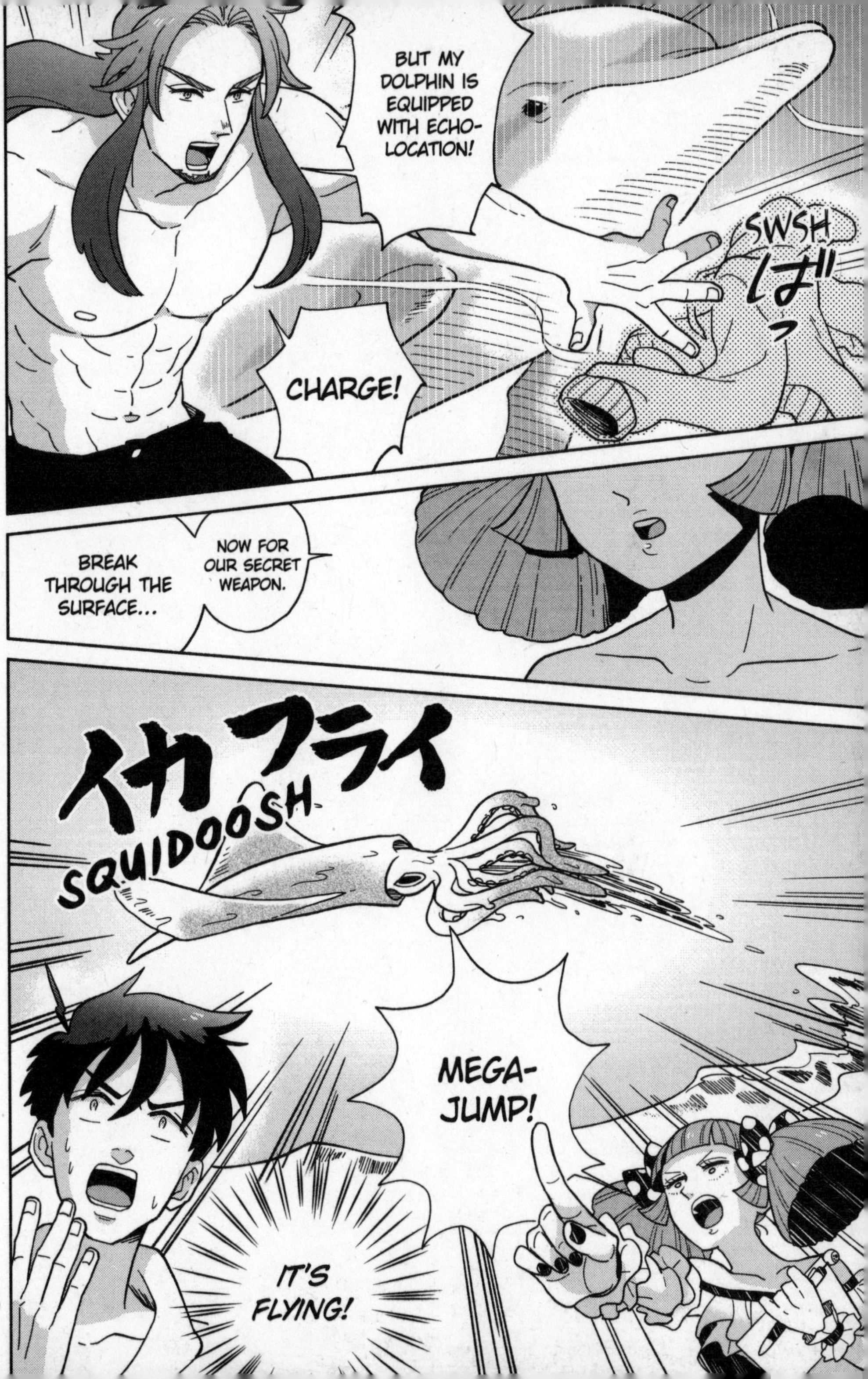
BUT MY DOLPHIN IS EQUIPPED WITH ECHO-LOCATION!
SWSH
ばっ
CHARGE!
NOW FOR OUR SECRET WEAPON.
BREAK THROUGH THE SURFACE...
イカフライ
SQUIDOOSH
MEGA-JUMP!
IT'S FLYING!

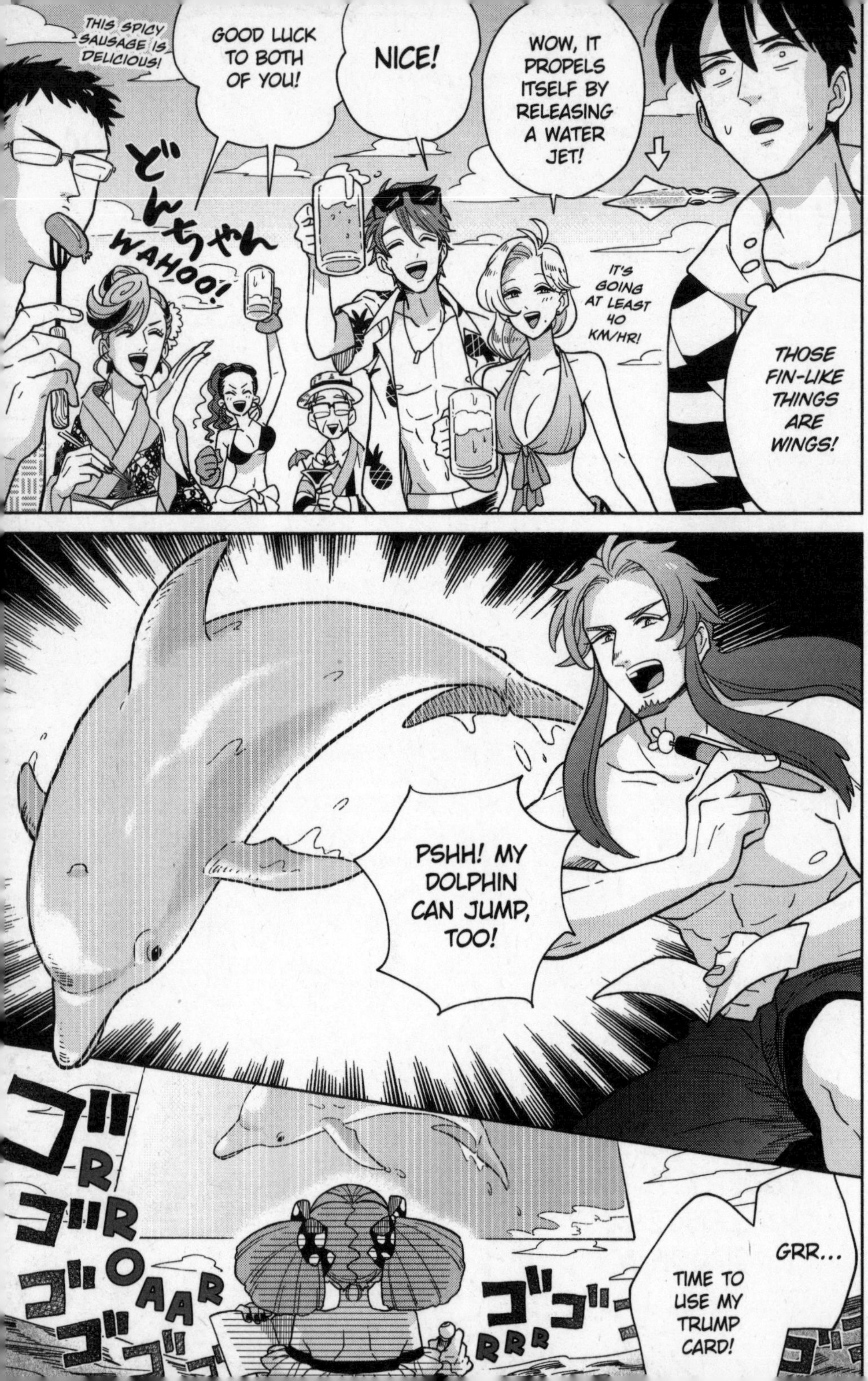
WOW, IT PROPELS ITSELF BY RELEASING A WATER JET!
IT'S GOING AT LEAST 40 KM/HR!
THOSE FIN-LIKE THINGS ARE WINGS!
NICE!
GOOD LUCK TO BOTH OF YOU!
THIS SPICY SAUSAGE IS DELICIOUS!
どんちゃん
WAHOO!
PSHH! MY DOLPHIN CAN JUMP, TOO!
GRR...
TIME TO USE MY TRUMP CARD!
ゴゴゴ RRR
ゴR ゴR ゴOAAR

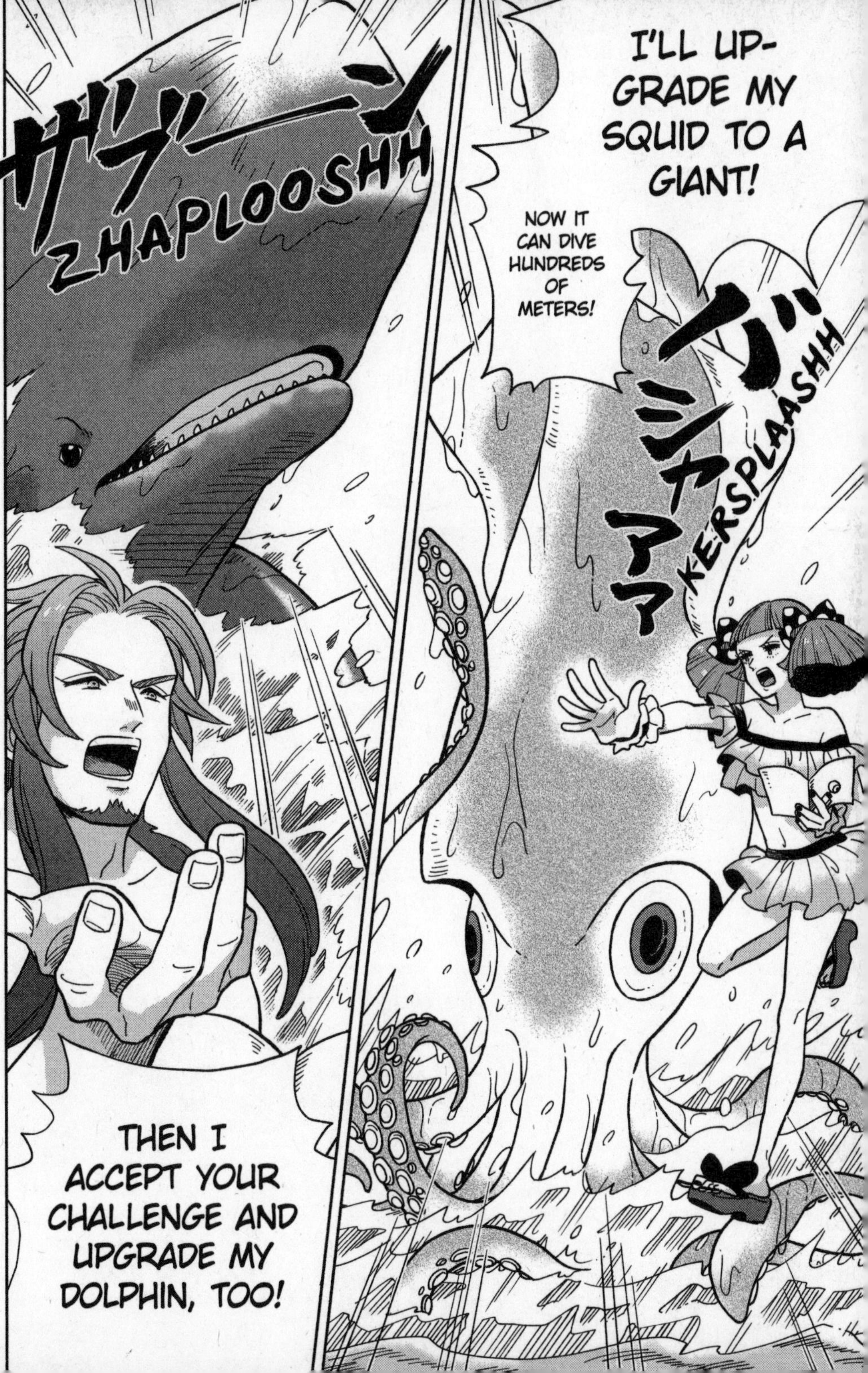
I'LL UP-GRADE MY SQUID TO A GIANT!
NOW IT CAN DIVE HUNDREDS OF METERS!
バシャアア
KERSPLAASHH
ザブーン
ZHAPLOOSHH
THEN I ACCEPT YOUR CHALLENGE AND UPGRADE MY DOLPHIN, TOO!

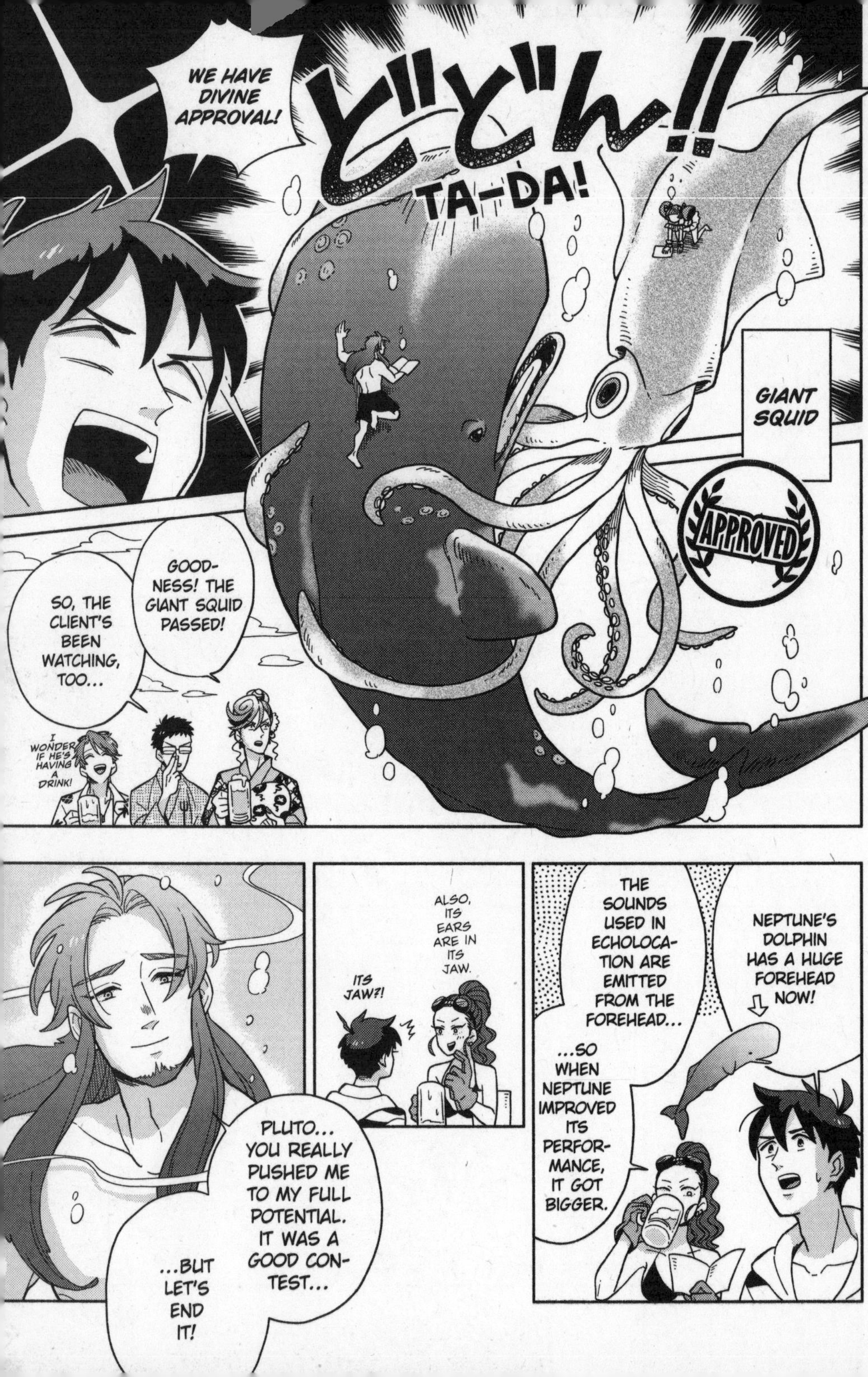
どどん!!
TA-DA!
GIANT SQUID
APPROVED
WE HAVE DIVINE APPROVAL!
GOODNESS! THE GIANT SQUID PASSED!
SO, THE CLIENT'S BEEN WATCHING, TOO...
I WONDER IF HE'S HAVING A DRINK!
NEPTUNE'S DOLPHIN HAS A HUGE FOREHEAD NOW!
THE SOUNDS USED IN ECHOLOCATION ARE EMITTED FROM THE FOREHEAD...
...SO WHEN NEPTUNE IMPROVED ITS PERFORMANCE, IT GOT BIGGER.
ALSO, ITS EARS ARE IN ITS JAW.
ITS JAW?!
PLUTO... YOU REALLY PUSHED ME TO MY FULL POTENTIAL. IT WAS A GOOD CONTEST...
...BUT LET'S END IT!

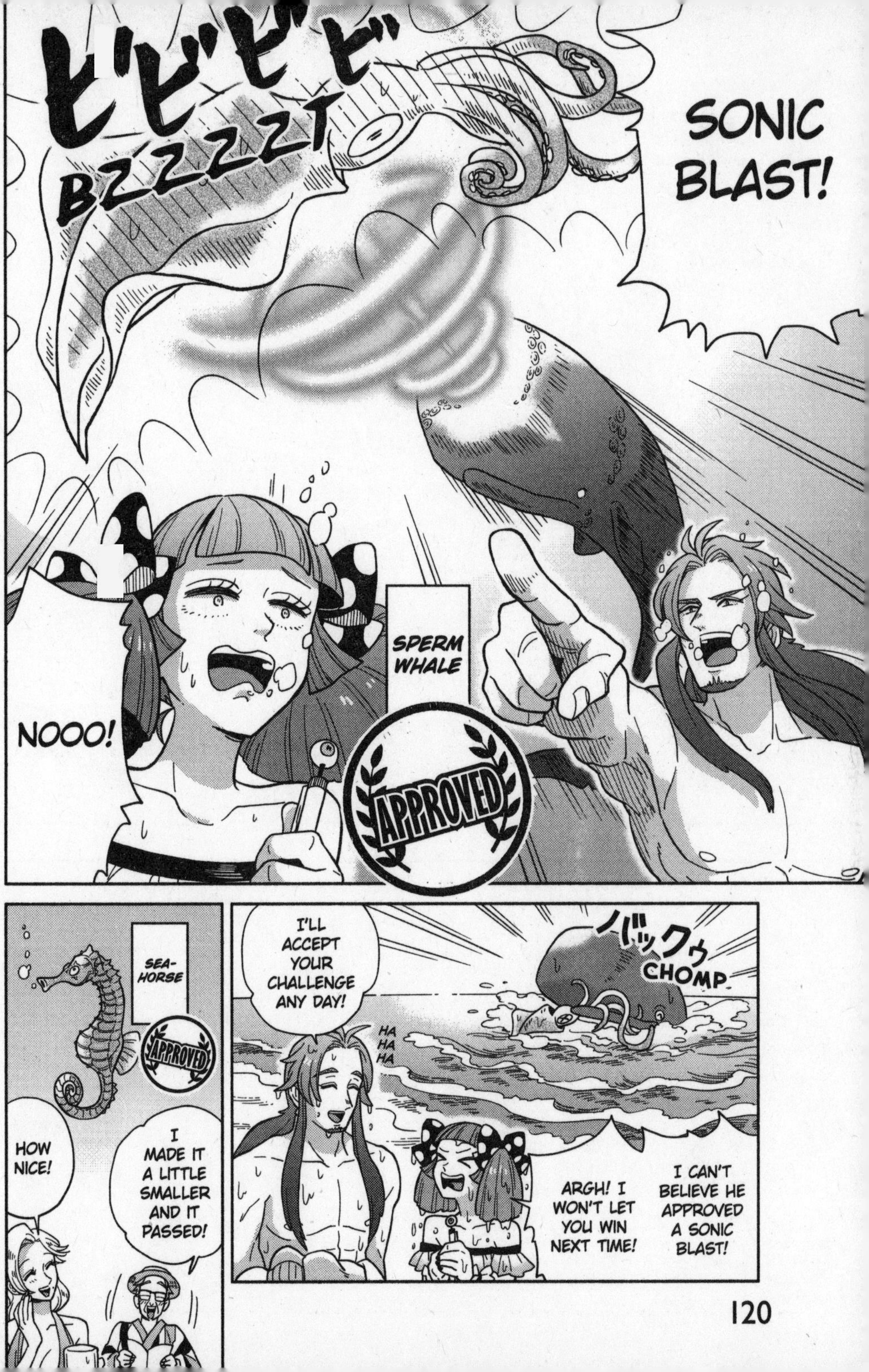
SONIC BLAST!
ビビビビビ
BZZZZZT
SPERM WHALE
APPROVED
NOOO!
バックゥ
CHOMP
I'LL ACCEPT YOUR CHALLENGE ANY DAY!
HA HA HA
I CAN'T BELIEVE HE APPROVED A SONIC BLAST!
ARGH! I WON'T LET YOU WIN NEXT TIME!
SEA-HORSE
APPROVED
I MADE IT A LITTLE SMALLER AND IT PASSED!
HOW NICE!

THE ENCYCLOPEDIA OF REAL ANIMALS 06

ANIMAL ENCYCLOPEDIA

ANIMAL 16 | SPERM WHALE

THE REAL THING

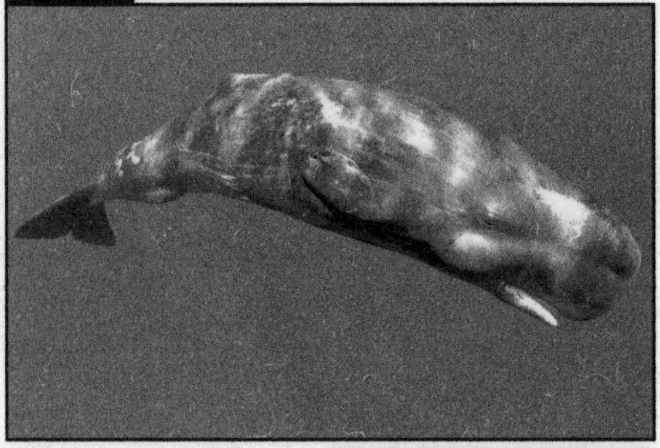

Often, sperm whales bear marks on their foreheads from battling giant squid.
Photo: Bluegreen Pictures/Aflo

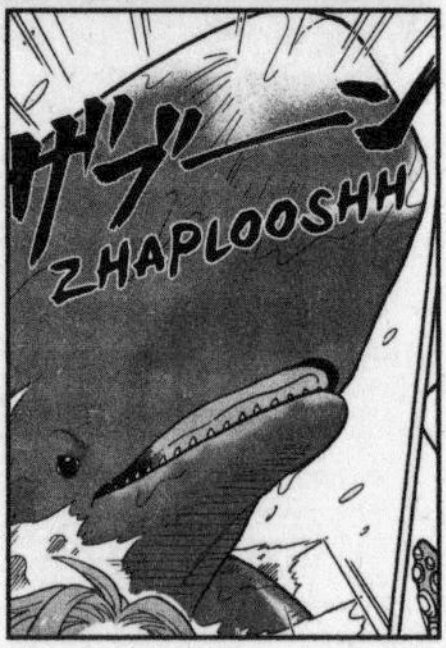
ZHAPLOOSHH

The sperm whale is the largest toothed animal in the world. It emits sound waves from its head, and its vocalizations are said to be as loud as 250 decibels (dB). Considering a jet engine heard from close by is approximately 120dB, one can only imagine the noise a sperm whale can make. Sounds louder than 200dB are fatal to small fish, and one theory claims that sperm whales use vocalizations to disable squid and other prey. The sperm whale can dive for over an hour because it can exchange around 90% of the air in its lungs per breath (whereas humans exchange only around 15%). It also has nine times the concentration of myoglobin (a protein that stores oxygen in muscle tissue) as humans, making its oxygen absorption highly efficient. The sperm whale dives directly down, perpendicular to the water's surface.

[Type species] *Physeter macrocephalus*
[Classification] Class: Mammalia
Order: Artiodactyla
Family: Physeteridae
Genus: *Physeter*
[Habitat] Deep oceans at depths of up to 3,000m (9,800 ft)
[Length] Up to 19 m (62 ft)

ANIMAL 17 GIANT SQUID

シャアア
KERSPLAASHH

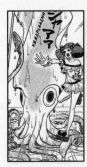

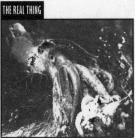

THE REAL THING

The first-ever live footage of a giant squid was taken in the waters south of Tokyo in 2006.

Photo: Tsunemi Kubodera/National Museum of Nature and Science/AP/Aflo

[Type species] *Architeuthis dux*
[Classification] Phylum: Mollusca
Class: Cephalopoda
Suborder: Oegopsina
Family: Architeuthidae
Genus: *Architeuthis*
[Habitat] Ocean at depths of 300-900 m (1,000-3,000 ft)
[Length] Over 10 m (33 ft); the largest known specimen, observed in Nov. 2017, was 14.3 m (47 ft)

It's thought that the giant squid evolved to such a great size to avoid being eaten by predators. It lives in the "twilight zone," a region that extends from a depth of 200 to 1,000 meters (650 to 3,300 feet) where some weak sunlight penetrates. It has been suggested that because the twilight zone doesn't offer many places to hide, growing to a giant size was the only means the squid had to escape its predators. It's also said that they can grow to up to 20 meters (65 feet), but this is debated and has not been documented.

ANIMAL 18 JAPANESE FLYING SQUID

Some relatives of the Japanese flying squid have been observed to glide for dozens of meters. The squid shoots out of the water with its fins held against its body, and then glides at 40 km (25 mi) per hour by spreading out its arms and fins. A subfamily of the bobtail squid uses the "smokescreen of light" mentioned in this chapter, while the Humboldt squid can communicate by changing color. Which tentacle is used for transferring sperm depends on the species of squid.

THE REAL THING

A Japanese flying squid swimming. They only live for one year.
Photo: Tsuneo Nakamura/Aflo

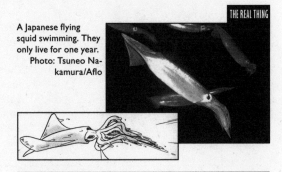

[Type species]: *Todarodes pacificus*
[Classification]: Phylum: Mollusca
Class: Cephalopoda
Order: Teuthida
Family: Ommastrephidae
Genus: *Todarodes*
[Range]: Northern Pacific Ocean
[Length]: Approximately 30 cm (1 ft)

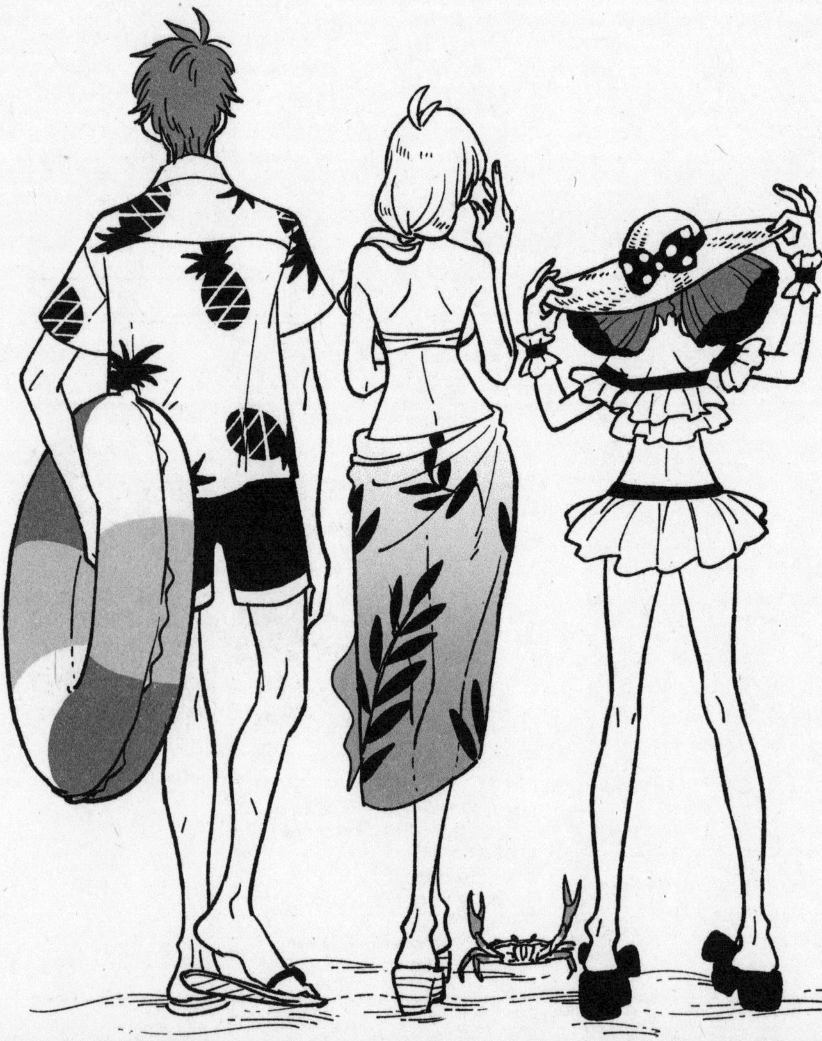

HEAVEN'S
DESIGN TEAM

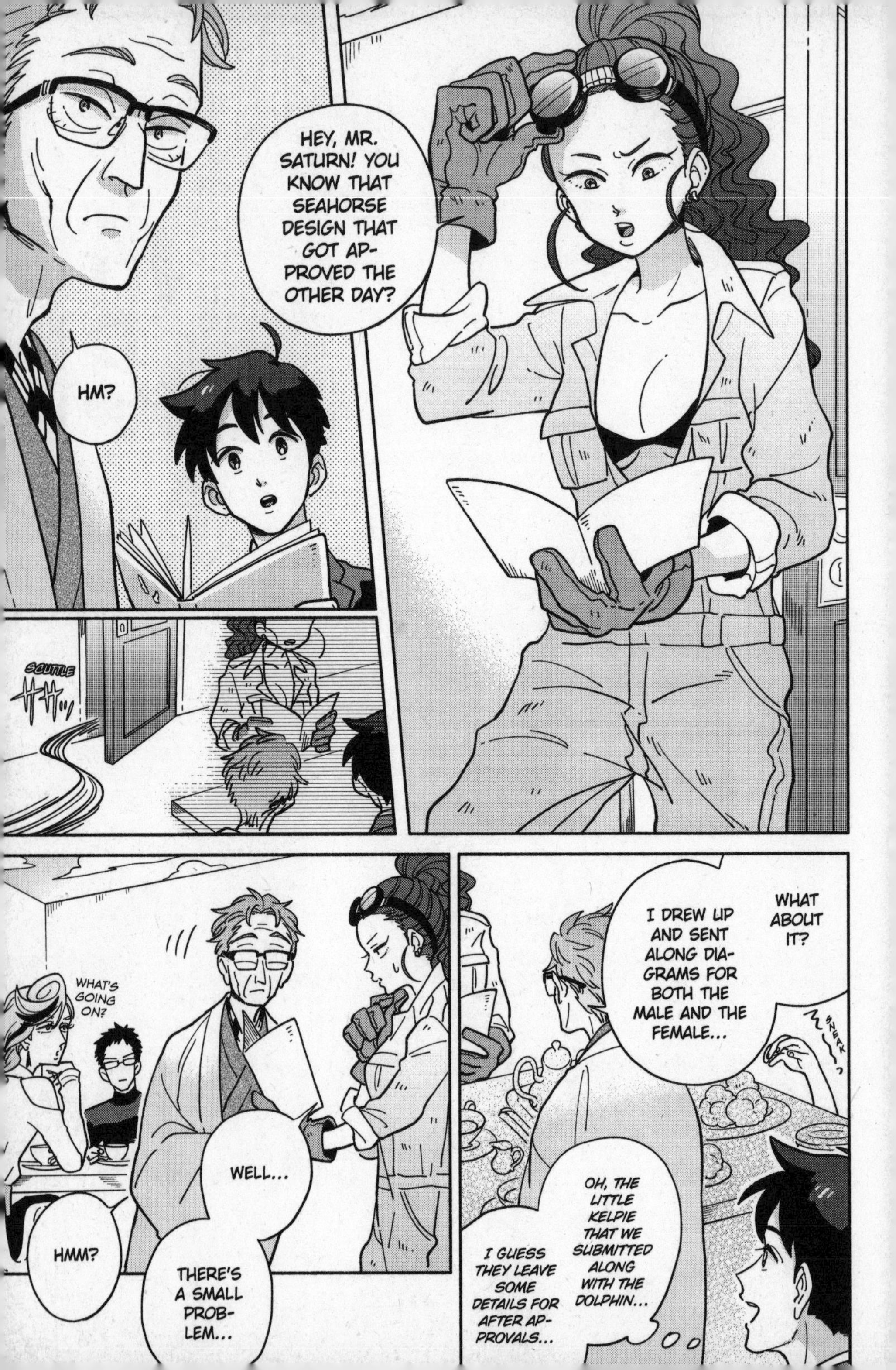

HEY, MR. SATURN! YOU KNOW THAT SEAHORSE DESIGN THAT GOT APPROVED THE OTHER DAY?
HM?
SCUTTLE
WHAT ABOUT IT?
I DREW UP AND SENT ALONG DIAGRAMS FOR BOTH THE MALE AND THE FEMALE...
SNERK
OH, THE LITTLE KELPIE THAT WE SUBMITTED ALONG WITH THE DOLPHIN...
I GUESS THEY LEAVE SOME DETAILS FOR AFTER APPROVALS...
WHAT'S GOING ON?
WELL...
HMM?
THERE'S A SMALL PROBLEM...

PROPOSAL 7 HEAVEN'S DESIGN TEAM

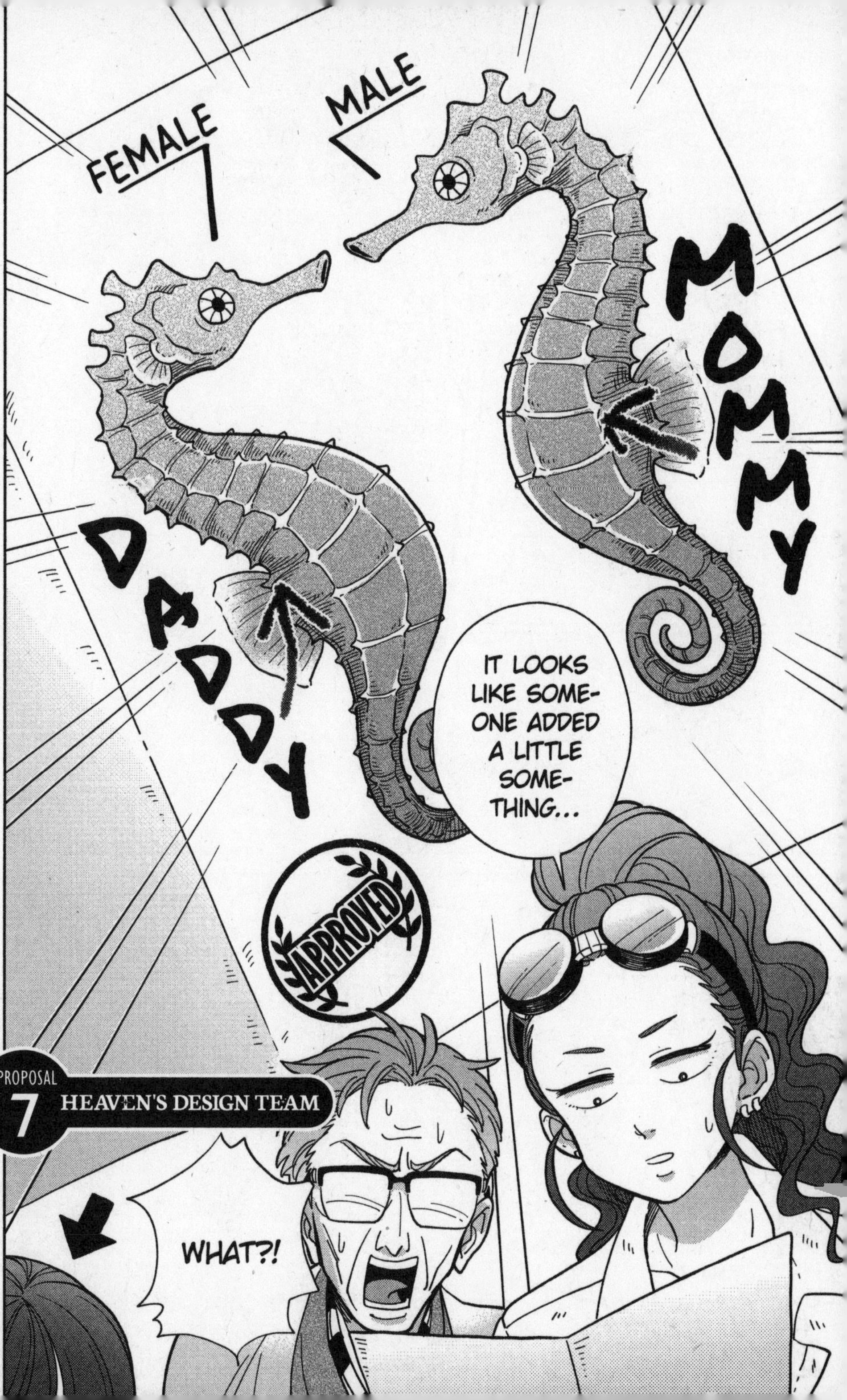
MALE
FEMALE
MOMMY
DADDY
IT LOOKS LIKE SOME-ONE ADDED A LITTLE SOME-THING...
APPROVED
WHAT?!

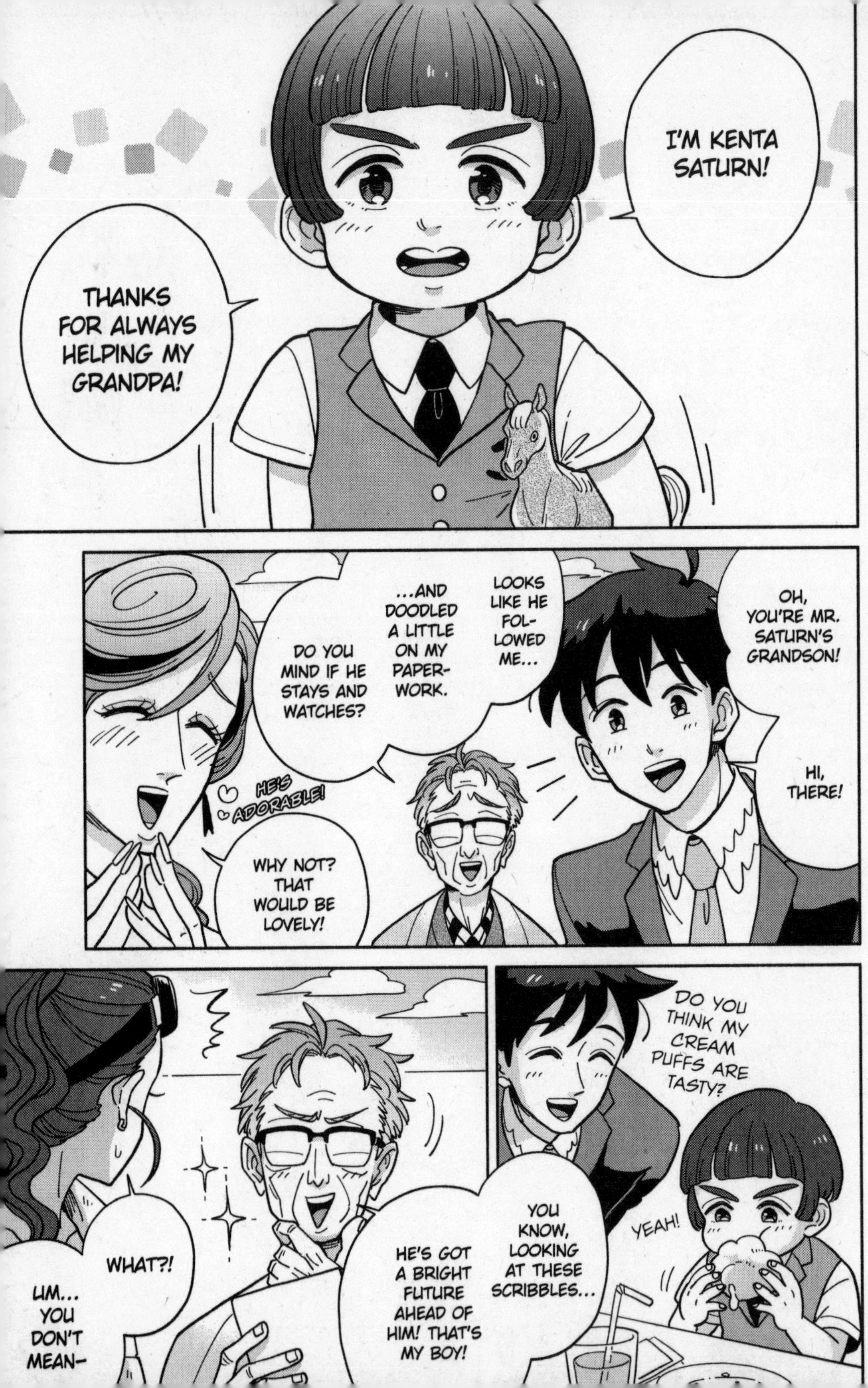
I'M KENTA SATURN!
THANKS FOR ALWAYS HELPING MY GRANDPA!
OH, YOU'RE MR. SATURN'S GRANDSON!
HI, THERE!
LOOKS LIKE HE FOL-LOWED ME...
...AND DOODLED A LITTLE ON MY PAPER-WORK.
DO YOU MIND IF HE STAYS AND WATCHES?
HE'S ADORABLE!
WHY NOT? THAT WOULD BE LOVELY!
DO YOU THINK MY CREAM PUFFS ARE TASTY?
YEAH!
YOU KNOW, LOOKING AT THESE SCRIBBLES...
HE'S GOT A BRIGHT FUTURE AHEAD OF HIM! THAT'S MY BOY!
WHAT?!
UM... YOU DON'T MEAN-

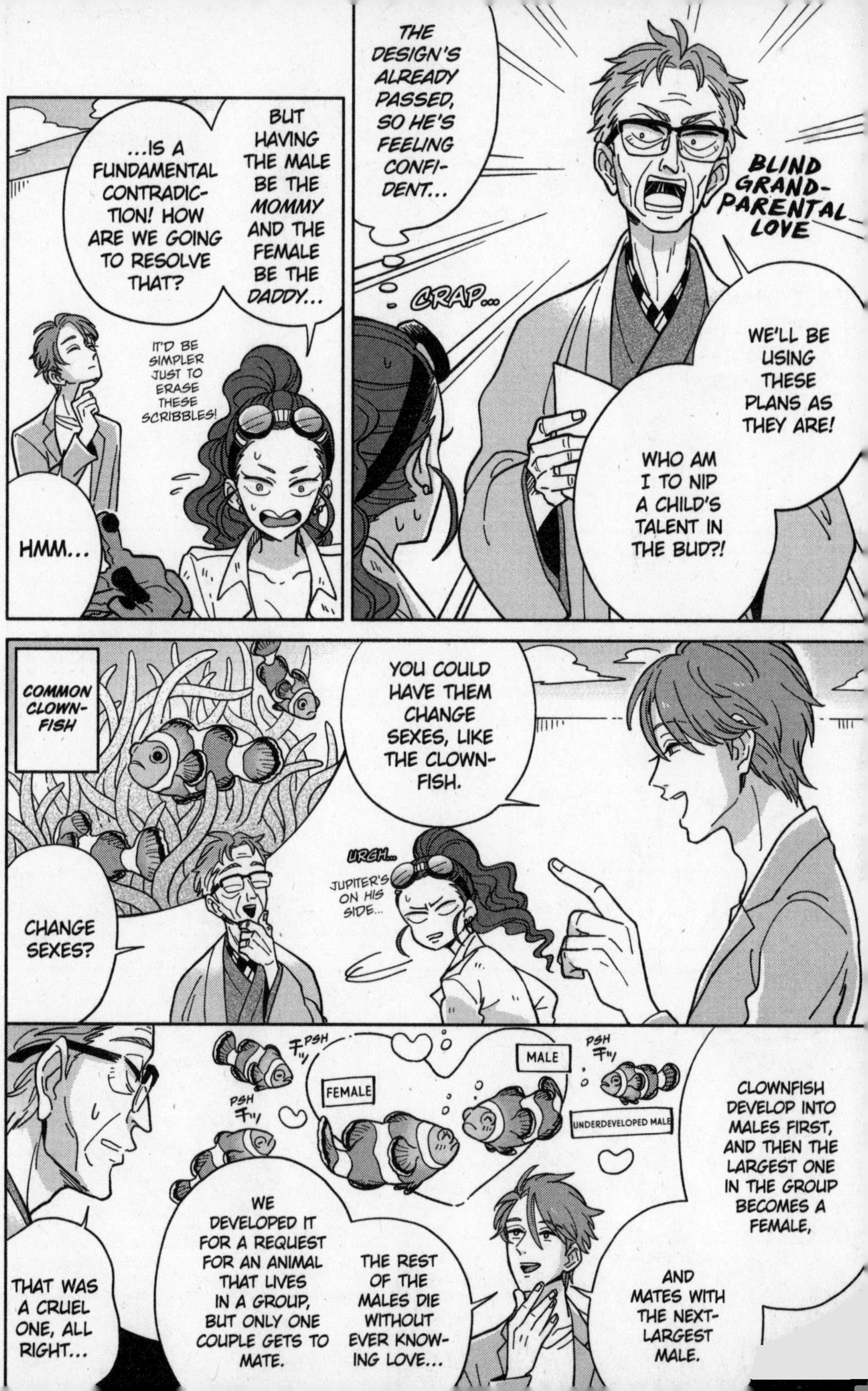
WE'LL BE USING THESE PLANS AS THEY ARE!
WHO AM I TO NIP A CHILD'S TALENT IN THE BUD?!
BLIND GRAND-PARENTAL LOVE
THE DESIGN'S ALREADY PASSED, SO HE'S FEELING CONFI-DENT...
CRAP...
BUT HAVING THE MALE BE THE *MOMMY* AND THE FEMALE BE THE *DADDY*...
...IS A FUNDAMENTAL CONTRADIC-TION! HOW ARE WE GOING TO RESOLVE THAT?
IT'D BE SIMPLER JUST TO ERASE THESE SCRIBBLES!
HMM...
YOU COULD HAVE THEM CHANGE SEXES, LIKE THE CLOWN-FISH.
COMMON CLOWN-FISH
URGH...
JUPITER'S ON HIS SIDE...
CHANGE SEXES?
CLOWNFISH DEVELOP INTO MALES FIRST, AND THEN THE LARGEST ONE IN THE GROUP BECOMES A FEMALE,
AND MATES WITH THE NEXT-LARGEST MALE.
PSH
MALE
UNDERDEVELOPED MALE
FEMALE
PSH
PSH
THE REST OF THE MALES DIE WITHOUT EVER KNOW-ING LOVE...
WE DEVELOPED IT FOR A REQUEST FOR AN ANIMAL THAT LIVES IN A GROUP, BUT ONLY ONE COUPLE GETS TO MATE.
THAT WAS A CRUEL ONE, ALL RIGHT...

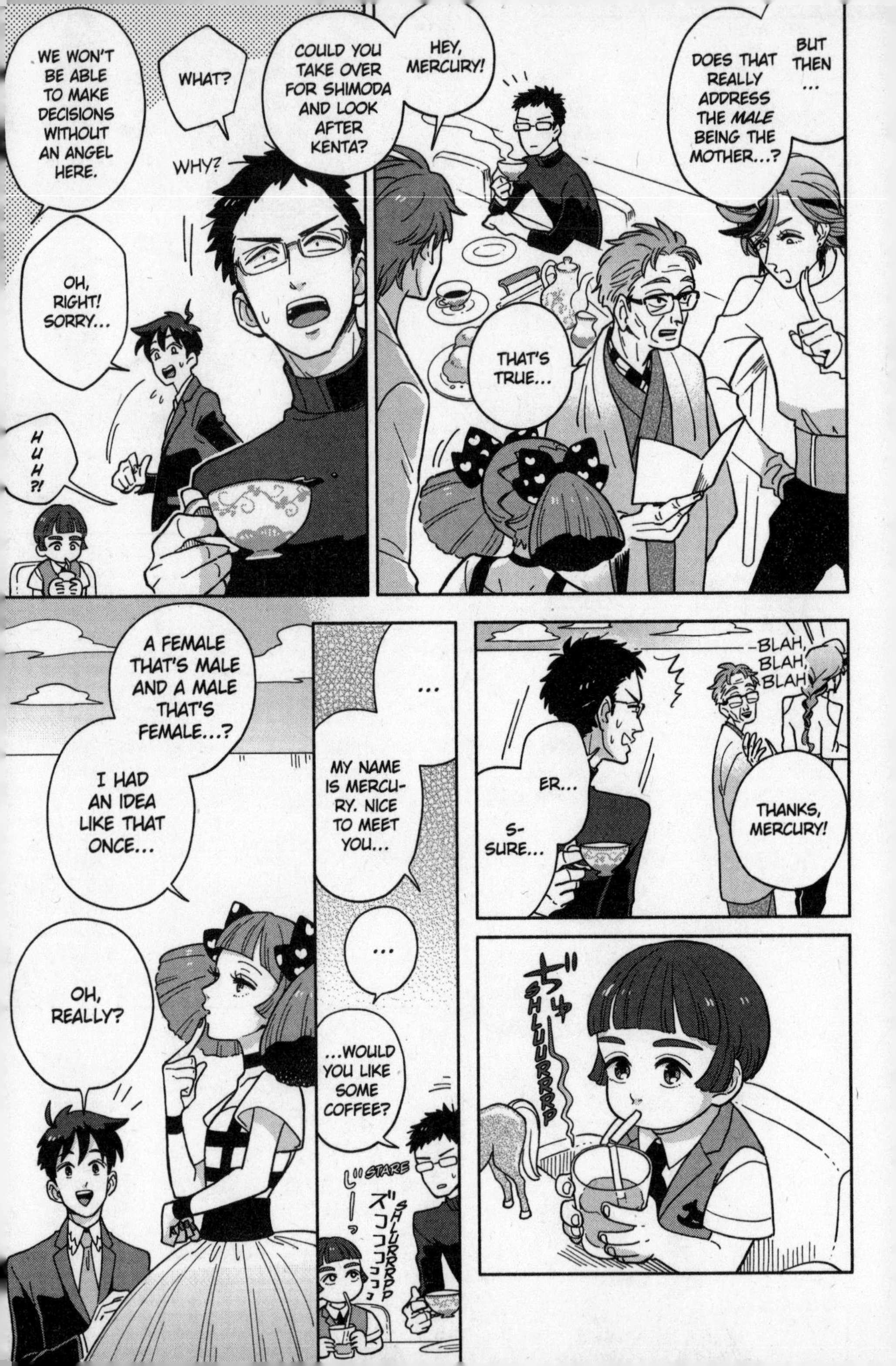

BUT THEN...
DOES THAT REALLY ADDRESS THE *MALE* BEING THE MOTHER...?
THAT'S TRUE...
HEY, MERCURY!
COULD YOU TAKE OVER FOR SHIMODA AND LOOK AFTER KENTA?
WHAT?
WHY?
WE WON'T BE ABLE TO MAKE DECISIONS WITHOUT AN ANGEL HERE.
OH, RIGHT! SORRY...
HUH?!
BLAH, BLAH, BLAH
THANKS, MERCURY!
ER...
S-SURE...
SHLUURRRP
...
MY NAME IS MERCURY. NICE TO MEET YOU...
...
...WOULD YOU LIKE SOME COFFEE?
STARE
SHLURRRP
A FEMALE THAT'S MALE AND A MALE THAT'S FEMALE...?
I HAD AN IDEA LIKE THAT ONCE...
OH, REALLY?

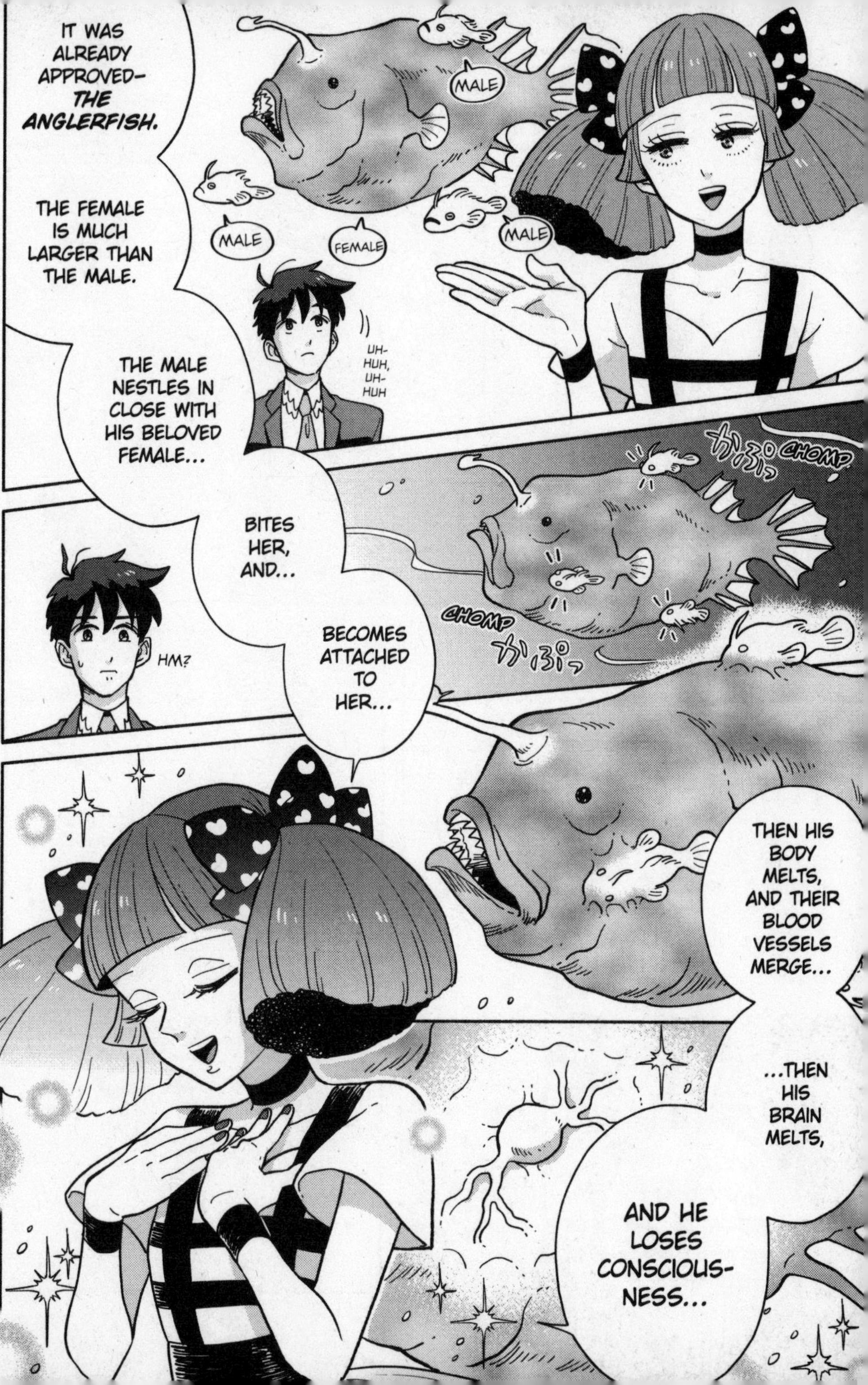

IT WAS ALREADY APPROVED- THE ANGLERFISH.
MALE
MALE
FEMALE
MALE
THE FEMALE IS MUCH LARGER THAN THE MALE.
UH-HUH, UH-HUH
THE MALE NESTLES IN CLOSE WITH HIS BELOVED FEMALE...
かぷっ CHOMP
CHOMP かぷっ
BITES HER, AND...
HM?
BECOMES ATTACHED TO HER...
THEN HIS BODY MELTS, AND THEIR BLOOD VESSELS MERGE...
...THEN HIS BRAIN MELTS,
AND HE LOSES CONSCIOUSNESS...

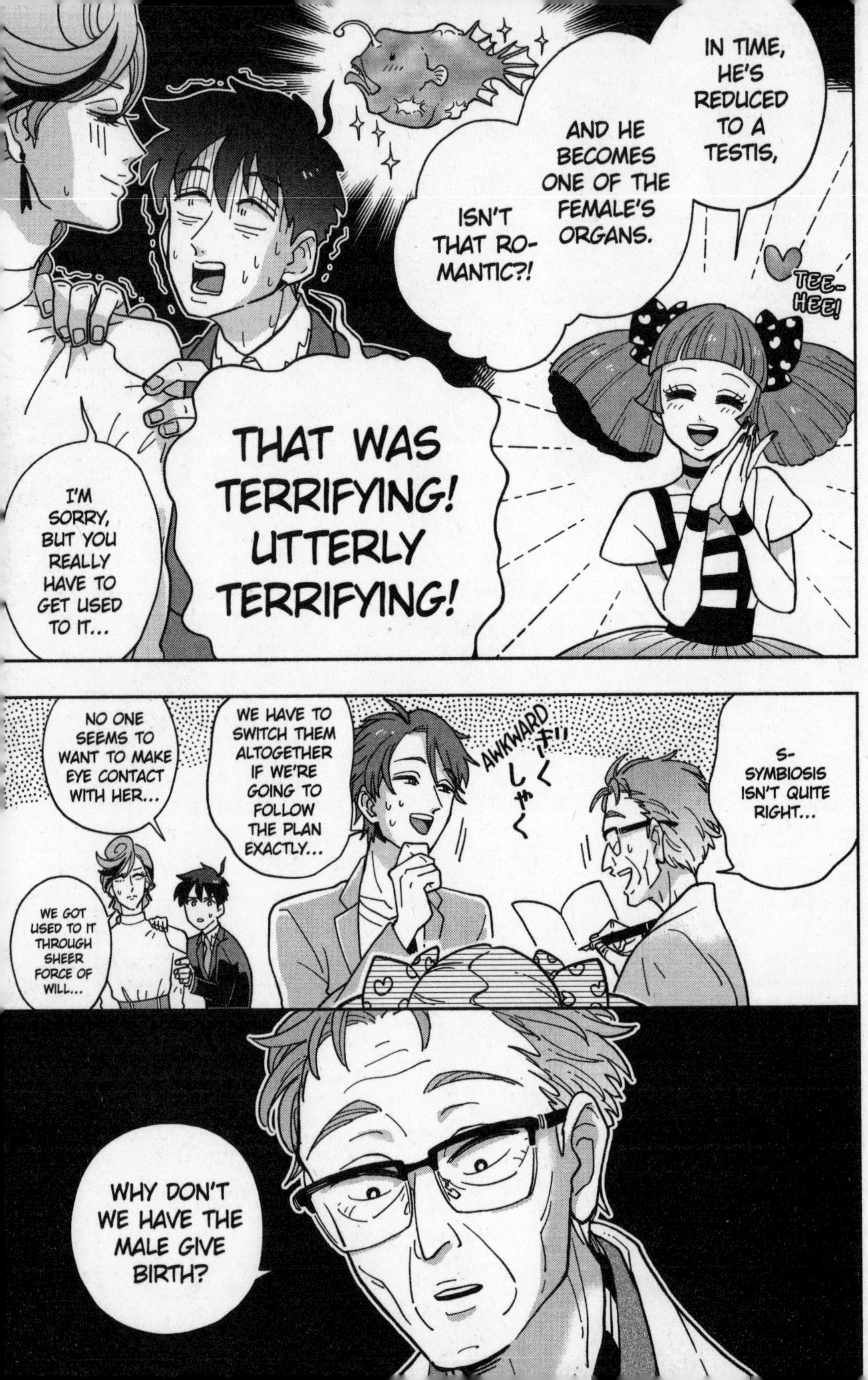
IN TIME, HE'S REDUCED TO A TESTIS,
AND HE BECOMES ONE OF THE FEMALE'S ORGANS.
ISN'T THAT RO-MANTIC?!
TEE-HEE!
THAT WAS TERRIFYING! UTTERLY TERRIFYING!
I'M SORRY, BUT YOU REALLY HAVE TO GET USED TO IT...
S-SYMBIOSIS ISN'T QUITE RIGHT...
AWKWARD
ぎくしゃく
WE HAVE TO SWITCH THEM ALTOGETHER IF WE'RE GOING TO FOLLOW THE PLAN EXACTLY...
NO ONE SEEMS TO WANT TO MAKE EYE CONTACT WITH HER...
WE GOT USED TO IT THROUGH SHEER FORCE OF WILL...
WHY DON'T WE HAVE THE MALE GIVE BIRTH?

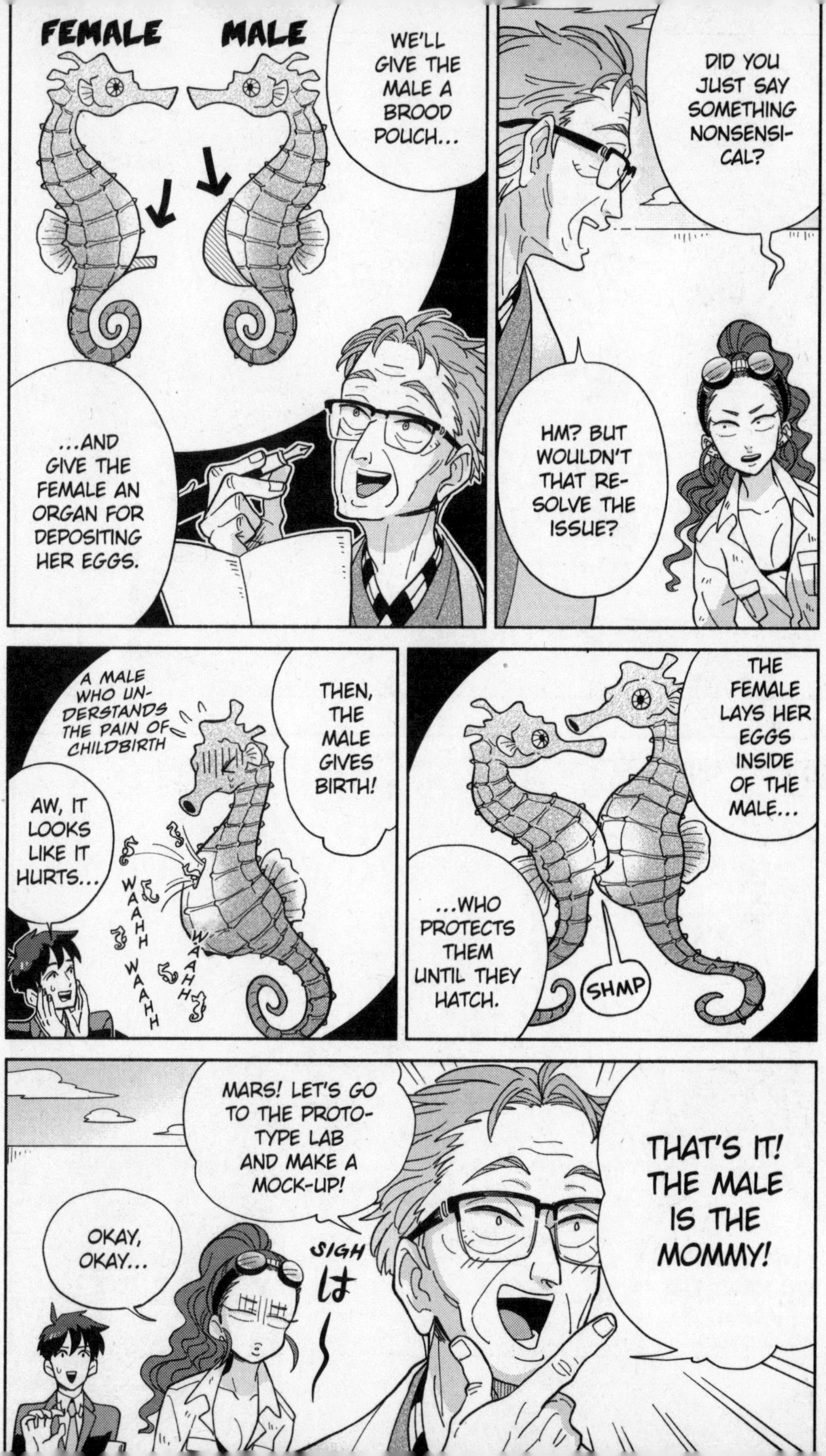
DID YOU JUST SAY SOMETHING NONSENSICAL?
HM? BUT WOULDN'T THAT RESOLVE THE ISSUE?
FEMALE
MALE
WE'LL GIVE THE MALE A BROOD POUCH...
...AND GIVE THE FEMALE AN ORGAN FOR DEPOSITING HER EGGS.
THE FEMALE LAYS HER EGGS INSIDE OF THE MALE...
SHMP
...WHO PROTECTS THEM UNTIL THEY HATCH.
THEN, THE MALE GIVES BIRTH!
A MALE WHO UNDERSTANDS THE PAIN OF CHILDBIRTH
AW, IT LOOKS LIKE IT HURTS...
WAAHH
WAAHH
WAAHH
THAT'S IT! THE MALE IS THE MOMMY!
MARS! LET'S GO TO THE PROTOTYPE LAB AND MAKE A MOCK-UP!
SIGH
は
OKAY, OKAY...

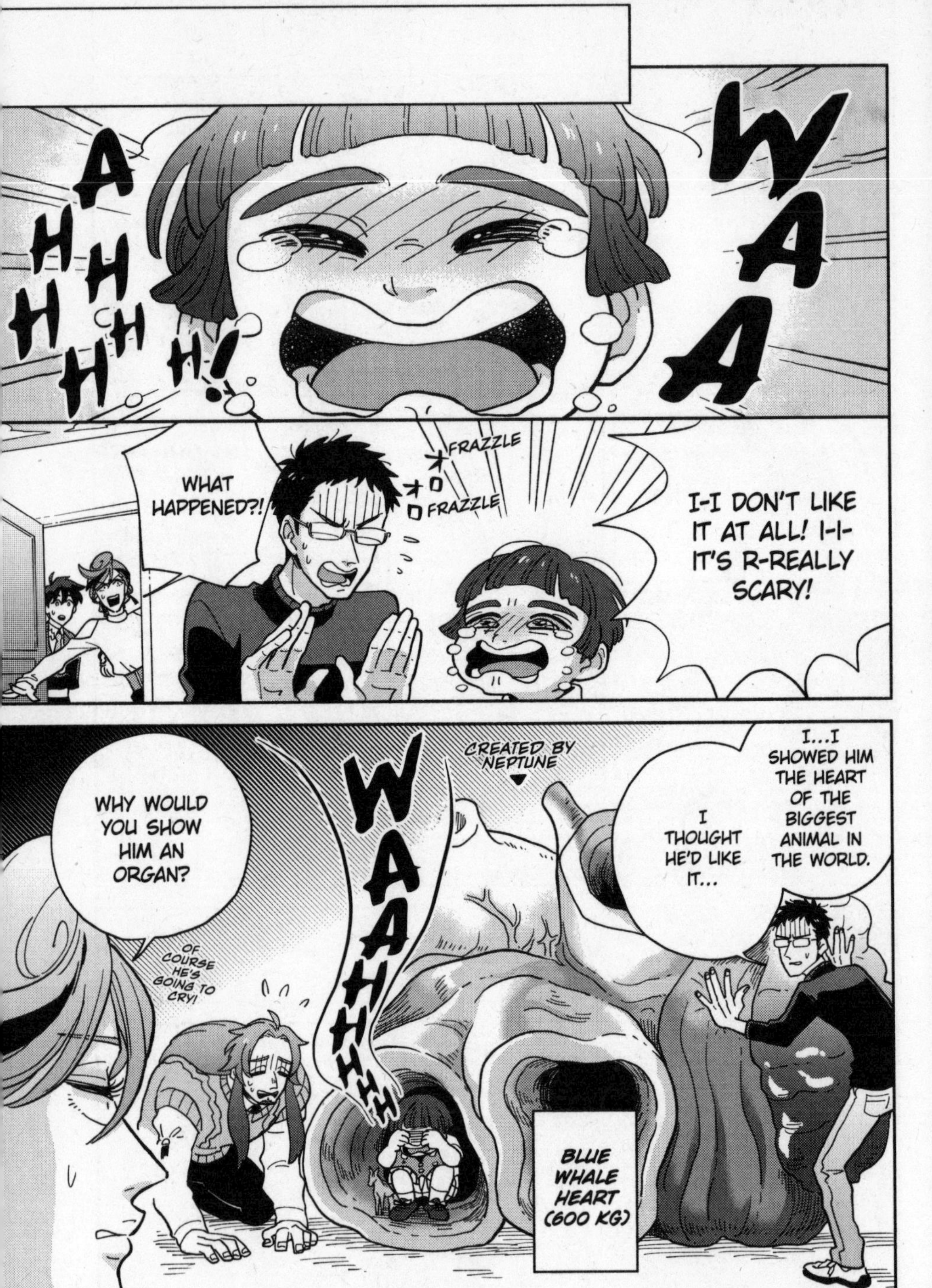
WAAA
AHHHHHHHH!
I-I DON'T LIKE IT AT ALL! I-I-IT'S R-REALLY SCARY!
FRAZZLE
FRAZZLE
WHAT HAPPENED?!
I...I SHOWED HIM THE HEART OF THE BIGGEST ANIMAL IN THE WORLD.
I THOUGHT HE'D LIKE IT...
CREATED BY NEPTUNE
WAAHHHHHH
WHY WOULD YOU SHOW HIM AN ORGAN?
OF COURSE HE'S GOING TO CRY!
BLUE WHALE HEART (600 KG)

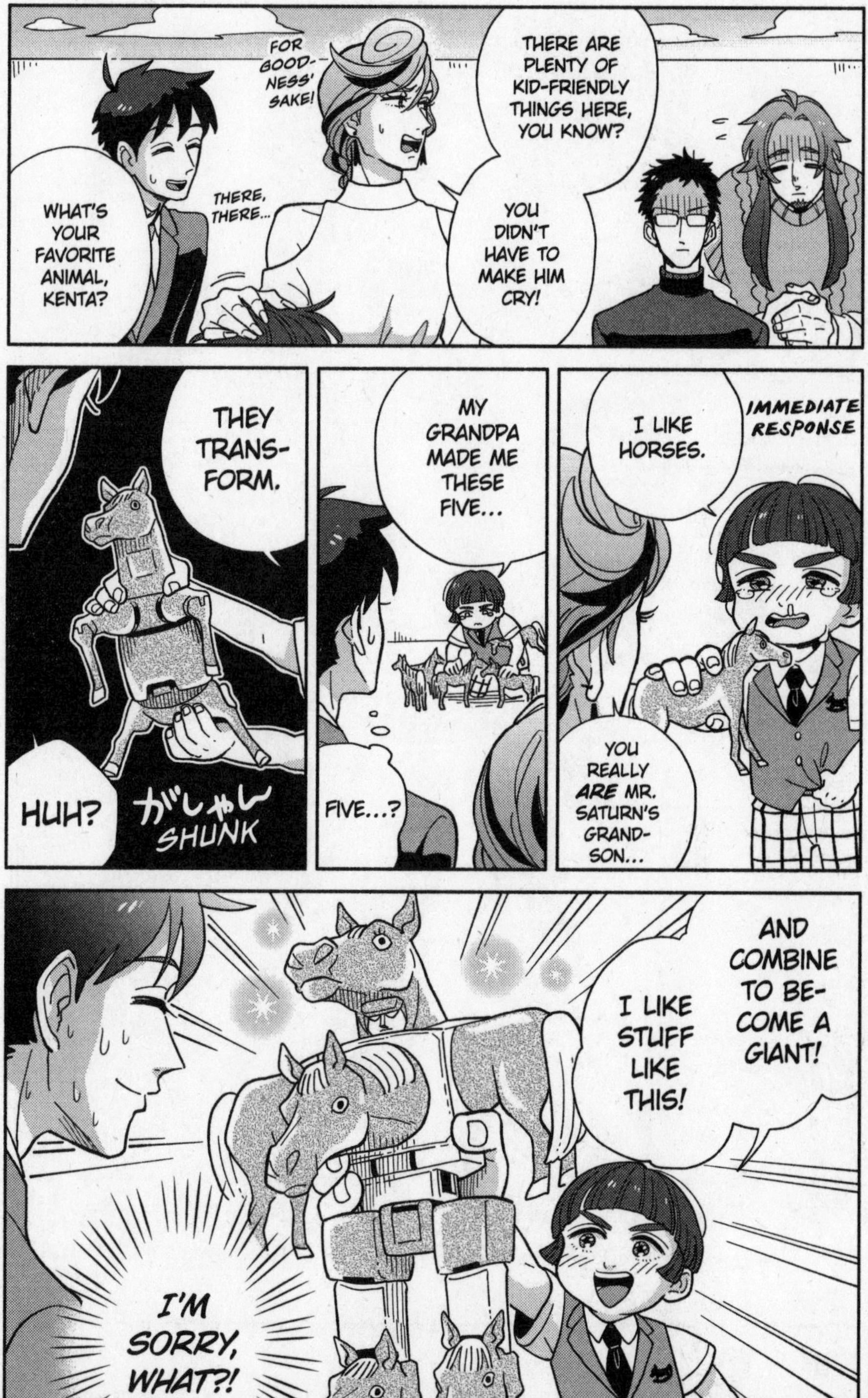
THERE ARE PLENTY OF KID-FRIENDLY THINGS HERE, YOU KNOW?
FOR GOOD-NESS' SAKE!
YOU DIDN'T HAVE TO MAKE HIM CRY!
THERE, THERE...
WHAT'S YOUR FAVORITE ANIMAL, KENTA?
IMMEDIATE RESPONSE
I LIKE HORSES.
YOU REALLY ARE MR. SATURN'S GRAND-SON...
MY GRANDPA MADE ME THESE FIVE...
FIVE...?
THEY TRANS-FORM.
がしゃん SHUNK
HUH?
AND COMBINE TO BE-COME A GIANT!
I LIKE STUFF LIKE THIS!
I'M SORRY, WHAT?!

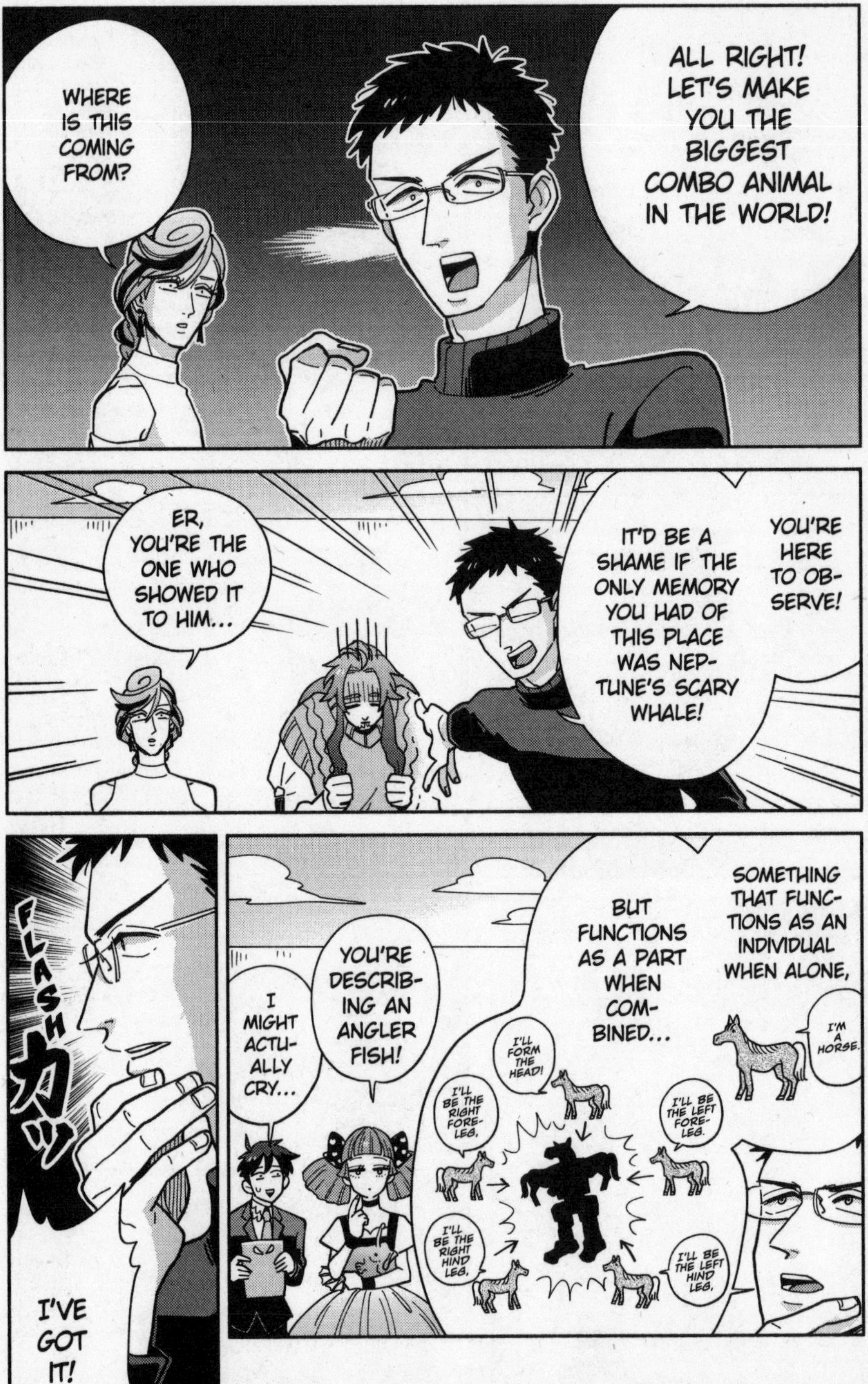
ALL RIGHT! LET'S MAKE YOU THE BIGGEST COMBO ANIMAL IN THE WORLD!
WHERE IS THIS COMING FROM?
YOU'RE HERE TO OB-SERVE!
IT'D BE A SHAME IF THE ONLY MEMORY YOU HAD OF THIS PLACE WAS NEP-TUNE'S SCARY WHALE!
ER, YOU'RE THE ONE WHO SHOWED IT TO HIM...
SOMETHING THAT FUNC-TIONS AS AN INDIVIDUAL WHEN ALONE,
I'M A HORSE.
BUT FUNCTIONS AS A PART WHEN COM-BINED...
I'LL FORM THE HEAD!
I'LL BE THE LEFT FORE-LEG.
I'LL BE THE RIGHT FORE-LEG.
I'LL BE THE LEFT HIND LEG.
I'LL BE THE RIGHT HIND LEG.
YOU'RE DESCRIB-ING AN ANGLER FISH!
I MIGHT ACTU-ALLY CRY...
FLASH
カッ
I'VE GOT IT!

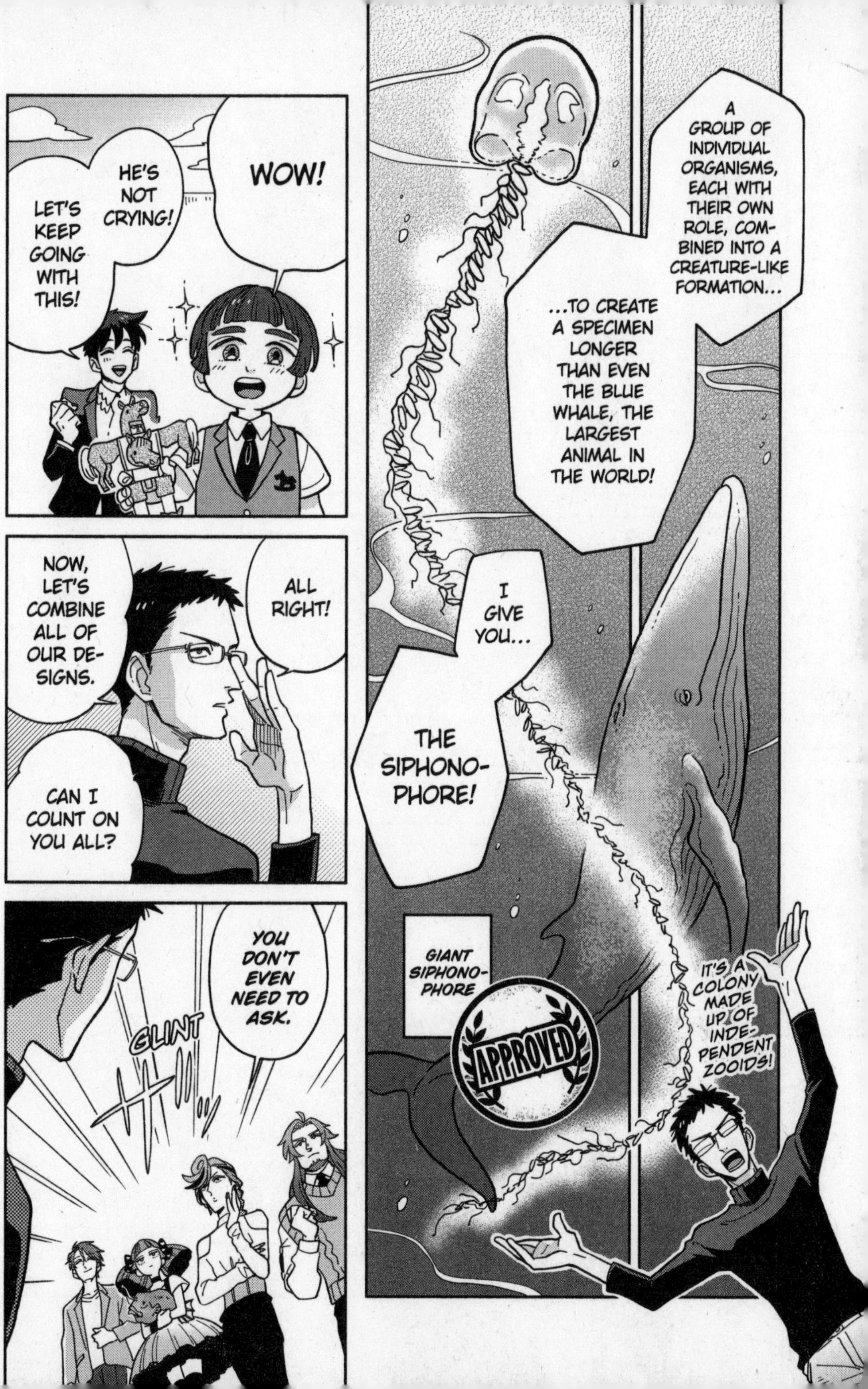
A GROUP OF INDIVIDUAL ORGANISMS, EACH WITH THEIR OWN ROLE, COMBINED INTO A CREATURE-LIKE FORMATION...
...TO CREATE A SPECIMEN LONGER THAN EVEN THE BLUE WHALE, THE LARGEST ANIMAL IN THE WORLD!
I GIVE YOU...
THE SIPHONOPHORE!
GIANT SIPHONOPHORE
APPROVED
IT'S A COLONY MADE UP OF INDEPENDENT ZOOIDS!
WOW!
HE'S NOT CRYING!
LET'S KEEP GOING WITH THIS!
ALL RIGHT!
NOW, LET'S COMBINE ALL OF OUR DESIGNS.
CAN I COUNT ON YOU ALL?
YOU DON'T EVEN NEED TO ASK.
GLINT

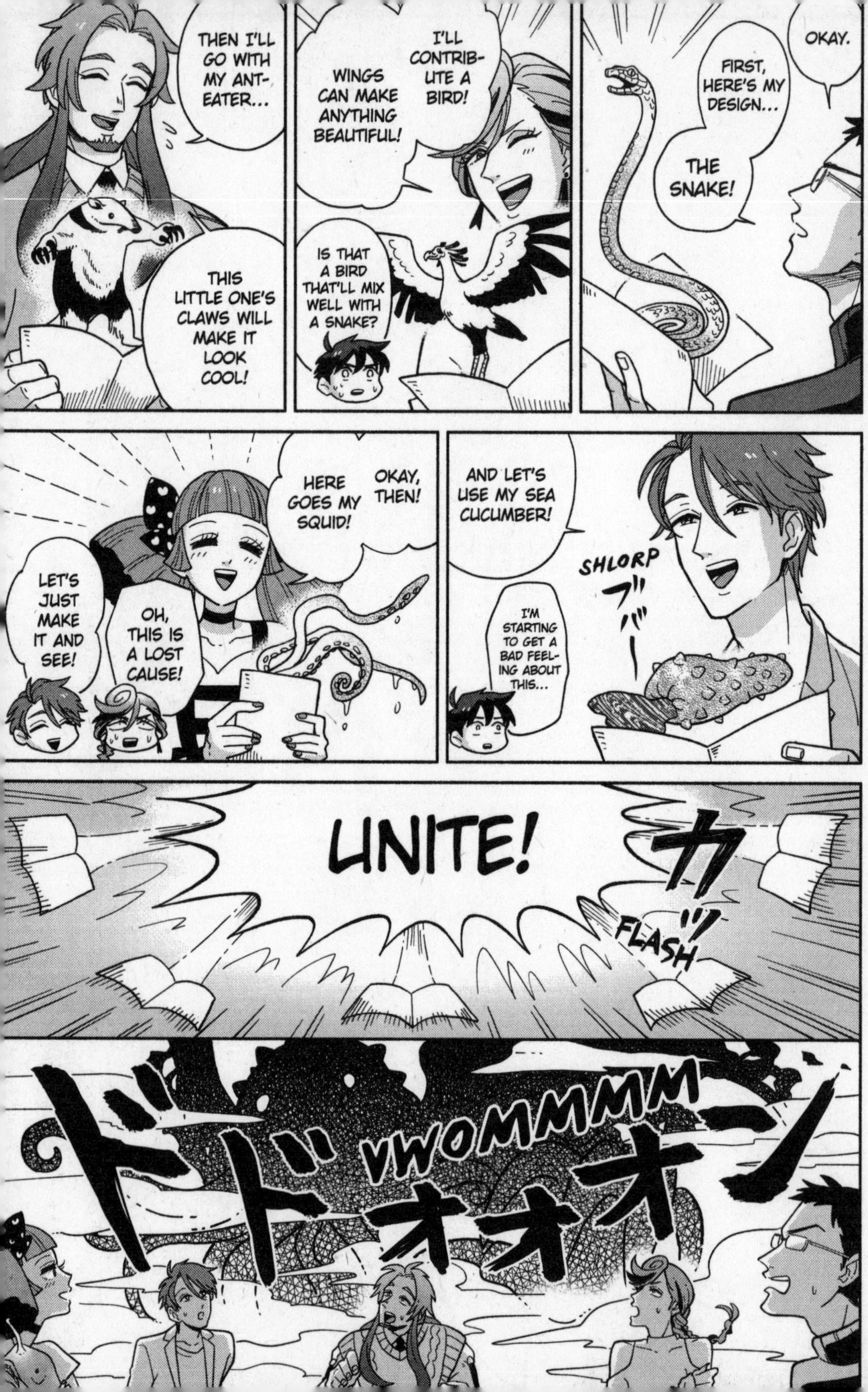

OKAY.
FIRST, HERE'S MY DESIGN...
THE SNAKE!
I'LL CONTRIB-UTE A BIRD!
WINGS CAN MAKE ANYTHING BEAUTIFUL!
IS THAT A BIRD THAT'LL MIX WELL WITH A SNAKE?
THEN I'LL GO WITH MY ANT-EATER...
THIS LITTLE ONE'S CLAWS WILL MAKE IT LOOK COOL!
AND LET'S USE MY SEA CUCUMBER!
SHLORP
I'M STARTING TO GET A BAD FEEL-ING ABOUT THIS...
OKAY, THEN!
HERE GOES MY SQUID!
OH, THIS IS A LOST CAUSE!
LET'S JUST MAKE IT AND SEE!
UNITE!
カッ
FLASH
ドドオオオン
VWOMMMM

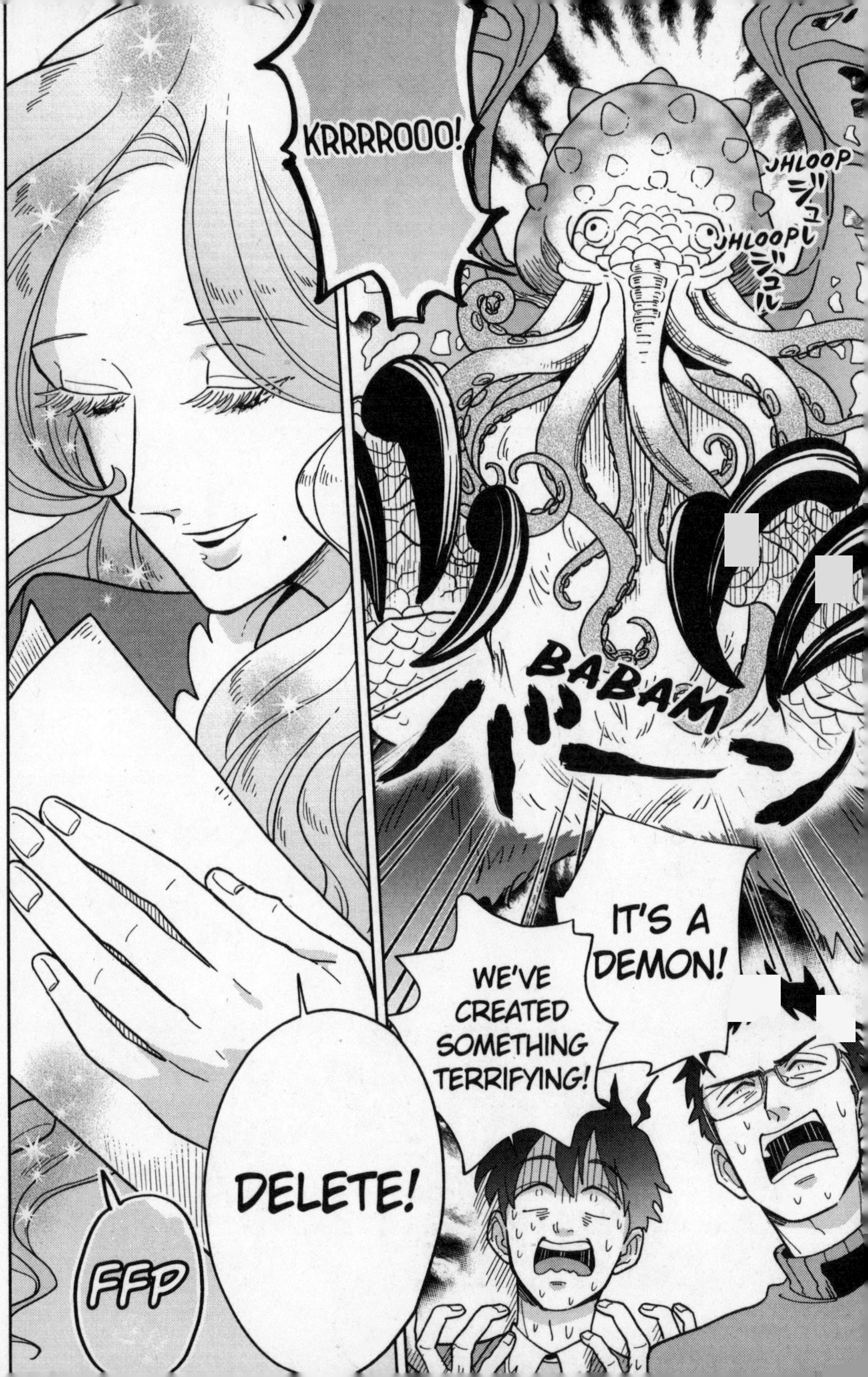
KRRRROOO!
JHLOOP
JHLOOP
BABAM
IT'S A DEMON!
WE'VE CREATED SOMETHING TERRIFYING!
DELETE!
FFP

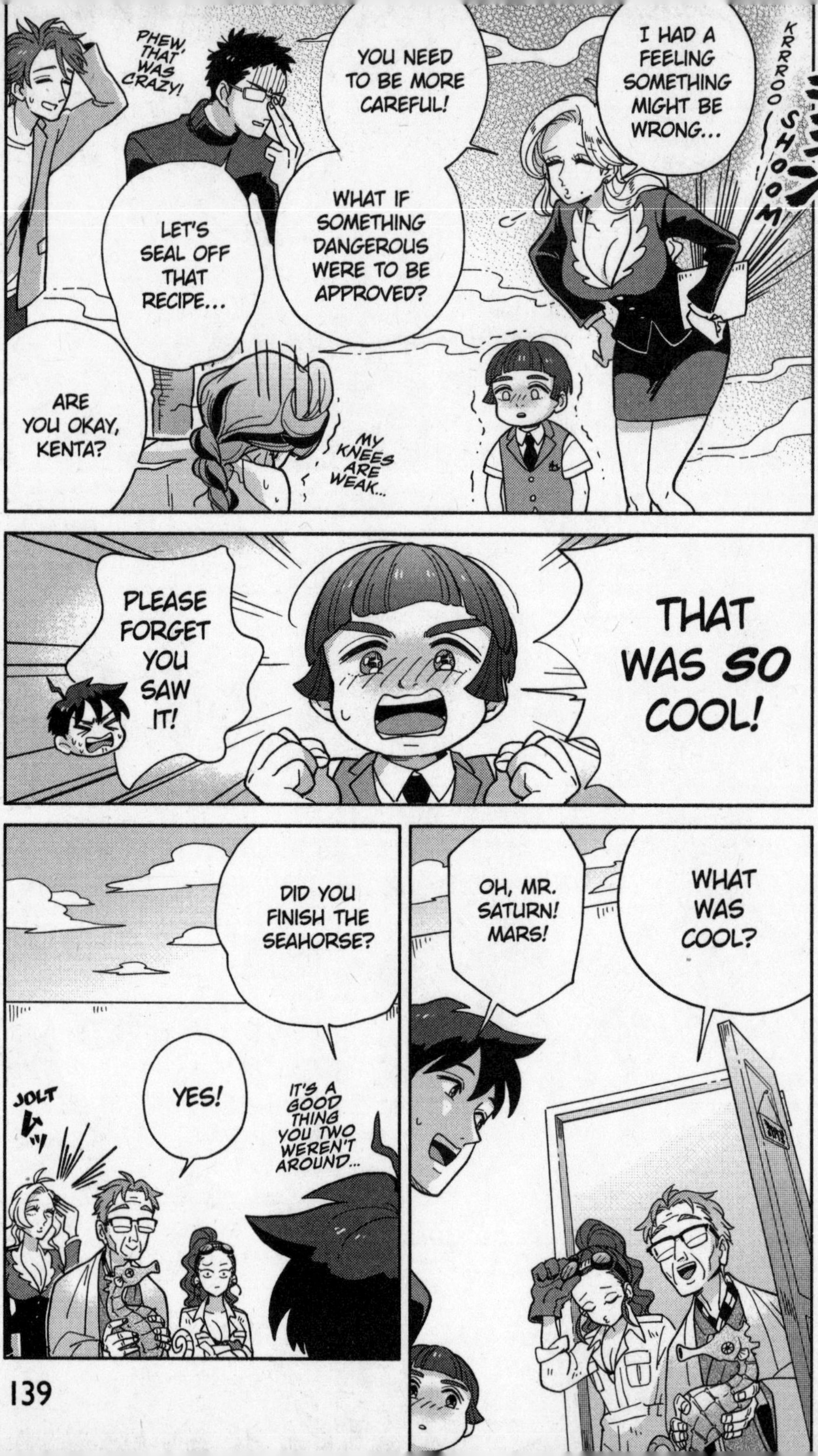
I HAD A FEELING SOMETHING MIGHT BE WRONG...
KRRROO SHOOOM
YOU NEED TO BE MORE CAREFUL!
WHAT IF SOMETHING DANGEROUS WERE TO BE APPROVED?
PHEW, THAT WAS CRAZY!
LET'S SEAL OFF THAT RECIPE...
MY KNEES ARE WEAK...
ARE YOU OKAY, KENTA?
THAT WAS *SO* COOL!
PLEASE FORGET YOU SAW IT!
WHAT WAS COOL?
OH, MR. SATURN! MARS!
DID YOU FINISH THE SEAHORSE?
IT'S A GOOD THING YOU TWO WEREN'T AROUND...
YES!
JOLT

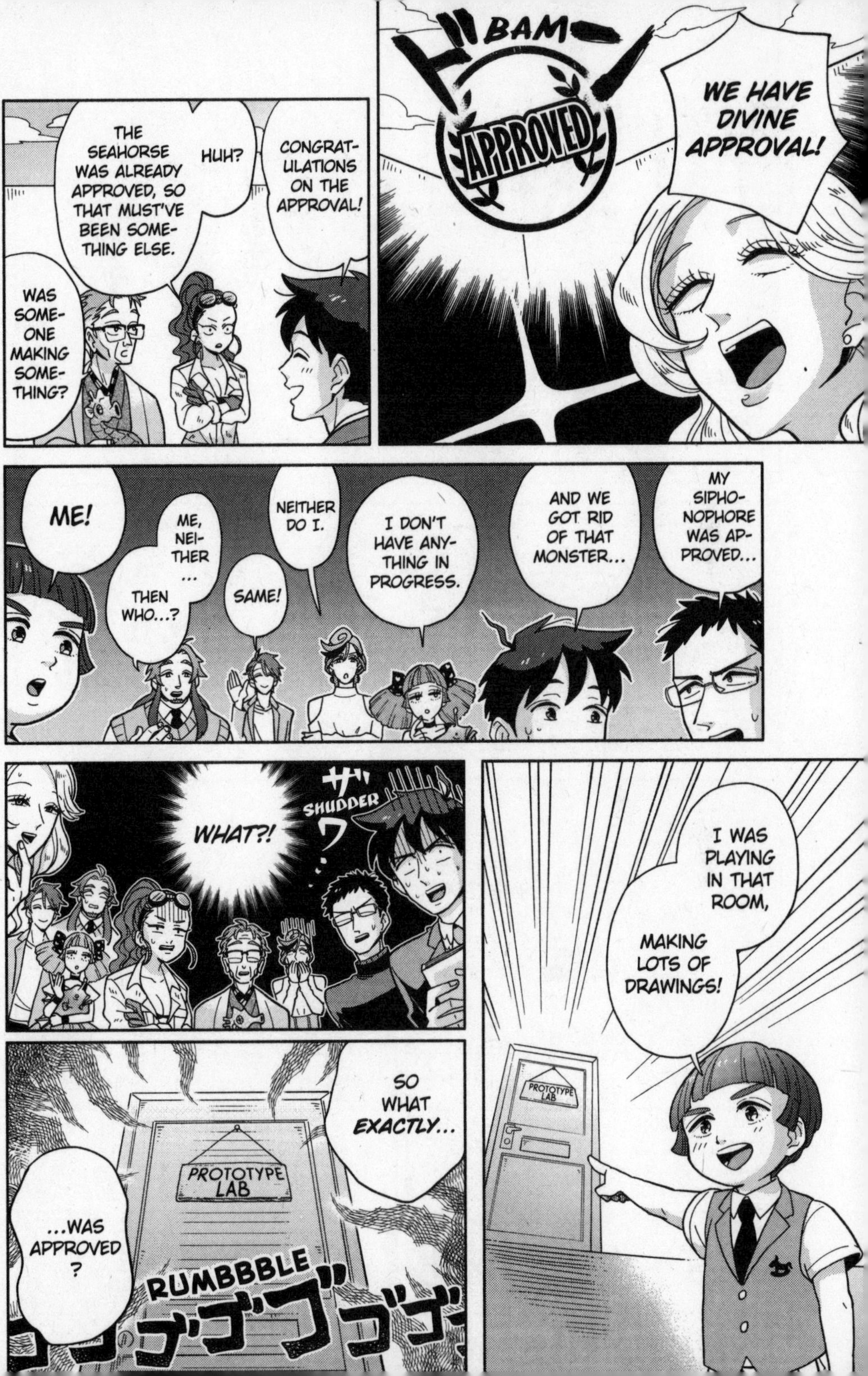
BAM
APPROVED
WE HAVE DIVINE APPROVAL!
CONGRATULATIONS ON THE APPROVAL!
HUH?
THE SEAHORSE WAS ALREADY APPROVED, SO THAT MUST'VE BEEN SOMETHING ELSE.
WAS SOMEONE MAKING SOMETHING?
MY SIPHONOPHORE WAS APPROVED...
AND WE GOT RID OF THAT MONSTER...
I DON'T HAVE ANYTHING IN PROGRESS.
NEITHER DO I.
SAME!
ME, NEITHER...
THEN WHO...?
ME!
I WAS PLAYING IN THAT ROOM,
MAKING LOTS OF DRAWINGS!
PROTOTYPE LAB
SHUDDER
WHAT?!
SO WHAT EXACTLY...
PROTOTYPE LAB
...WAS APPROVED?
RUMBBBLE

THE ENCYCLOPEDIA OF REAL ANIMALS 07

ANIMAL ENCYCLOPEDIA

ANIMAL 19 | GIANT SIPHONOPHORE

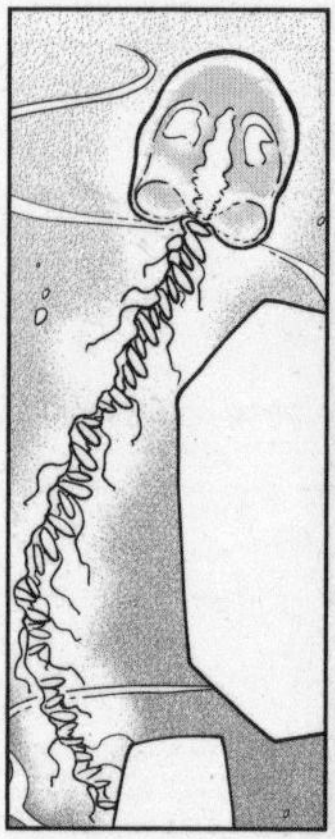

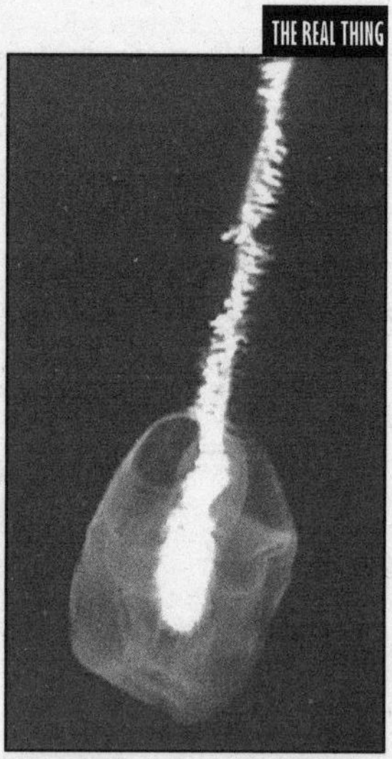
THE REAL THING

A rare image of a live giant siphonophore.

Provided by the Japan Agency for Marine-Earth Science and Technology

The giant siphonophore is a colonial animal made up of individual hydrozoans, which are each specialized for different functions, like feeding or defense. It functions more like a corporation with a variety of specialized departments than a combiner robot. The giant siphonophore can grow to be more than 40 meters (130 feet) long, and if the colony is considered to be one single creature, it surpasses the blue whale as the longest animal in the world. Its rival for this world record is the Portuguese man o' war. The Portuguese man o' war is another colonial animal of the Siphonophorae order, so as long as you remember that the world's longest animal is a siphonophore, you should do well during your next trivia night. The giant siphonophore is very delicate, and can break apart at the slightest touch, but it's able to grow to great lengths because of the calm of the deep sea.

[Type species] *Praya dubia*
[Classification] Class: Hydrozoa
Order: Siphonophora
Family: Prayidae
Genus: *Praya*
[Habitat] Deep ocean
[Length] Around 40 m (130 ft), a world record!

| SEAHORSE

FEMALE   MALE

THE REAL THING

When seahorses mate, the female (left) inserts her ovipositor into the male.
Photo: Aflo

The males of this genus, literally called "sea horse" in both Japanese and English, have a sac called a brood pouch in which they care for the eggs deposited by the female until they are fully developed. The males have a round belly and a hole from which they birth their babies, while the females have bumpy bellies. The female's penis-like ovipositor, which she inserts into the male, is typically stored within the body.

[Name] Seahorse
[Classification] Phylum: Chordata
Class: Actinopterygii
Order: Syngnathiformes
Family: Syngnathidae
Genus: *Hippocampus*
[Habitat] Shallow tropical and temperate waters
[Height] Several centimeters to several dozen centimeters

| ANGLERFISH

As is not uncommon in the world of anglerfish, the male triplewart seadevil is significantly smaller than the female. The male attaches to the female as a parasite, and eventually becomes a part of her after all of his own systems, except for the reproductive organs, degenerate. Sometimes, multiple males will attach to one female, as was the case with one female specimen found with eight male parasites.

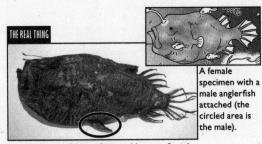

THE REAL THING

A female specimen with a male anglerfish attached (the circled area is the male).

Provided by the Marine Science Museum, Social Education Center TOKAI University

[Type species] *Cryptopsaras couesii*
[Classification] Phylum: Chordata
Class: Actinopterygii
Order: Lophiiformes
Family: Ceratiidae
Genus: *Cryptopsaras*
[Habitat] Oceans at depths of 500-1,250 m (1,600-4,100 ft)
[Length]: Around 30 cm (1 ft) (females) and several centimeters (males)

References

Pat Senson. (2010). "Nasty, Brutish, and Short: The Quirks and Quarks Guide to Animal Sex and Other Weird Behaviour. Asuka Shinsha Popular Science". (Tamura Genji, Trans.). Asuka Shinsha. (Original publisher: The Canadian Broadcast Corporation).

Hokkaido University CoSTEP Science Writers. (2007). "The Evolutionary Process: Unraveling Animal Mysteries Through Their Evolution". Gijyutsu-Hyoronsha.

Satō Katsufumi. (2011). "Could Pterosaurs Fly? The Zoology of Size and Movement". (Heibonsha Shinso vol 568). Heibonsha.

Douglas J. Emlen and David J. Tuss. (2015). "Animal Weapons: The Evolution of Battle". (Yamada Yoshiaki, Trans.). X-Knowledge. (Original publisher: Picador).

Bruce Bagemihl. (1999). "Biological Exuberance: Animal Homosexuality and Natural Diversity". Profile Books, Ltd.

National Astronomical Observatory of Japan (ed.). (2004). "Chronological Scientific Tables (Heisei 17)". Maruzen.

Kawada Yukiaki. "Stories Close to the Heart (Number 54): The High Blood Pressure of Giraffes, the Giant Hearts of Elephants". <https://www.jhf.or.jp/bunko/mimiyori/54.html>

Todd McLeish. (2014). "Narwhals: Arctic Whales in a Melting World". (Nakamura Yui, Trans.). X-Knowledge. (Original publisher: University of Washington Press). Harashobo.

Iwahori Nobuharu. (2014). "An Illustrated Guide to the Evolution of Organs". (Blue Backs, 1853). Kodansha.

Ker Than. (2008). "Barnacles Can Change Penis Size and Shape". <http://news.nationalgeographic.com/news/2008/02/080213-barnacle-penis.html>

Kellie Whittaker, Sierra Raby, David Wake, and Michelle Koo. (2017). "Agalychnis callidryas". <http://www.amphibiaweb.org/cgi-bin/amphib_query?where-scientific_name-callidryas>

Karen M. Warkentin. (2002). "Hatching Timing, Oxygen Availability, and External Gill Regression in the Tree Frog, Agalychnis callidryas". Physiological and Biochemical Zoology 75, no. 2 (March/April 2002) p. 155-164.

Ross Piper. (2007). "Extraordinary Animals: An Encyclopedia of Curious and Unusual Animals". Greenwood Publishing Group.

Ann Moyal (2008). "Koala: A Historical Biography". CSIRO Publishing.

Shiraishi Taku (2006). "Crazy Creatures: Why Don't Fish Freeze at the South Pole?!". Takarajimasha.

Imaizumi Tadaaki. (2008). "Top 50 Scariest Venomous Animals: What's More Venomous than a Cobra or a Tarantula?". (Science Eye Shinso SIS-083). SB Creative.

Takayama Vikki and Matsuhashi Toshimitsu. (2013). "The Encyclopedia of Fantastic Frogs". (Book for Discovery). Yama-kei Publishers.

Nakamura Fumi and Yoshino Toshiyuki. (2014). "The Encyclopedia of Brilliant Birds". (Book for Discovery). Yama-kei Publishers.

Nippon Veterinary and Life Science University, Department of Food Science and Technology, Meat Section. "The Basics of Meat, Number 59: The Characteristics of Chicken". <http://www.agr.okayama-u.ac.jp/amqs/josiki/59-9804.html>

Ikeda Kiyohiko. (2015). "Truth and Lies in Zoology: The 88 Newest Mysteries of the Animal Kingdom". Shinchosha.

University of Tokyo Communicators of Science & Technology. (2016). "Animal Trivia by University of Tokyo Students". Energy Forum.

"Encyclopedia of Australian Wildlife". (Published October 31, 2005). Reader's Digest (Australia) Pty Ltd.

Mizuguchi Hiroya. (1998). "The Encyclopedia of Whales and Dolphins". TBS Britannica.

Minemizu Ryo. (2000). "Crustaceans of the Sea". (Nature Guide). Bun-ichi Sogo Shuppan.

Yamagiwa Jyuichi, Supervisor. (2011). "Kodansha Interactive Encyclopedia Series MOVE: Animals". Kodansha.

Imaizumi Yoshinori. (1982). "Mammals (IV): Hippopotamuses, Deer, Giraffes, Cows, Whales, and Others". (Animals of the World: The Picture Encyclopedia of Animals 10). Kodansha.

Mark Carwardine. (1996). "Whales, Dolphins, and Porpoises (Natural World Handbook)". Nihon Vogue Corporation.

"Strange Animals: Sperm Whales" (Newton) February 2014 Issue. Newton Press.

Kodansha (ed.). (2016). "Kodansha Interactive Encyclopedia Series WONDER MOVE: Exposed". Kodansha.

Kubodera Tsunemi. (2013). "Giant Squid: A Fateful Encounter". Shinchosha.

Okutani Takashi. (2009). "Squid That Talk and Fly: A Beginner's Guide to their Fascinating World (Special Edition)". (Blue Backs, 1650). Kodansha.

Sakurai Yasunori. (2015). "Strange Squid: Japanese Flying Squid, Seasonal Travelers". Hokkaido Shinbunsha.

NHK Special Deep Sea Project Correspondent, Sakamoto Shiho. (2013). "Document: The Hunt for the Gigantic Deep-Sea Squid!". (Kobunsha Shinsho). Kobunsha.

Murayama Tsukasa. (2013). "The Mammals that Returned to the Sea: Mysterious Dolphins". (Blue Backs, 1826). Kodansha.

Nature Pro Editing Room (ed.). (1998). "100 Questions and 100 Answers: The Mysteries of Whales and the Secrets of Dolphins". Miyazaki Nobuyuki, Supervisor, Kawade Shobo Shinsha.

Seidosha Editing Department (ed.). (1997). "The Psychology of Whales and Dolphins". Seidosha.

Fukui Atsushi, Supervisor. (2017). "Kodansha Interactive Encyclopedia Series MOVE: Fish" (Hardcover edition). Kodansha.

Kodansha (ed.). (2017). "Kodansha Interactive Encyclopedia Series EX MOVE: Deep-Sea Creatures". Okutani Takashi, Amaoka Kunio, Supervisors, Kodansha.

jfish. (2006). "The Bizarre Underwater World of Jellyfish". Gijyutsu-Hyoronsha.

Knut Schmidt-Nielsen. (1995). "Scaling: Why Is Animal Size So Important?". (Ohara Masahiro, Trans.). Corona Publishing. (Original publisher: Cambridge University Press).

* All websites accessed on October 25, 2017.

Special thanks:

Yoshimi Takuwa-san

Kamome Shirahama-san

Saba-san

Ame Toba-san

Japan Agency for Marine-Earth Science and Technology (JAMSTEC)

HOW HDT WAS BORN

HEBI-ZOU

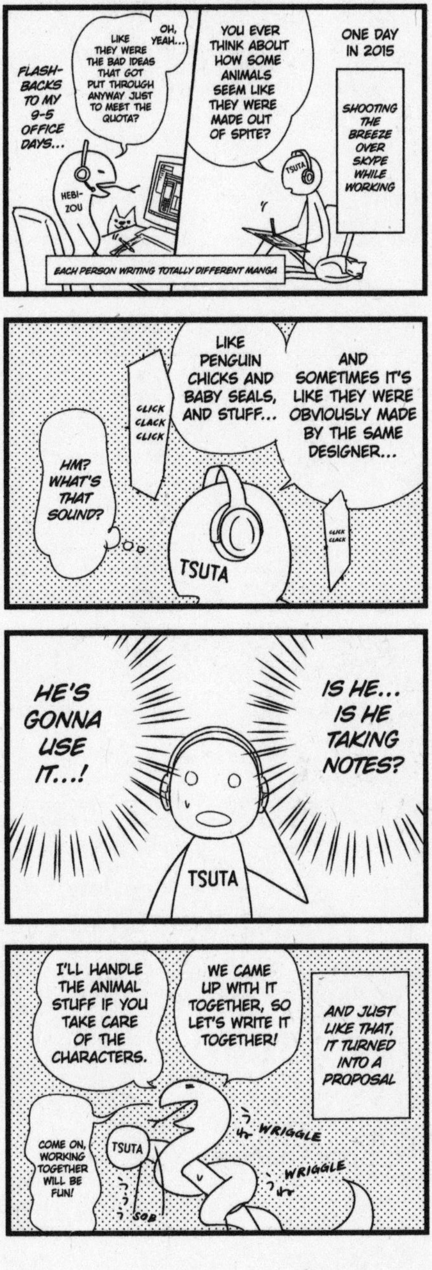
ONE DAY IN 2015
SHOOTING THE BREEZE OVER SKYPE WHILE WORKING
YOU EVER THINK ABOUT HOW SOME ANIMALS SEEM LIKE THEY WERE MADE OUT OF SPITE?
TSUTA
OH, YEAH... LIKE THEY WERE THE BAD IDEAS THAT GOT PUT THROUGH ANYWAY JUST TO MEET THE QUOTA?
FLASH-BACKS TO MY 9-5 OFFICE DAYS...
HEBI-ZOU
EACH PERSON WRITING TOTALLY DIFFERENT MANGA
AND SOMETIMES IT'S LIKE THEY WERE OBVIOUSLY MADE BY THE SAME DESIGNER...
LIKE PENGUIN CHICKS AND BABY SEALS, AND STUFF...
CLICK CLACK
CLICK CLACK CLICK
HM? WHAT'S THAT SOUND?
TSUTA
IS HE... IS HE TAKING NOTES?
HE'S GONNA USE IT...!
TSUTA
AND JUST LIKE THAT, IT TURNED INTO A PROPOSAL
WE CAME UP WITH IT TOGETHER, SO LET'S WRITE IT TOGETHER!
I'LL HANDLE THE ANIMAL STUFF IF YOU TAKE CARE OF THE CHARACTERS.
WRIGGLE
WRIGGLE
TSUTA
COME ON, WORKING TOGETHER WILL BE FUN!
SOB

LAYOUTS EDITION

HOW HDT IS CREATED

TSUTA SUZUKI

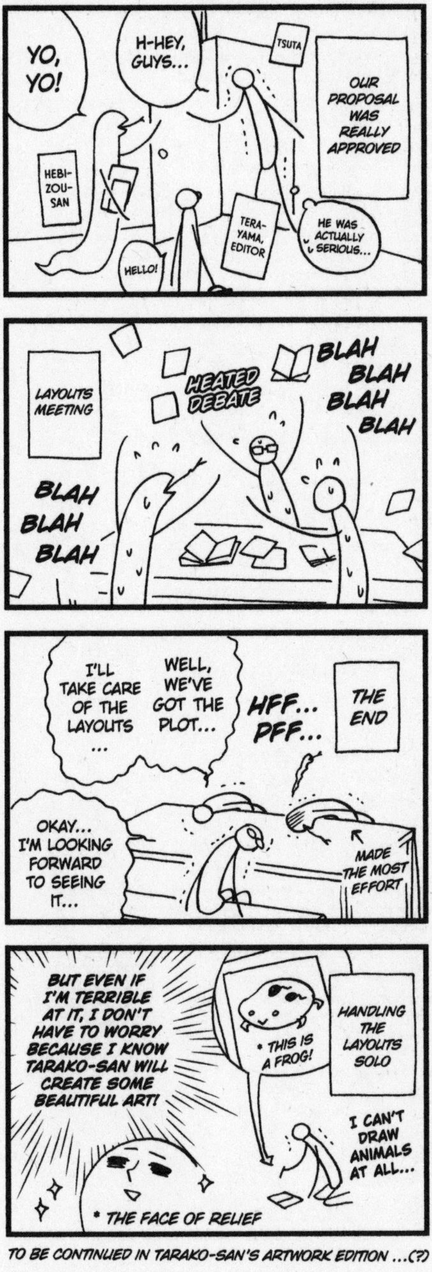
TSUTA
OUR PROPOSAL WAS REALLY APPROVED
H-HEY, GUYS...
YO, YO!
HE WAS ACTUALLY SERIOUS...
TERA-YAMA, EDITOR
HEBI-ZOU-SAN
HELLO!
BLAH BLAH BLAH BLAH
HEATED DEBATE
LAYOUTS MEETING
BLAH BLAH BLAH
THE END
HFF... PFF...
WELL, WE'VE GOT THE PLOT...
I'LL TAKE CARE OF THE LAYOUTS ...
MADE THE MOST EFFORT
OKAY... I'M LOOKING FORWARD TO SEEING IT...
HANDLING THE LAYOUTS SOLO
* THIS IS A FROG!
BUT EVEN IF I'M TERRIBLE AT IT, I DON'T HAVE TO WORRY BECAUSE I KNOW TARAKO-SAN WILL CREATE SOME BEAUTIFUL ART!
I CAN'T DRAW ANIMALS AT ALL...
* THE FACE OF RELIEF

TO BE CONTINUED IN TARAKO-SAN'S ARTWORK EDITION ...(?)

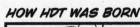

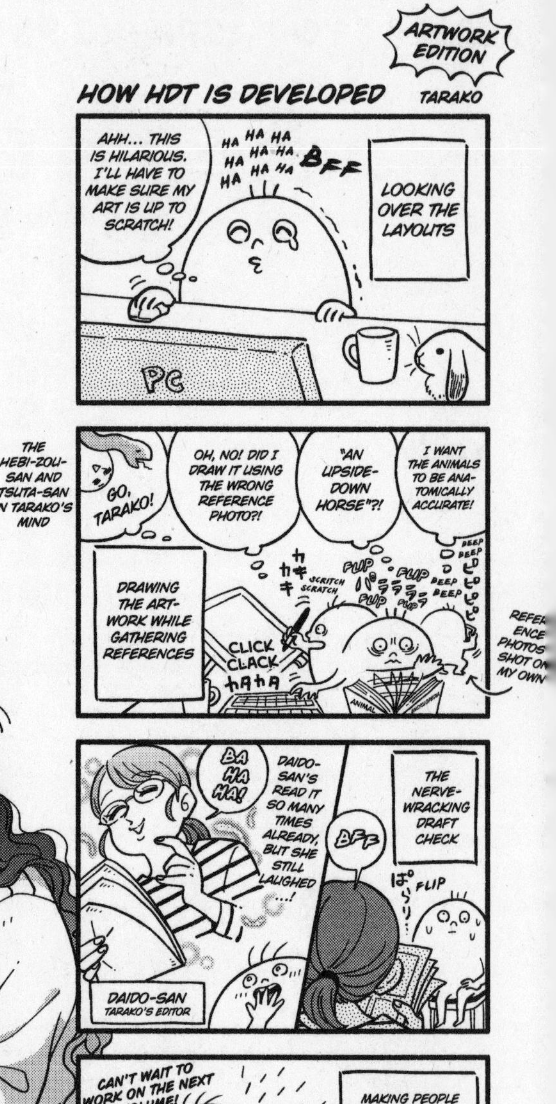
ARTWORK EDITION
HOW HDT IS DEVELOPED
TARAKO
LOOKING OVER THE LAYOUTS
AHH... THIS IS HILARIOUS. I'LL HAVE TO MAKE SURE MY ART IS UP TO SCRATCH!
HA HA HA HA HA HA HA HA HA
BFF
PC
I WANT THE ANIMALS TO BE ANATOMICALLY ACCURATE!
"AN UPSIDE-DOWN HORSE"?!
OH, NO! DID I DRAW IT USING THE WRONG REFERENCE PHOTO?!
GO, TARAKO!
THE HEBI-ZOU-SAN AND TSUTA-SAN IN TARAKO'S MIND
DRAWING THE ART-WORK WHILE GATHERING REFERENCES
BEEP BEEP BEEP BEEP
FLIP FLIP FLIP FLIP
SCRITCH SCRATCH
CLICK CLACK
REFERENCE PHOTOS SHOT ON MY OWN
THE NERVE-WRACKING DRAFT CHECK
DAIDO-SAN'S READ IT SO MANY TIMES ALREADY, BUT SHE STILL LAUGHED...!
BA HA HA!
BFF
FLIP
DAIDO-SAN
TARAKO'S EDITOR
MAKING PEOPLE LAUGH WITH MY ART, EVEN WITHOUT THE WORDS – THE ULTIMATE JOY FOR ME AS AN ARTIST!
CAN'T WAIT TO WORK ON THE NEXT VOLUME!
HERE ARE MY EDITS.
BEING LAUGHED AT (?!) HELPS HDT EVOLVE!

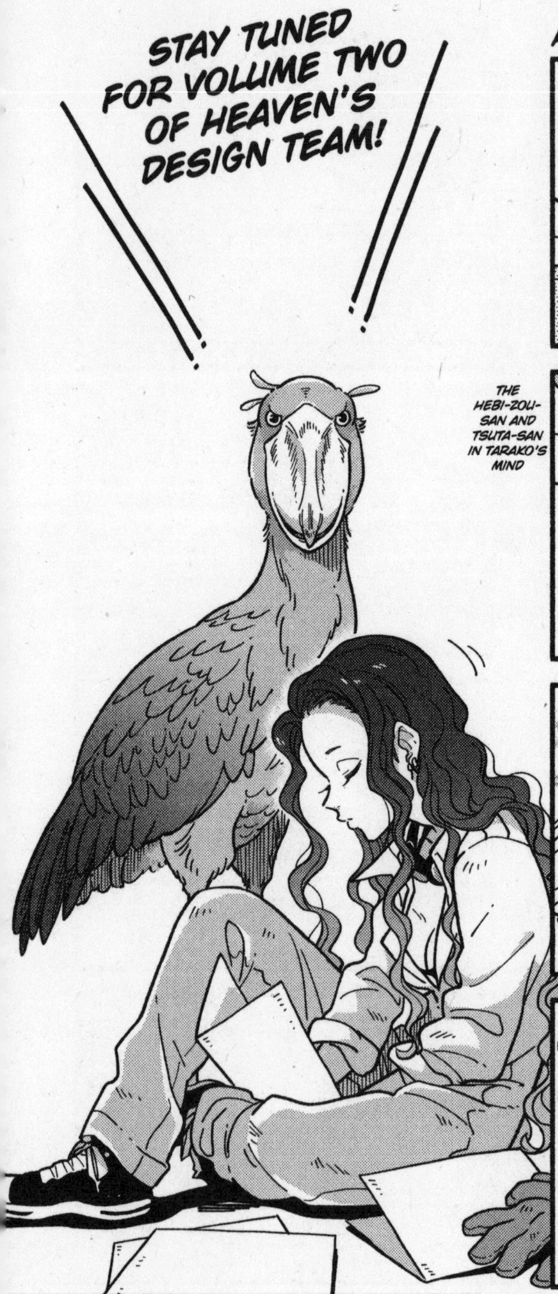
STAY TUNED FOR VOLUME TWO OF HEAVEN'S DESIGN TEAM!

The adorable new odd-couple cat comedy manga from the creator of the beloved *Chi's Sweet Home*, in full color!

Sue & Tai-chan

Konami Kanata

Sue is an aging housecat who's looking forward to living out her life in peace... but her plans change when the mischievous black tomcat Tai-chan enters the picture! Hey! Sue never signed up to be a catsitter! *Sue & Tai-chan* is the latest from the reigning meow-narch of cute kitty comics, Konami Kanata.

KC KODANSHA COMICS

Young characters and steampunk setting, like *Howl's Moving Castle* and *Battle Angel Alita*

A boy with a talent for machines and a mysterious girl whose wings he's fixed will take you beyond the clouds! In the tradition of the high-flying, resonant adventure stories of Studio Ghibli comes a gorgeous tale about the longing of young hearts for adventure and friendship!

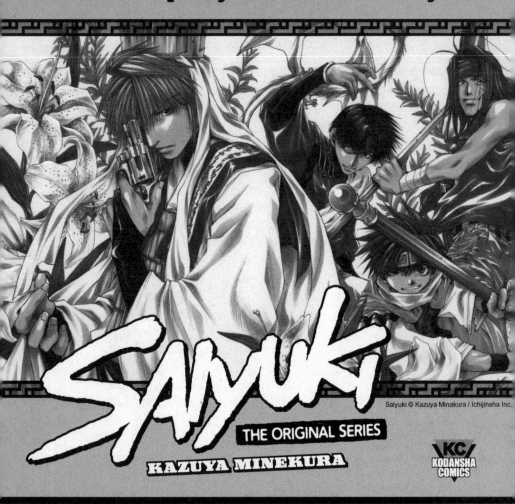

A SMART, NEW ROMANTIC COMEDY FOR FANS OF *SHORTCAKE CAKE* AND *TERRACE HOUSE*!

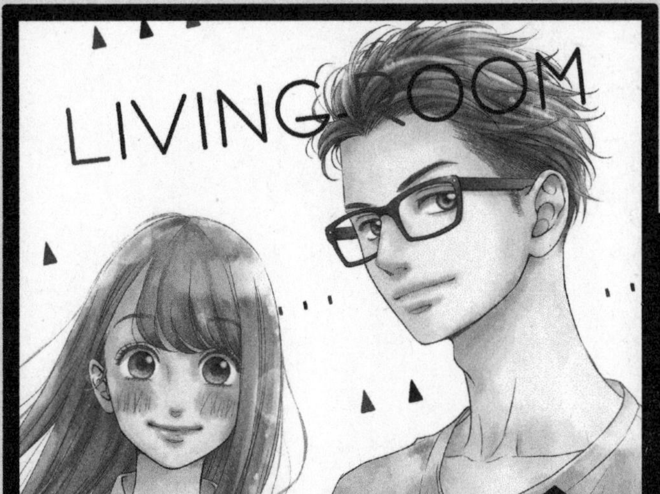
LIVING-ROOM
1
Keiko Iwashita
MATSUNAGA-SAN

A romance manga starring high school girl Meeko, who learns to live on her own in a boarding house whose living room is home to the odd (but handsome) Matsunaga-san. She begins to adjust to her new life away from her parents, but Meeko soon learns that no matter how far away from home she is, she's still a young girl at heart — especially when she finds herself falling for Matsunaga-san.

KC KODANSHA COMICS

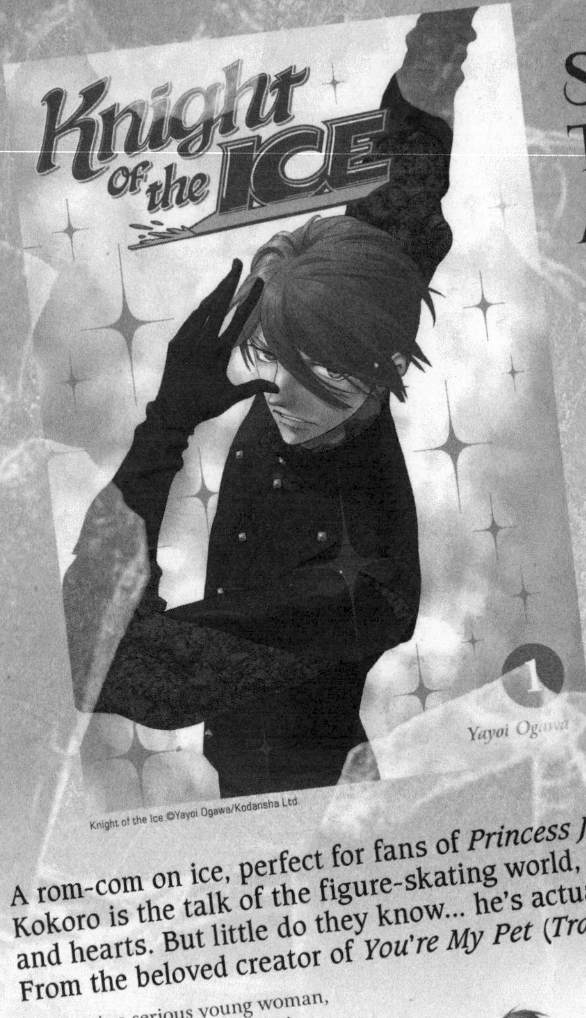
Knight of the ICE
1
Yayoi Ogawa

Knight of the Ice ©Yayoi Ogawa/Kodansha Ltd.

SKATING THRILLS AND ICY CHILLS WITH THIS NEW TINGLY ROMANCE SERIES!

A rom-com on ice, perfect for fans of *Princess Jellyfish* and *Wotakoi*. Kokoro is the talk of the figure-skating world, winning trophies and hearts. But little do they know... he's actually a huge nerd! From the beloved creator of *You're My Pet* (*Tramps Like Us*).

Chitose is a serious young woman, working for the health magazine *SASSO*. Or at least, she would be, if she wasn't constantly getting distracted by her childhood friend, international figure skating star Kokoro Kijinami! In the public eye and on the ice, Kokoro is a gallant, flawless knight, but behind his glittery costumes and breathtaking spins lies a secret: He's actually a hopelessly romantic otaku, who can only land his quad jumps when Chitose is on hand to recite a spell from his favorite magical girl anime!

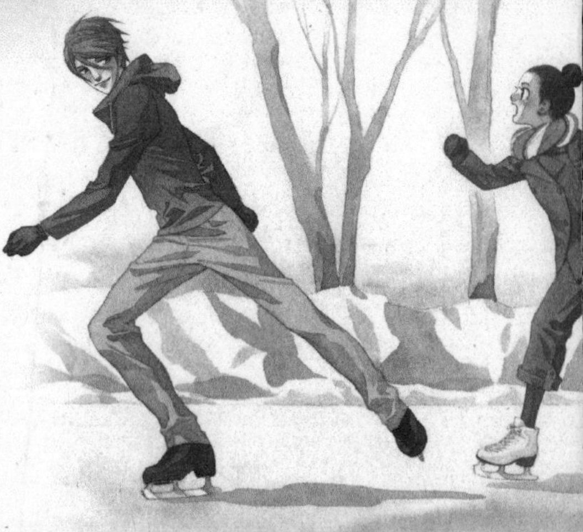

KC KODANSHA COMICS

A Kodansha Comics Trade Paperback Original
Heaven's Design Team 1 copyright © 2017 Hebi-zou&Tsuta Suzuki/Tarako
English translation copyright © 2020 Hebi-zou&Tsuta Suzuki/Tarako
All rights reserved.

Published in the United States by Kodansha Comics, an imprint of
Kodansha USA Publishing, LLC, New York.

Publication rights for this English edition arranged through
Kodansha Ltd., Tokyo.

First published in Japan in 2017 by Kodansha Ltd., Tokyo
as *Tenchi sozo dezainbu*, volume 1.

ISBN 978-1-64651-113-6

Original cover design by SAVA DESIGN

Printed in the United States of America.

www.kodanshacomics.com

9 8 7 6 5 4 3 2 1
Translation: JM Iitomi Crandall
Lettering: Ean Scrale
Editing: Z.K. Woodbridge, Vanessa Tenazas
YKS Services LLC/SKY Japan, INC
Kodansha Comics edition cover design by My Truong

Publisher: Kiichiro Sugawara

Director of publishing services: Ben Applegate
Associate director of operations: Stephen Pakula
Publishing services managing editor: Noelle Webster
Assistant production manager: Emi Lotto, Angela Zurlo
Logo and character art ©Kodansha USA Publishing, LLC